NEVER
SMILE
AT A
CROCODILE

Confessions of a Tax Traveller

Paul DioGuardi

Brilliant Idea Books

The information contained in this book is non-technical and meant for general readership. The author and publisher disclaim all liability for any damages resulting from the application of the information provided. In publishing this book, the author is not engaged in rendering legal, accounting, or other professional service. If you are contemplating applications to federal or provincial tax amnesty programs, notices of objection, taxpayer relief submissions, tax appeals, rectification, or other topics covered, you should seek specific, updated advice from experienced, legal tax counsel before proceeding.

DioGuardi Tax Law case histories used herein have been altered to protect lawyer-client confidentiality.

ISBN (Paperback): 978-0-9938387-0-5
ISBN (e-Book): 978-0-9938387-1-2
First Printing

Printed in Canada.

Publishing Consultant: **Brilliant Idea Books**

Story Mentor: Patricia Plant
Editor: Catherine Leek of **Green Onion Publishing**
Interior Design: Kim Monteforte for **WeMakeBooks.ca**
Electronic Page Composition: Beth Crane for **WeMakeBooks.ca**
Cover Concept: Jacky Wan of **Thoughtform Digital**
Crocodile Illustration: Maria Bell for **CEO Media Group Inc.**

MIX
Paper from
responsible sources
FSC® C107923

To Carmen, *ma douce moitié,*
and to Patti, my muse and Amanuensis,
for their patience in bringing to life
the most extraordinary group of tales ever told
by an old tax traveller.

Sincere thanks also to the colleagues, clients, friends and family
whose participation along the way has enriched the voyage.

Contents

Not Always Tax

An Indulgence

No Place to Hide

Travels for Tax

The Tax Games

Crocodile Tactics

Crocodile Chess

The Crocodile on Your Doorstep

Insatiable Appetite

A Necessary Preamble

"BEFORE SEVENTY WE ARE MERELY RESPECTED, at best, and we have to behave all the time, or we lose that asset; but after seventy we are respected, admired, revered, and don't have to behave unless we want to 'because we are recognizably old.'"

So said the delightfully irascible Samuel Clemens, popularly known as Mark Twain. Whether there is truth to the foregoing or not, having passed the milestone of threescore and ten, I choose to forego convention and write down what I remember of the journey as it comes to mind, and in no particular order.

As you skip from one account to another at will, my hope is that you enjoy what is, by convention, the most unusual group of tales ever told by a tax traveller.

Paul DioGuardi
Queen's Counsel
Tax Lawyer
May 2014

Pirates of the Caribbean

Dread Pirate Vince and a Tale of Seven Mile Beach

BEAUTIFUL SEAS. SANDY COVES. BLUE LAGOONS. CAYMANS.

Caymans are first cousins to the crocodile. Like crocodiles, caymans love the warm lazy waters of the Caribbean islands. So do sharks. And somewhere between these live the pirates who seek refuge in the islands to shelter their wealth from tax.

It's only fitting, then, to begin my tales and confessions in the land of the caymans and pirates.

I've had many adventures there, some related to tax and some not.

Let's begin with this tale from Grand Cayman.

In the 1970s, Grand Cayman and Little Cayman were the hidden gems of island paradises. They had only recently set themselves up as a world-class tax haven and, compared to the established havens of Switzerland, Lichtenstein and Luxembourg, and the like, were rather unsophisticated.

The journey from Canada to the Caymans was an adventure in itself. First you flew to Miami, where you embarked on an American Airlines flight over Cuba. Given the frosty nature of U.S./Cuban relations, it was forbidden to take photographs of Cuba while flying over the island in an American plane. Violations could result in the plane being forced down by the Cuban authorities. I don't know how they would have checked, and certainly I never had that experience, but the airline staff was always very vigilant in enforcing the no-photo-graphs rule. It added a *frisson* of intrigue to the Canada-Grand Cayman flight path.

My first landing in Grand Cayman was an even greater adventure. The runway was short and bumpy, and the terminal was something out of a Hollywood B movie. A wizened old man sat by a tin shack near where luggage was unloaded from the plane. As suitcases were tossed out from the belly of the plane, his job was to mark an X on them with a piece of chalk. Apparently that meant your bag was cleared for customs. So you picked your bag up and carried it to customs, where, after a cursory look at your passport, the customs officer waved you on. Nobody bothered to ask any questions. How times have changed!

From the airport, it was a short ride into Georgetown, the capital of the Cayman Islands.

This first time, I was travelling to Grand Cayman on an interesting mission. Months earlier, a lady had consulted with me in my Ottawa office. Her son, Vince, had just won a million dollars in the Lotto Canada. He didn't have to pay tax on the windfall. Surely, she asked me, there must be a way her son could continue to avoid tax on his wealth.

At that time, a million dollars was a real fortune. Today it would take a prize of at least 8 to 10 million dollars to equal it. This lady's quest for intelligent tax planning could have a tremendous impact on her son's windfall of wealth over the long term. I agreed to take on Vince as a client, and scheduled a meeting.

Sheltering wealth from tax is not easy if you continue to live in Canada. So I explored Vince's appetite to become a non-resident. The Cayman Islands was a new tax haven, but much closer to Canada than the established European options.

If Vince became a non-resident, under Canadian tax law he could invest his wealth in Canada, where it would be safe, in a special class of government bond which would pay him interest tax free. This way the Canadian Tax Crocodile (aka Revenue Canada) could never take a bite out of his $1,000,000, or the investment growth on those funds. Back in the seventies, interest rates were very good. I believed Vince would be able to live quite comfortably in the Caymans on his interest income, while preserving, and even increasing, his base of capital.

The special government bonds to which I referred are offered by our federal government, and by some of the provinces, to entice foreign investment in Canada. These bonds provide a safe haven for foreign investors to "park" their money tax-free because, for non-residents of Canada, the interest earned on these special bonds is not taxed in Canada.

This may not seem fair to the hard-working Canadians who live and invest here, and pay tax on the growth of their investments. Money is a competitive business, and Canada is eager to capture its share of the world's investment market. As a tax lawyer, I am aware of these opportunities and advise clients of the options available.

After lengthy discussions, and some research into eligible island paradises, Vince opted to become non-resident. He was in his prime. Winning a million dollars had changed his life. He had no interest in regular employment, and a move to the islands could be exciting.

All of which brought me to Seven Mile Beach, and the reason for my first trip to Grand Cayman.

I flew down to get Vince organized as a resident. I stayed at a small hotel on Seven Mile Beach. It was, and still is, the most beautiful beach on the island. Back then it boasted little more than The Buccaneer, the dilapidated hotel where I was staying. There were also a few private homes, including, notably, the Governor's residence. Every morning you could see the Governor driving along the beach road in his white Rolls Royce en route to his office. Seven Mile Beach was a lovely spot for Vince to find his island legs, as it were.

I had to admit to a tiny bit of jealousy that Vince could enjoy such an idyllic lifestyle while I would be returning to the cold winters of Canada and my law practice.

My first impression of Grand Cayman was that it was a little island trying to be financially sophisticated. The ex-pats (British and Canadian, mostly) were like the caymans in the lagoons, lying low, but always on the lookout for opportunities to make money to feed their desired lifestyle.

It took several days for me to get Vince properly organized. Down there, business moves at island speed – slowly, and with a rhythm as inalterable as the lapping of the waves on the beach. Thus I came to spend many hours on the beautiful beach, and in the lobby bar at The Buccaneer.

I had many conversations, and a few "greenies" (island slang for a bottle of Heineken beer) with the locals. The realtors would regale me with tales of fantastic land bargains to be had. At that time the island was undiscovered territory, which means there were some truly remarkable opportunities to buy beachfront land at reasonable rates. I was intrigued.

On my return to Ottawa, I discussed the beach and the opportunity to buy property on the island with my good friend, Chris.

Chris and I had known each other since our early teens. Aside from being my best friend, he had a nose for a good business deal. My descriptions of Grand Cayman captured his imagination, and he agreed to scout out the real estate opportunities with me. And we did discover some great deals. All we needed was the cash.

Back home in Ottawa, Chris went to work, recruiting a group of Canadian investors to raise seed capital for a potential purchase of beachfront real estate. A prominent local judge was among the group. (The significance of this detail will become apparent later.) Within a few months Chris had raised enough seed money to get us into the game, so we journeyed back to Grand Cayman in search of a property.

Once arrived, we called on Vince. He was nicely settled on the island and knew his way around. We asked if he had come across any good buys. He recommended Villas Pappagallos, a condominium project still under construction. It was on the beach and, since Vince knew the owners, the price would be right.

We made a cash offer on a condo unit and the builders accepted. The purchase price was over $160,000 USD, plus closing costs. At the time, that was big money. But timing and opportunity are everything, and the investors were pleased with the deal.

Now we turned to the business of managing the beginning of a new real estate enterprise. Since Vince was already living on the island, he was a logical choice to manage our condo, and any other units that the group might buy in the future. And so we began.

For several years, all went well. The condo was rented out to tourists and produced a reasonable income. Vince collected the rents, deposited the money in the investors' account at the bank in Georgetown, and reported directly to Chris on the operation of the property. For practical reasons, Vince had been given signing authority on the investors' account at Barclay's Bank.

Then Murphy's Law struck and things suddenly went very wrong.

It was February, and Chris and I were at dinner with our wives. Chris, then only in his mid-40s, looked very ill. He told me the doctors in Ottawa could not diagnose what was wrong. His illness could not have come at a worse time. He was an investment advisor, and he couldn't afford to step away from his firm's sales activity until the end of RRSP season. His health issues would have to wait. Come March, he would go to Florida to rest and recuperate.

He was a young man, and I expected to see him hale and hearty after a few weeks in the sunny south.

It came as a stunning surprise when, a few weeks later, in late March, my phone rang and it was Chris' father calling me from Tampa. Chris, he said, had been taken to the hospital and, unexpectedly, had passed away.

Bad news often seems to come in batches. Shortly after the funeral, Vince called me from the Cayman Islands.

"Sorry to hear about Chris," he said. "Since I can't tell him, I'm telling you. I've sold the condo."

This was news to me. I said so.

"Chris knew all about it," Vince replied. "We couldn't agree on managing the property, and he and I had one argument too many. So he told me to sell. It's a done deal."

I couldn't ask Chris to verify any of this, so I jumped to the only relevant question.

"What did you sell it for?" I asked.

"Seventy-one thousand," Vince said.

"Seventy-one?" I was almost speechless. That was less than half of the original purchase price. I found voice enough to ask, "Where is the money?"

Vince didn't answer. I started to realize that now that the deal was done, Vince probably had no intention of getting the money to the investors.

But I kept asking questions until Vince finally shouted he was keeping the money and we would never find it. It was payback for his arguments with Chris, he said, and he had a foolproof plan.

Then he hung up.

I was stunned. Clearly we had been robbed. What was I to do from Canada? Pirate tactics were in play in the islands and I was a long way away.

I shared the story with my law practice partner, Hamilton. As luck would have it, he reminded me that his brother-in-law, Reilly, was chief legal counsel to the RCMP. Perhaps Reilly could help me. Hamilton and Reilly were both top-notch lawyers, more seasoned, and senior to me at the bar. They were also Irish. They had fight in them. Hamilton used to tell me that an Irishman will fight you over a nickel. Well, I had much more than a nickel at stake here. If these two had a plan, or at least an "in" with the police, I was happy to follow their lead.

Hamilton set up the meeting and I told Reilly the facts as I knew them: Vince had sold the property without authority, had sold it at a huge undervalue, and, it appeared, had absconded with the money.

We mulled over the problem, and Reilly recommended I report it officially to the RCMP. Up we went to "A" Division in Ottawa. If you're not from Ottawa, you won't be impressed. I was born and raised in Ottawa and, at that time, "A" Division at the RCMP meant I was pretty much deep in HQ. This was big.

I explained to the senior police official that, in addition to the basic facts of the unauthorized sale and potential theft of funds, one of the investors in the group project was a prominent local judge. The other investors were well-known in the local community. If word got out, the matter would be big media news in Ottawa. We could not just walk away and let it be.

That did the trick. The RCMP responded as quickly as if they were ancient Irish warriors rebuffing an English attack on the Blarney Stone. In a flash we were on the phone and speaking to Detective Superintendent Bryan Martin of the Cayman Islands Police, Commercial Crime Branch. I was impressed. I didn't stop to think why the RCMP in Ottawa had the number of the Cayman Islands Police practically on speed dial. Maybe this happened a lot. Detective Superintendent Martin was delighted to be of assistance.

"Best you come down here in person," he said. "We'll need you to visit your bank in Georgetown and see if there's any trace of the money."

I was game. And angry. If I had any chance of catching up with Vince I had to move fast. I caught the next flight to Grand Cayman.

I went straight to Barclay's Bank in Georgetown and presented my credentials to the assistant manager. He went away to find the records of the bank account and then returned with the bad news. The account was empty. No money had been deposited recently. To make things worse, the books and records of the property investment business had been removed from the vault.

It was the beginning of proof. I went straight from the bank to the office of Detective Superintendent Martin and, on behalf of the investment group, made a formal complaint of theft.

The police swiftly laid criminal charges against Vince. I suggested they grab his Canadian passport so he couldn't leave the island. They did and it worked. Vince was a virtual prisoner on the Island. So much for us never catching him.

I continued to grapple with the mystery of why? Why would Vince stoop to such blatant theft? Surely he didn't need the money. He had won a million dollars and was living in a tax-free jurisdiction. He should be flush with cash. I knew he had bought several properties on Seven Mile Beach. This would have depleted his capital, but why would he resort to stealing from people he knew? Compared to a million dollars, seventy-one thousand was pocket change. There had to be something else.

I tried to phone Vince, hoping I could talk some sense into him and settle this between us. He did not return my calls. The plot thickened. I let loose my next arrow.

I had done my homework before I left Ottawa. Looking for a way to keep Vince from liquidating his assets, I vaguely remembered, from law school or some extra-curricular reading, that there was a way to get a court order to prevent a debtor from liquidating assets before creditors had secured a judgment. It was called a Mareva Injunction. If I could get the courts in Grand Cayman to issue a Mareva – or something like it – I could keep Vince from disposing of his island properties. That would at least give me a chance to try to recover some of our group's investment.

From the police station I went to the nearest law chambers in search of legal counsel. I engaged the services of a Cayman lawyer on behalf of the investors, and briefed him on my strategy. He was not familiar with the "Mareva," but he was smart and a good lawyer. He did his own research and discovered a similar type of application, which he made forthwith to the Grand Court of the Cayman Islands. The court granted an *ex parte* injunction restraining Vince from disposing of his assets within the jurisdiction.

Vince must have been very surprised to find that all of his Cayman properties were effectively "frozen." There was no way he could liquidate any of them.

However, I was thinking beyond the islands, and with a couple of phone calls I had similar injunctions registered on the property he owned in Ontario.

The culprit was now pinned down with little hope of escape. He couldn't leave the island. His assets in two countries were frozen. He was trapped. He would need the stolen money now more than ever.

In due course, the Cayman police found and arrested Vince, and threw him in jail. Contrary to the beauty of the island, the jail, I was told, was an abomination. It was small, dirty, crowded and full of bugs. One assumes that Vince, to say the least, was not a happy camper. With his properties frozen, he wasn't even able to raise bail. Eventually a family member came up with funds, and Vince was released pending trial.

I went back to Ottawa to practice law and placate our group of investors.

In time, the criminal trial was due for hearing. The prosecuting attorney requested that I appear as his witness. I agreed to give evidence and flew to Georgetown.

The Grand Court of the Cayman Islands is very British. The case was heard before a judge and jury. It was a courtroom scene out of a classic movie. Not quite the set of *Witness for the Prosecution*, but close. Lawyers were in robes, a British judge was on the bench in robes and a wig. Overhead fans spun in a desultory attempt to keep the air circulating. The lawyers and the judge must have been hot in their robes and wigs. I was hot enough in my summer-weight suit.

During examination-in-chief, the Crown prosecutor asked me to recount the details of my telephone conversation with Vince. In particular he wanted to know what Vince had said about the disposition of the property.

Crown counsel was greatly surprised – and likely elated – when I produced the handwritten notes that I had taken during my telephone conversation with Vince. In court, contemporaneous notes, being much better than a witness's recollection, are very powerful evidence. My notes indicated that Vince had said he had accepted a deal to sell the property for less than it was worth. I had also noted Vince's comment that this was payback for his arguments with Chris. Finally, I had noted, Vince had said we, the investors, would never see the money. My handwritten notes also contained my own personal comment: "I can't explain what has happened to Vince. The whole thing borders on lunacy. Vince seems to have done a very stupid thing here. He may have gone somewhat mad. ..."

In the Cayman Islands, you are either a "Belonger" or you're not. Belongers are citizens of the islands. Everyone else is just a tourist. Vince was not a Belonger.

The jury, however, were all Belongers. They were further impressed by my designation as a Queen's Counsel, or QC. In Britain, a QC is highly regarded, and bestowed on only the most favoured of the legal profession. Cayman still honoured its British heritage, especially in matters of law. My Queen's Counsel designation was about to stand me in good stead.

Vince's defence lawyer stepped up to attempt to cross-examine me. I think he thought it would be easy to discredit me, a mere tourist testifying before a jury of Belongers. His first questions inadvertently handed the balance of power to me.

"Sir," he asked, "you are a Queen's Counsel."

"I am," I replied.

"But a Queen's Counsel can tell a lie. Is that not true?"

"Yes," I answered. "I could tell a lie. But I am here under sworn oath to tell the truth, and I will not lie."

Watching the jury out of the corner of my eye, this response seemed to go over very well with them.

Defence counsel then made his second major mistake.

"Well," he asked rhetorically, "aren't the investors in this property all wealthy Canadians? One of them is even a judge." He said it as if these wealthy Canadians could sustain the loss of their investment with no harm.

He may have thought that the jury, who looked like they were all ordinary folk, might feel less sympathy for people who were well to do, and thus sway them to pity his client and acquit him.

Again, the tactic was misdirected. I turned to the judge, Mr. Justice David Hull, who was seated beside my perch in the witness box.

"As Your Honour well knows," I said, "not all judges are wealthy. The Canadian judge is certainly not wealthy, nor are the other investors. They are all ordinary people who invested their money in a piece of property – money that the accused has stolen."

Justice Hull gave a big smile and nodded his head. It was a signal that he, as a judge, most likely did not have huge personal wealth. That was my cue to look again at the jury's reaction. They were nodding their heads in accord with the judge.

When my testimony had ended, the defence lawyer tried to argue that Vince had given the money from the sale to Chris before he died. The prosecution countered with powerful testimony from Chris's widow, the relevant portion of which deserves to be quoted:

> Prior to his decease my husband … informed me that he had learned that Vince had sold the sole asset of the company, a one-bedroom condominium in Villas Pappagalos in Grand Cayman, for what he told me was less than half its value, and appeared to have pocketed the money. … My husband and I travelled from our home to Tampa Florida for our winter vacation. Shortly thereafter, he became quite ill and entered hospital where he died. …
>
> During the time he was in hospital he indicated to me on several occasions that he was angry at this breach of trust and that he wanted to go to the Cayman Islands when he was better to ascertain exactly what had happened.
>
> I understand that the accused has given a statement to the Royal Cayman Islands Police indicating that he came to Canada and gave the money from the sale of the condominium to my husband. I know this to be untrue. I am certain that I would have been informed had he spoken to or met my husband. Knowing my late husband's feelings on the matter I do not believe that Vince would have escaped unscathed if he dared to meet with my husband.

Chris had stood over 6-foot-2-inches tall, and was a former football player. I agreed with his widow. It was unlikely Vince would have had the temerity to face him in person.

After this evidence, the defence attorney wilted. His case was falling apart.

I was not present for the rest of the trial. The local newspaper reported that Vince was asked to disclose the location of the money from the sale of the condo. He refused to answer. The judge then threatened Vince with contempt of court if he did not answer. After hemming and hawing, Vince said he didn't know. That sealed his fate.

The jury's verdict was front page news in the *Caymanian Compass*. The headline read: "Canadian Millionaire Convicted of Theft." Vince was thrown in jail pending sentencing, but this time there would be no bail, since he was now a convicted felon. In due course, he was sentenced to 2.5 years in prison.

Back in Ottawa I reported to the investors that Vince had been convicted and was now sitting in jail. His Cayman and Ontario real estate remained frozen by the *ex parte* injunction. Vince would be unable to dispose of anything. There was still hope that, in time, we could recover some of the losses.

Vince appealed his conviction to the Court of Appeal in Jamaica. Predictably, the appeal failed. Appeal Courts do not lightly overturn the findings of fact of a jury, and this case was no exception.

In due course, Vince's wife asked if I could assist in having Vince released from prison. My response to her was that all the investors wanted was their money back, plus costs. Although he had "ripped us off," no one wanted to see Vince rot in a Caribbean jail. If the money was repaid, I promised to make a plea for clemency to the authorities.

Apparently, the failure of his "foolproof plan" and several months in jail made Vince see the light. Vince miraculously located the money from the condo sale, and it was repaid, with additional recompense to cover all costs and expenses, to the investors, none of whom lost a cent. Then, with the group's approval, I made a plea to the court for Vince's release. The plea was accepted and Vince was set free. Eventually he returned to Canada, thus ending his island adventures. Mine, however, continued for many years in the Caymans and other islands.

As to the Tale of the Dread Pirate Vince, my only regret was that my friend, Chris, was not with us to see justice served.

Undiscovered Country
– Turks and Caicos

I CAME TO KNOW THE REGULARS in the bar of the Buccaneer Hotel on Seven Mile Beach on Grand Cayman Island. One of these fellows was a Canadian businessman who had come there from Jamaica. His name was Robert, and over several meetings and even more greenies (slang for Heinekens), he shared his story.

Robert's family were prominent in the jewellery business in Jamaica. Life was good, and the business, as well as the island, prospered under British rule. Independence changed all that. Economic pressures and the enormous gap between the haves and the have-nots led to an ever-increasing atmosphere of violence. Eventually it forced Robert and his family to leave Jamaica, hence his presence on Grand Cayman.

For Robert, the breaking point had come one night when he was at home relaxing after a long day's work. Several local men approached the house. The windows and doors had bars on them, and Robert had locked up for the night. The group of men was nonetheless intent on burglary. The story, while heartbreaking, had its irony.

"What are you doing here?" Robert asked the men, from behind his barred window.

"Well, sir," said one of the men politely. "We're going to take things. If you open the door and let us in, no one will be harmed. If we have to break in ... well," the man sighed, "we will be very angry. We might have to kill you. Your choice, man."

Robert knew better than to doubt them. Crime on the island, particularly in the cities, was out of control. The police were unreliable. And he knew that if he made a move to call police, he'd be dead before he reached the phone. He let the men in. They ransacked the place while he watched, but, true to their word, he was not harmed.

The next day Robert and his family left Jamaica forever and made a new home in the Cayman Islands.

A few months later, when I came back to Georgetown to look for more property to buy, I met Robert by chance at the airport.

"I'm on my way to the Turks and Caicos Islands," he said. "My plane is fuelling up now. Why don't you come along?"

Turks and Caicos, like the Caymans, are a British tax haven. The beauty of the islands and its beaches was unequalled in the Caribbean, according to Robert.

But its greatest attraction, Robert said, was that "nobody knows about them."

I was aware that Robert now was becoming uneasy in Grand Cayman. He had told me that he could see a change in locals of late. They called themselves "Belongers" as if to challenge anyone else to stand in their way. They were difficult to deal with, and prices for their services were escalating rapidly. Robert, who had already fled Jamaica, had sensed a similar change pending in the Caymans. He was going over to Turks and Caicos to scout it out as a potential new home.

While recounting this, he renewed his invitation for me to come along. The flight would only take a few hours. Why not hop on board and look the place over?

There's not a lot to do in Georgetown, even at the best of times. I had the time. And Robert was determined to give me the motive. So I said yes and followed Robert onto his twin engine plane.

We took off for Grand Turk Island, where the seat of government is situated. Robert let me try my hand at flying the twin engine plane. I had told him I, too, was a pilot. I was only certified for single engine aircraft. Flying the twin engine was a step up.

I've already told you in "Dread Pirate Vince" my opinion of the Georgetown airport. Next to Grand Turk airport, Georgetown airport was state of the art. Robert landed us on a very rough and short landing strip, parked the plane, and we made our official entry into the Turks and Caicos.

Somehow we managed to hail a cab, and we were driven into Cockburntown, the capital. The drive from airport to capital was essentially a tour of the island. It's that small.

Cockburntown's main claim to fame is that it was a former U.S. naval base. John Glenn's first manned American spaceflight splashed down in the sea near here, as did several of those that followed. The U.S. Navy would proudly steam out from its base in Grand Turk to recover the astronauts and space capsules while the world watched on television

It took only a couple of hours for us to take the measure of the island, so Robert suggested we saddle up again and fly over to Providenciales, another island in the Turks and Caicos chain.

"The future real estate development will be over in Provo," Robert predicted. He was right.

Providenciales, or "Provo," as it was called by the locals, was an undiscovered paradise. The airport runway had been freshly paved by a group of wealthy Americans, headed by a member of the Dupont family, in return for large grants of land on Grace Bay Beach.

Grace Bay surpassed the Cayman's Seven Mile Beach. It was stunning. Azure seas, pristine sand, and at that time virtually no development. The sunsets were breathtaking. The world had yet to discover this halcyon spot. Today, *Condé Nast Traveller* lists Grace Bay as one of the three best beaches in the world.

At that time, Grace Bay boasted a newly built Club Med, and a few private homes. Otherwise, it was undeveloped. And for some unfathomable reason, land was for sale at ridiculously low prices. That's why Robert was checking it out.

My focus at the time was still on Grand Cayman, so I missed out on the opportunity to pick up Provo beachfront land at bargain prices, and have kicked myself ever since. Prices on Grace Bay beach properties today are many hundreds of thousands of dollars per acre. "If only" have to be the two saddest words in the English language. If only I had done this or not done that … .

That's the nature of life. We can't take advantage of all the bargains as they come along.

Back to earlier days … .

Further along the coast from Grace Bay lay Turtle Cove. This was the crème de la crème of Provo, and the only hotel was the quaint, but very elite, The Third Turtle Inn. It was a beautiful little jewel set on turquoise waters. The Dupont-led American investment group had built it to serve as a place for their enjoyment of this unknown paradise. The best of its hotel rooms were on piers right over the water. Large yachts owned by some of the American and European glitterati were anchored there, and the parties, reputedly, were fantastic and non-stop.

The parties must have been pretty hot because, a few years later, the hotel mysteriously burned to the ground one night. It was never rebuilt, and the good time group moved on to new playgrounds.

At the end of the afternoon, Robert and I returned to Grand Cayman.

Back in Ottawa, I shared my adventures with Chris and I described the Turks and Caicos. Always game for a good deal, we made our own exploratory trip together to Provo. Robert was not available to provide a private flight, so the journey was even more adventurous; Ottawa to Miami, then on to Grand Turk, with a final plane change to Provo. But it was safer than the other alternative – a small plane out of Fort Lauderdale. That small plane was, putting it kindly, past its prime and decidedly decrepit. We both preferred the safety of the American Airlines route.

While Provo was attractive, at the time Chris and I were focused on Grand Cayman. Alas, we did not have the time to venture back to Provo together. But I never forgot the beauty of that island. Years later, on my own, I made a small investment in a condominium on beautiful Grace Bay, and my wife Carmen and I still spend time there each winter.

I have also been called to the local Bar – the law society bar, not the Third Turtle Inn facility.

During one of my many visits to the Turks I had become friends with Terrence, a local lawyer who had recently served as the Attorney General of the Turks and Caicos Islands. On the basis of my standing as a Queen's Counsel in Canada, he suggested I join the Turks and Caicos Bar Association, and offered to act as my sponsor. I decided to do so since it could be of assistance in my tax practice, especially when dealing with off-shore matters.

I agreed to present myself as a candidate for the Bar, and awaited the next visit of the presiding judge from the United Kingdom.

During the swearing-in ceremony, the British judge reviewed my credentials and asked if I was a permanent resident of the islands. My sponsor, Terrence, said no, but told the judge I had come all the way from Canada in order to be sworn in as a member of the local Bar. The judge agreed to my call, likely because the request came from the former Attorney General. He advised, however, this would be the last time anyone who was not a full-time resident of the Turks and Caicos Islands would be permitted to join the Turks and Caicos Bar.

I had squeaked in just under the wire, and maintain my membership in good standing to this day.

Swimming
with Sharks

DURING MY EARLY DAYS IN THE Caymans, it seemed like a good idea to get SCUBA certified. My son, Philippe, and I signed up together for a 3-week open water diver course. After completing the mandatory early training, the day came for our first dive in what I called deep water. We were going down about 60 feet.

Our instructor had a special surprise for us. Perhaps we should have realized he had something up his wetsuit when he offered some advice on what to do if a shark was sighted. For the record, if you see a shark, the rule is to get to the bottom and lie very still.

Philippe and I both thought the warning was routine. With the rest of the class, we donned our masks and breathing gear and went down into the deep.

We didn't know that an Italian film crew had just wrapped up an underwater shoot for a scene where divers were attacked by sharks. They hadn't removed the props yet. So when we came upon the mangled and bloody remains of several divers, we all went straight to the bottom and lay very still. For a moment. Until we looked closer and saw that the mangled torsos and limbs were mannequins. And the blood was fake. And there were no sharks swimming about.

It's hard to laugh when you're wearing scuba gear. But later, when the dive was over and we were out of the water, we let our instructor enjoy the joke, and laughed along with him. Talk about getting thrown in the deep end.

At the end of the course we came to our final test – a night dive. It was going to be an adventure.

About 70 feet down, at the bottom of the reef, lay the wreck of the *Oro Verde* (Green Gold). As the locals tell it, the ship was a drug runner that had been loaded to the gunwales with ganga. One night it struck the reef and sank. Word spread like wildfire. It was a race between the locals and the police to see who got to the ganga first.

Legend has it the locals won, and there was one great glorious smoke up on the beach.

We explored the ship on our night dive, but the ganga, apparently, was all long gone.

We were awarded our scuba certificates in a smoke-free ceremony.

The Sting

SWIMMING WITH SHARKS WAS my long-winded way of saying drugs have long been a factor in the Caribbean.

When first I starting going to the Turks and Caicos, there were downed aircraft littering many of the islands in the chain.

I've shared my assessment of the paved landing strip they called a runway in Provo in a number of my Island tales. It was navigable in daylight. Until about 1983, however, the lack of proper lighting made it unsafe to land there at night. Not so on South Caicos, another island in the chain.

The South Caicos airport had a long paved runway, good lighting, and a Shell Oil aviation fuel distributor located right at the airport. It was easy for drug runners from Columbia to land and refuel there on their way to Florida. They were always well served because they paid the locals with fistfuls of U.S. dollars. Under cover of darkness, the refuelled drug planes cruised at an altitude a few feet above the waves, literally under the radar, as they shuttled their cargo to its destination.

It turned out that the Shell Oil distributorship at the South Caicos Airport was owned by the Saunders family. Norman Saunders was also the Chief Minister of the Turks and Caicos Islands. He was a competent politician and bureaucrat, and was well liked by the locals. Unfortunately the British officials apparently did not hold him in the highest regard.

Terrence, my friend who was formerly the Islands' Attorney General, was also Norman's friend and attorney. After dinner one evening at a beach restaurant, Terrence and his wife invited Carmen and I to their home for a nightcap. After a few drinks Terrence relaxed and grew eloquent. He was renting this huge house on the beach, he confided, from Chief Minister Norman Saunders, who was presently serving time in a Florida jail.

And he shared this very sad story of the Chief Minister.

The FBI, Terrence said, had been watching the drug runs out of the South Caicos Island for some time. They knew that Chief Minister Saunders' family owned the fuel depot there.

The FBI watched and waited, and when Saunders flew to south Florida for a conference, the FBI set up a sting and arrested him. They alleged that they had received information that Saunders had been offered big money by the drug cartels to arrange refuelling on South Caicos for planes en route to the U.S.

Saunders' trial was held in the U.S. Terrence was unable to defend him because he was not licensed to practice there.

To this day, we were informed, the true source of the allegations is far from clear.

Terrence, and most of the "Belongers" in the Turks and Caicos, believed that the British Governor of the islands had set up Saunders. Of course, this was vehemently denied and could never be proven. And so Saunders was convicted of being an accomplice to drug trafficking, and sentenced to jail time in a U.S. federal prison.

Terrence had reason for his suspicions. It was common knowledge in the Caribbean that the South American drug cartel had moved in on the Bahamian island of Norman's Cay, and were using it as their main base to run cocaine into the U.S. The Prime Minister of the Bahamas, Lyden Pindling, was believed by them to be "on the take" to the tune of at least $60 million. The Drug Enforcement Agency repeatedly tried to extradite Pindling to the U.S. to face charges, but he was well protected by the drug lords.

The Iran-Contra scandal eventually revealed that the CIA, Colonel North, and some other high officials in the U.S. administration had closed their eyes, and even facilitated the drug trade, to provide funds to finance their war against the Sandinistas in Nicaragua.

Terrence told me that at a time when the Americans were calling for heads, it would have been easier for the British Governor in the Turks and Caicos to sacrifice Norman Saunders in the name of international cooperation. The Norman's Cay drug lords were too dangerous to take down.

Even today the relationship in the Turks and Caicos between the locals and the British government is not the best. Michael Misick, a subsequent Chief Minister, was removed from office by the British over allegations of secret profiteering on land deals. In fact, the situation got so serious that U.K. officials came in, and booted out the governing locals. Then they took over the direction of the island's government. This is greatly resented today and much talk of independence is in the air.

Early in 2014 this same Michael Misick was extradited from Brazil and returned to Turks and Caicos to face charges of corruption and acceptance of unlawful inducements while serving as a minister of the government. His bail was set at $10 million. It was posted, of course. As of the time of writing, he is still awaiting trial.

Shootout at the Provo Corral

PROVO, THE MAIN ISLAND OF TURKS and Caicos, has developed much since the mid-80s. There are condominiums, resorts, shopping centres and restaurants. Nevertheless life can still be wild and woolly.

My good friend, Charley, an ex-pat Scot and now a practicing lawyer in Providenciales, opened my eyes with this true tale of what I call the "Shootout at the Provo Corral."

Charley is married to a local, which makes him a "Belonger." As such, he has all the benefits of a full citizen of the islands. He also is very well connected and, has a good relationship with the authorities and the locals.

A few winters ago, I had the chance to catch up with Charley over a meal and some "greenies" (Heineken). He told me life on Provo was much changed, and that the influx of displaced Haitians in the aftermath of the 2010 earthquake was becoming dangerous. He went on to tell me he had obtained a permit to carry a concealed weapon.

"Why did you do that?" I asked him. "Is it getting that bad?"

"You tell me," Charley replied, and shared the following story.

He had been in a local bar, having a quiet drink with the owner, whom he knew quite well. They were sitting at a table at the far end of the barroom. Two Haitians wandered in, and approached the bartender. One of them pulled out a pistol and the other brandished a sawed-off shotgun. They demanded cash, but the bartender said he didn't have any. The two men looked around the bar, and saw the owner sitting at the back with Charley. Charley looked like a businessman, and they decided he was a better target. The man with the shotgun stomped over to their table, pointed his weapon at Charley, and demanded money.

Charley is a large man, tall and sturdy. You don't take on Big Charley without expecting repercussions. He stared back at the gunman for a moment, then whipped out his concealed pistol and fired a shot. The bullet narrowly missed its target, but the two men didn't wait around for a second shot. They fled post-haste.

Later they were picked up by the police and jailed.

Certainly, our undiscovered paradise was growing up.

Sadly, I cite the headline in the March 1, 2014, edition of *The Turks & Caicos Weekly News*: "Crime Leaps by 24% in 2013."

It's easy for Haitians to get on a boat and land at night on the beaches of the islands in the Turks and Caicos Archipelago. Once there, they work for cash and try to scrape out a living. Or they turn to crime.

The priest of the local Catholic church in Provo has jokingly mentioned to me, in conversation, that he sees many new parishioners each and every week. According to him, while the Haitian men aren't all that religious, their wives and children usually show up for Sunday Mass. Despite their poverty, they come to church dressed in their best. As more and more people flee the devastation in Haiti, the local parishes are growing in ways church authorities had not foreseen.

Today, even my friend Charley, the big Scottish-born lawyer, carries a gun. In the words of Bob Dylan, "Oh the times, they are a-changin'...."

Hotel Dominican Republic

YOU MAY REMEMBER ROBERT, my acquaintance from The Buccaneer Bar in Grand Cayman, who introduced me to the beauties of
Providenciales.

After the debacle with Vince, and the death of my close friend
and co-investor, Chris (see "Dread Pirate Vince"), there was nothing
to draw me back to Grand Cayman. The investment group no longer
had any property there. Land bargains appeared to be better in Provo.
Even Robert had decamped for the Turks and Caicos. He was living
full time on Grand Turk Island, had acquired a real estate franchise,
and was ready to point out the bargains. Robert had also started a
trust company that provided corporate services to non-residents.
(This will become important in a future chapter.)

Ever the entrepreneur, Robert also had real estate interests in the
Dominican Republic, which brings me to the story at hand.

It was a blustery winter day. I was in my Ottawa law office when
Robert called from the bar he owned in Sosua, a small resort town in
the Dominican Republic.

"Paul," he said, "do you feel like a trip to the sunshine?"

The temperature in Ottawa that day was about 20 degrees below
Celsius – before the wind chill. Sunshine sounded good. I said so.

"Well, I have an opportunity for you," Robert said. "I'm working
with some fellows from Ottawa on a land deal here in the Dominican.
They're going to build a hotel, and they want some tax advice. From a
Canadian lawyer. Are you interested?"

I asked who they were, and Robert told me that the group was headed by an Ottawa businessman named Nathan.

I knew Nathan by name. He was reputed to be a straight shooter with a good nose for a business opportunity. Robert gave me Nathan's phone number and I got in touch with him.

I will say right here that Nathan and his gracious wife Marisa have become our very great friends. We met shortly after that first phone call, and I liked both Nathan and the nature of his investment very much. So much so, that I asked to join the group as an investor. In return I would provide my tax advice *pro bono*.

Nathan was delighted. His group of investors agreed to let me join. And so began a new friendship and a new set of adventures.

Our investment group had a great strength in the person of Tony, an ex-pat Canadian who was both a partner in the group, and "Our Man in Sosua." Tony had a great deal of Canadian construction experience. As Our Man in Sosua, he would be able to supervise the work teams building the hotel on beachfront land already acquired.

Tax and travel make for great fun and I do like to get my hands in the pizza dough. I viewed the Dominican hotel project as an exciting undertaking, and was not about to let the experience pass me by. Nathan was of the same mind, and so we travelled together to Sosua to get the ball rolling.

Construction had just begun, but no big contract had been signed yet. We knew that without a trustworthy business network on the island, we would be at the mercy of rogues and pirates who think nothing of taking the "gringos" to the cleaners.

Nathan knew exactly where to start.

"We'll go to the synagogue," he said, "and seek help there. Trust me, my community will look out for us."

Nathan himself was the son of Jewish/Russian parents, who had immigrated to Canada when Nathan was young. He had become a leader in the Jewish community in Ottawa. I trusted his judgement in this matter. And so I went with him to the synagogue.

There we met Samuel, an elderly gentleman who was a successful businessman in Sosua and a respected elder.

SAMUEL AND THE VOYAGE OF THE ST. LOUIS

Samuel was most interested in our project, and in us as Canadians. I shared my surprise at the size of the Jewish community in Sosua. I had not expected to find such a large group in the Dominican Republic.

Samuel smiled and told us the tale of the *St. Louis*. Before the Second World War, the Nazis permitted some prominent Jews to board this ship and set sail in search of asylum. It was a cruel propaganda ploy. Their plan was to have the ship visit a number of countries, including Canada and the United States, where the German Jews on board would ask for refugee status or asylum. Herr Goebbels believed that no one would accept them, and they would have to return to Germany. Indeed, the Nazis used their influence behind the scenes to ensure that these nations would not permit the Jews to land. When the would-be refugees returned, rejected, the Nazis would be able to say nobody wanted the Jews, and that Germany was really quite reasonable by comparison.

It is shameful that Canada, the United States and Cuba turned away a ship of people in such need. As the ship left Cuba, the dictator of the Dominican Republic, whose wife, local rumour had it, was of the Jewish faith, unexpectedly sent word that he would permit the Jews on the *St. Louis* to buy land in Sousa and settle on the island. The story was that the dictator strong-armed a U.S. fruit company to give him the land for free, and then made a large profit selling the land to the refugees, who were happy to buy it.

Of course, not all the passengers on the *St. Louis* had the means to buy land. They, unfortunately, ultimately sailed home to Germany, where many later perished tragically in the horror that was the Holocaust.

Samuel and his family were among the lucky ones who settled in the Dominican Republic. Life in their new land was daunting. Most of the refugees had come from large cities in Europe and knew nothing about farming. Sosua was far from any sizeable urban centre, on an island that was well off the beaten path. The settlers had little time to learn how to support themselves by working the land.

It was quite a story, and Samuel was enjoying the telling of it. A man after my own heart.

The settlers ordered tools and farm implements from Sears Roebuck in the United States he said. And it was a great day when the packages arrived.

Once armed with farm tools, the pioneers went to work. Their first project was the building of a beautiful wooden synagogue – the one we were sitting in.

Next they plowed fields, planted their crops, and built homes. Through dint of hard work, everyone managed to survive. Some grew prosperous, and Samuel eventually started a dairy, with great success. We were shown films documenting the history of the settlement in Sosua, which brought the people of the *St. Louis* to life for us.

Nathan had been correct. The local Jewish community became our unofficial "sponsors" on the island, introducing us to people of good character and reputation who helped us throughout the building of our hotel.

With their help, and the management of Tony, we had no problems during construction, with one glaring exception, when we literally had to call out the army.

But that tale is yet to come.

HANDS-ON CONSTRUCTION

During the months of construction, Nathan and I were back in Ottawa. As it was our custom to holiday in the islands in the winter months, Dominican would be the obvious choice of destination.

Carmen and I flew down to check the progress of our investment. The flight was its own adventure.

Nobody dislikes flying in bad weather. We hit a very bad storm as we came over Haiti. The lights in the plane cabin were flashing on and off. The plane itself was tossed around like an empty tin can in a windstorm. We were hanging on to the seat backs in front of us, and both of us were desperate to get off. When we made a stopover in Port au Prince, Haiti, my wife begged me to leave the flight there. She suggested we could drive across the island into the Dominican Republic and Sosua.

I knew better. Haiti was lawless and crime ridden. A Canadian couple on their own would not be safe, even in a car. I could not risk our safety for the sake of one more short flight, however unpleasant. Reluctantly, we agreed to stay on the plane, and soon after were airborne again and en route for Sosua.

Luck was with us, and we reached our destination safe and sound.

After the storm, of course, the new day dawned sunny and warm, and we ventured forth to visit the construction site of our new hotel.

Construction in the Dominican is largely done by labourers. They use very little machinery because, as one of the Dominican engineers explained, "Machines are expensive and they break down. And we have lots of men who want to work."

The job site appeared very well organized, but we had never seen so many men working on a single construction site.

Tony had engaged Dominican engineers to run the crews. They were promised a bonus if the construction finished on time and on budget. Tony knew it was better for Dominicans to run their own people, rather than "gringos" from North America. He was right. Construction was on schedule and there were no cost overruns.

Our investment group had provided for open-air kitchens on site, where local women would feed the men in rotation as construction progressed. The project was well funded and we were able to get goods and services at lower cost because Tony, by paying cash on the barrel head at the gate as materials were delivered, got a 10% discount.

All went swimmingly well, as the British would say. The hotel was finished on time, and on budget. It was christened "Sosua by the Sea."

The baptism by fire came later.

We opened our doors for business and guests started to arrive. Tony, still Our Man in Sosua, switched his hat from construction over-seer to the operator of the hotel. It looked like we would have smooth sailing. Many toasts were proposed and drunk.

Then a pirate ship figuratively pulled alongside us and we were boarded by modern-day buccaneers. That's when the real fun began. We, the Canadian investors, soon discovered what Tony already knew. In the Dominican you did not operate on the same business standards as we do here in Canada.

The Dominican is a poor society and people need money. They will do almost anything to get it. Tony had made sure he got to know the local authorities well because, if anything went wrong, he knew that going through the courts would be a nightmare.

His foresight paid off in spades. Unbeknownst to us, some wild and crazy things were about to happen.

One day Tony called Nathan in Ottawa, all in a panic.

"We have a problem," he said. "It's about the doors and windows."

"What's the problem?" Nathan asked. "We paid the supplier months ago. The doors and windows should be installed by now."

"That's the problem," Tony said, and went on to explain that the contractor was leveraging him for more money, even though the job was finished and paid for. If Tony didn't come up with something extra, the contractor warned that things would not go well. Tony had tried to bluster it out, and that's when, as the saying goes, the excrement hit the oscillating unit, Dominican-style.

The hotel was full of guests when several trucks arrived suddenly. The contractor and his men jumped out and started ripping out doors and windows. Needless to say, the guests were not happy and Tony panicked. Hence his call to Nathan.

Nathan instructed Tony to get help from our local friends forthwith. Tony called his best resource, who happened to be a retired general in the Dominican Army. To our great relief, the general agreed to help.

I can only imagine the scene. Angry men tearing the windows and doors out of a newly completed hotel. Hotel guests screaming at the men and at management to stop it. Suddenly several Jeeps and trucks with armed soldiers (and the retired general) arrive. Guns were pointed at the looters. Nothing needed to be said. The contractor and his men dropped everything and ran for the hills. The guests cheered. Tony thanked the general, and broke out the booze.

The soldiers partook in the liquid refreshments. The guests did, too. The hotel staff, with some additional hired hands, put back the windows and doors. Calm was restored, and the hotel's stock of liquor was severely depleted, but the guests were happy and tipsy at the same time. Always a good recipe.

Welcome to the Dominican Republic.

Gangster Takeover

SOSUA BY THE SEA WAS SUCCESSFUL from the day it opened. There were few hotels in the area, and little competition then. It was the lull before the tempest.

Nathan called me out of the blue one day. He was calm; Nathan was always calm. But I sensed a slight edge in his voice.

"We've got trouble, Paul," he said. "Those Americans have taken possession of the hotel."

Some months before, Tony had been approached by a group of Americans who offered to buy the hotel at an attractive cash price. We conferred, and instructed Tony to accept the deal. The paperwork was signed, but the money never materialized. As far as we were concerned, the deal was dead.

"They don't have title," I responded. "They have no right to the property."

"It's an extortion ring," Nathan said, still remarkably calm. "They're saying they paid Tony the money, and he's stolen it. When Tony told them there was no deal, they pulled out guns and told him they were staying."

"Is Tony still at the hotel?" I asked.

"No, they forced him out at gunpoint," Nathan said. "I told him to stay out and stay safe until we find an answer. It's not worth a man's life."

I agreed, but now Nathan and I had to figure out what to do.

Nathan suggested we try Foreign Affairs in Ottawa. (We're Canadian. We always try to solve things through government.) Nathan made the call. Foreign Affairs suggested helpfully that we speak to the Canadian representative in Santo Domingo, the capital of the Dominican Republic.

Nathan and I determined to go down to the Dominican. I don't think our wives were very happy at the thought of us flying into danger. Or maybe they just wanted in on the adventure. In any case, they both elected to come with us. We had to get our hotel back.

Once on the island, we drove to Santo Domingo to meet the Canadian bureaucrat. He was very nice to us, and truly wanted to help. Alas, it quickly became obvious that this man had no power to assist us.

We were living something out of a bad Hollywood movie. Our hotel had been seized by gangsters, who were now running it for their own benefit. They had managed to convince the Dominican authorities that they had paid Tony cash for the property, and that Nathan and Tony had absconded to Florida with the money. According to them, the hotel belonged to them and they weren't leaving.

This would have been a good time for my Provo friend Big Charley and his gun (see "Shootout at the Provo Corral").

Nathan and I weren't gun fighters. We both trusted the rule of law. And so we sought out a prominent Dominican lawyer, thinking we could start a lawsuit to oust the gangsters and recover our hotel.

The lawyer looked at us for a few moments before he spoke.

"I recommend you find $10,000 and give it to me to bribe the judge," he said.

Under my breath I muttered to Nathan "Run, don't walk, to the nearest door."

Needless to say, we didn't retain that lawyer. Instead, Nathan spoke to his contacts on the island, and we were referred to other counsel, who agreed to file a lawsuit on our behalf.

The gangster's lawyer filed a bogus defence to our suit. He alleged that that there had been an agreement of purchase and sale between Tony and his client, and that millions in cash had indeed been paid.

We could prove the gangsters never paid us the sale price. Litigation, however, takes time, and if the right palms were greased along the way, the court could too easily be convinced to rule in the gangsters' favour. We were at, as they used to say in the old Western movies, a Mexican standoff.

True to form, Nathan had an ace up his sleeve.

"We must get back to Sosua," he said. "I understand the synagogue roof is badly in need of renovation. Bring your wallet."

I had no idea what the synagogue's roof had to do with our hotel. Nevertheless, I drove back to Sosua with Nathan and off we went to the synagogue. Apparently Nathan was planning a petition to a force even mightier than prayer.

He introduced me to the Chairwoman of the synagogue restoration fund. I didn't need his elbow in my side to prompt me to offer to make a large donation.

As I was emptying my wallet, Nathan whispered in my ear, "Her husband is the American Consul here. He's in thick with the President of Dominican. I'm hoping he can influence the right people for us."

It hit me like a bolt of lightning. Of course. The Canadian government was powerless here. But the Americans! The Yankee dollar gave them a lot of clout in the Dominican. Perhaps they really could help us out.

After I made my very generous contributions to the building fund, Nathan and I shared our tale with the Consul's wife.

She was most sympathetic. "Certainly you must speak to my husband," she said. "Come to the Skyhorse Ranch Sunday at 10 AM. He'll be free then."

Skyhorse Ranch was the official residence of the American Consul.

Bright and early Sunday morning Nathan and I arrived at Skyhorse Ranch. We had coffee and conversation with the American Consul. As the senior American diplomat on the island, he had a direct line to the island's President. It was our best chance and, at that point, our only chance to get our hotel back.

We told him how American gangsters had defaulted on their offer to purchase, and then seized our hotel at gunpoint, alleging that they had paid us in cash. We gave him their names and descriptions so he could check them out. He agreed that it was likely these men were criminals, and undertook to see what he could do.

God and the Americans work in mysterious ways. We heard nothing more from the American consul. Then one day the Dominican police swooped in on the hotel and arrested the gangsters, who were deported – or maybe even extradited – to the United States. What happened thereafter we were never told. In any event, we were more interested in restoring Tony to run Sousa by the Sea.

Tony did return to the hotel, and managed it well for our little group of investors. Several years, and many adventures later, a Canadian conglomerate offered to buy our hotel at an attractive price. Their offer was accepted, and this time the money materialized and the deal was properly closed.

Thus my Dominican chronicles came to an end.

Swan Song

DURING ONE OF MY MANY TRIPS to the Dominican Republic on hotel business, I encountered my friend Robert, who had introduced me to Nathan and the other hotel investors.

He had a very sad tale for me. Robert had just moved away from the Turks and Caicos after a harrowing experience in the Canadian courts.

Among his business interests in the Turks, Robert had started a trust company. A number of Canadian clients sent money down to him, which his company held in trust for them.

One of his Canadian clients was suspected of criminal activity by the RCMP. This made any funds Robert's company held in trust for him subject to scrutiny and even seizure. Robert, of course, was unaware of any of this.

In an extraordinary turn of events, the RCMP, together with the Turks and Caicos Islands Police, surreptitiously entered the premises of Robert's trust company at night, without a warrant, and copied all the records.

Robert was none the wiser. It was business as usual, until he journeyed to Canada to visit family As soon as he landed on Canadian soil, he was charged with aiding and abetting in money laundering. Robert was flabbergasted.

He retained Canadian criminal counsel, of course, and his lawyer pleaded that any information that had been obtained in Grand Turk was against Robert's Canadian *Charter* rights, since there had been no search warrant, and the raid had been surreptitious. Defense Counsel moved to exclude the evidence. On the basis of our law at time, he should have been successful.

Inexplicably, our courts at the very highest level decided that it didn't really matter if the entry by the RCMP and the Turks and Caicos Islands police was illegal. They were going to allow the evidence to be used against Robert, anyway. The basis for the decision related to the way in which the raid had been conducted.

Robert's defense lawyer argued that the RCMP had enlisted the assistance of the Turks and Caicos Island Police, and then staged the raid. The Crown argued that the raid was conducted by the Turks and Caicos police, who were the only enforcement agency on the island with the authority to take such an action. The court decided that since the evidence seized was the product of an action by another enforcement agency, and not a direct action of the RCMP, Robert's *Charter* rights to exclude the evidence did not apply.

Robert's case has set a dangerous precedent for any Canadian doing business in a foreign jurisdiction. It was a powerful warning to many bankers and investment advisors, as well as to their clients.

As a result of this decision, some offshore bank investment advisors got cold feet and suggested that their clients repatriate their investments.

More than one client came my way as a result, and we were able to negotiate many tax amnesties for protection from prosecution and penalties under the terms of the Voluntary Disclosures Program.

Robert was not so lucky.

As a lawyer it is not my place to criticize the decision of our judiciary. I am allowed to say, however, that in my opinion, the court's reasoning was unsound, and Robert should never have been convicted, on the basis that the evidence was illegally obtained.

After Robert's unfortunate legal debacle, he withdrew from the Turks and Caicos entirely. Where he moved I know not. I have neither seen nor heard from him since that chance meeting in the Dominican. Perhaps he hadn't the heart to maintain his Canadian friendships.

Robert's situation exposes how vulnerable any of us can be to the whims of fate.

Of course the RCMP would pass any information it gathers over to the Canada Revenue Agency. Anyone can get caught in the jaws of the Tax Crocodile at any time.

And sometimes this crocodile can't be convinced to let go.

I've Looked
at Tax from
Both Sides Now

Why Tax?

AFTER COMPLETING MY SECOND YEAR at Queen's Law School, I was offered a summer job by Stuart Willoughby, a litigation lawyer who ran a general practice in Kingston, Ontario. (By this time I was the father of a precocious toddler, my son Philippe, who now practices tax law with me). This made life busy for my wife and me, coping as we were in modest accommodations befitting a young law student surviving on the kind support of his family.

As luck would have it, after I reported for work, Stu broke his leg. He was reduced to hobbling around on crutches. Thus it was one of my duties to drive him, in his large green Cadillac, to his court appearances in Kingston and the surrounding judicial districts. This gave me the opportunity to sit with him in court and observe how he argued his cases. My duties also included preparing briefs and digging up case precedents.

Stu was a superb litigator, and usually won his cases. He was a gifted orator who spoke compellingly, with confidence and wit. My colleagues today suggest a bit of his influence rubbed off on me. Certainly I have used whatever skills he imparted to great advantage in court. (See "To Every Cloud a Silver Lining" later in this book.)

As my summer work term ended, Stu and I enjoyed a last beer together. After some kind and confidence-boosting words of praise, which my mentor graciously shared, most likely to keep me inspired to continue in law, he asked what area of law was of interest to me for my own practice. When I said, "Tax," Stu was astounded. "Lawyers don't *practice* tax law!" he shot back.

He had a point. Remember, this conversation took place in 1962. This was before the creation of the Tax Court of Canada as a formal legal body. Tax cases were argued in front of the Tax Review Board, usually presided over by a senior lawyer, rather than a judge. Anyone, including friends, bookkeepers or accountants, was permitted to represent a taxpayer in front of the Board. So if Stu thought there wasn't much opportunity for a *real* lawyer in tax, he wasn't alone.

You must understand that I was born and raised in the Ottawa Valley, and close enough to the federal seat of power to understand that the administration and enforcement of income tax – unquestionably a government cash-grab since the *War Income Tax Act of 1917* invented this new way of thrusting the hands of government into the pockets of the nation – would undoubtedly and increasingly become more and more the domain of lawyers.

To my mind, a young tax lawyer could carve out a niche in this relatively uncharted field. Leave the centuries old litigation matters and real estate deals to the old or unadventurous. I wanted excitement. Tax law was gaining prominence in the United States, where the Internal Revenue Service (IRS) was already legendary for its merciless pursuit of tax cheaters.

The indictment and conviction of Al Capone for tax evasion was still discussed, and recent high profile cases involving movie stars like Judy Garland made tax seem rather interesting, if not glamorous. I knew that where the IRS led, Canada would be sure to follow. (Fifty years later nothing has changed. The Canada Revenue Agency (CRA) today boldly follows in the footsteps of the IRS. Very Canadian. But more on that later.)

So with all the conviction and courage of youth, I stood my ground and told Stu tax law was my choice, and I expected to be very successful in that field.

Stu just shook his head. I knew he was thinking that easier money was to be made in the traditional areas of practice, and what on earth was I thinking when I had a wife and child to support.

Maybe Stu was right, but I had my sights set on starting a tax practice. After completing my third year of law school, followed by articling with a respected Ottawa law firm – where I tasted real estate, estates, litigation, and other general law assignments – I investigated the possibility of joining the Department of National Revenue. (That's what the CRA called itself at that point. It actually was a government department, not the agency it is today.) I was at Osgoode Hall in downtown Toronto by then, completing the Bar Admission Course as the final step before I would be called to the Bar. It was high time I found a means of supporting my family.

Carmen, my beloved wife, is French-Canadian, born and raised in Wrightville on the Quebec side of the Ottawa River. Her family is among the oldest in the province. As her first language is French, we wished to raise our children in both official languages. In order to be perfectly bilingual, French must be their mother tongue. What can I say? Children are always closer to their mother. Toronto, or even Kingston, where I went to law school, were too far removed from "la belle province" for the happiness of my better half. As the saying goes, "Happy wife, happy life."

Tax. Language. Family. Opportunity. It simply all came together in one neat package.

Thus, during the last months of the Bar Ad course, I applied for a position at the federal tax department, and was requested to attend at Ottawa head office for an interview.

Inside the Crocodile

IN 1966, THE TAX CROCODILE – the Department of National Revenue HQ – lived in Ottawa on Sussex Drive, where the Embassy of the United States of America now stands. The Prime Minister's official residence is farther along the river on Sussex Drive.

Back then, National Revenue was in a "temporary" wooden building thrown up during World War II, still doing yeoman service more than 20 years later.

The first time I entered into the jaws of the crocodile was when I attended at National Revenue's head office for my job interview. I was ushered into a rather small office where two old lawyers sat waiting. (I was all of 27, so anyone over 45 would have looked old to me, but I think they were quite senior and seasoned. They were certainly old enough to be intimidating to me, a fresh soon-to-be member of the Bar.)

My academic credentials spoke for themselves, but the National Revenue lawyers seemed mystified as to why a young lawyer would want to start his legal career in the tax department, which was hugely dominated by accountants. I don't know how many other lawyers were at National Revenue then. These two likely represented the lion's share of the legal staff.

My goals were unchanged since my conversation with Stu a few years earlier. I told them that I saw great potential for a lawyer in tax, and that National Revenue was the only place to get hands-on experience, and would be far superior to taking the textbook-dry in-depth tax course offered by the schools.

They looked at each other and smiled. "Quite right," one of them said. "We consider this the equivalent of a post graduate course in taxation. You've come to the right place. You're hired."

The jaws of the crocodile snapped shut on me, and there I was, on the inside looking out.

As soon as I completed the Bar Admission course in Toronto, I was to start there as an appeals assessor. In due course I was called to the Bar, sworn to secrecy in the service of National Revenue, and handed a copy of the Department of National Revenue "Assessing Guide."

It was quite a ride. I went from Toronto, as an appeals assessor, to assisting in other sections of National Revenue to gain on-the-job insights, and then on the road with senior tax litigators following the Tax Review Board across Canada, pleading the Crown's case.

To put all this in perspective, a bit of history is required.

The Tax Review Board was essentially an administrative tribunal whose members were often lawyers. It was intended to be an informal forum for resolving tax disputes. Its decisions could be appealed *de novo* to the Federal Court, which permitted appellants to present a nominal case before the Board in the knowledge that, if they failed, it was possible to present a full case before the Federal Court. A smart taxpayer could bypass the Board entirely and appeal straight to the Federal Court – Trial Division. This trick became so popular, eventually the Federal Court became overwhelmed. To address this problem, the Tax Court of Canada was formed in 1983 as a court of record, and later it became a superior court of record.

IN COURT FOR THE CROCODILE

The lessons I learned at the Tax Review Board, from my first mentor, Frank, a senior tax litigator, served me well. Over time I found my sea legs and gained increased confidence by attending hearings and pleading cases, under his tutelage.

In tax matters, unless the proceedings are criminal in nature, the *onus probandi* – the burden of proof – is on the taxpayer. At the start this was very helpful. Once I had a few cases under my belt, however, it became evident that too many taxpayers came to court poorly prepared, or were assisted by accountants or lawyers who had no idea how to argue a tax case.

When the wins became too easy, I sometimes helped appellants put forward the basis of their case to the adjudicator presiding over the hearing. This was frowned upon. My role was to represent the Crown. But sometimes compassion for a beleaguered soul whose case had merit got the better of my good judgement, and I offered "coaching" as far as possible while still arguing for the "other side."

Litigators were accorded little respect in these hearings, and sometimes a young lawyer had to bite his tongue. This brings to mind the time a hearing member tried to put me down and was startled when I barked back.

I was in Fredericton, New Brunswick, appearing before Colonel Fordham, who was reputed, by all accounts, to be condescendingly arrogant. In person, the Colonel exceeded his reputation.

It is customary in court for a lawyer to introduce himself to the Bench at the outset of his or her appearance. I did so, saying, "Paul DioGuardi, for the Crown."

One hundred years ago, Colonel Fordham might have held up a monocle or some such haughty accessory and peered at me through it. In 1967, in New Brunswick, such affectations were no longer in fashion. Colonel Fordham didn't need a monocle to stare me down and snap, "DIOGUARDI? What kind of a name is that! How do you spell it? It is too hard to say."

I was young, and still wet behind the ears. Yet I, too, was a member of the Bar. The Colonel was many years my senior, but he was, after all, only another lawyer – and an arrogant son of a bitch at that. I looked right back at him and answered, "What do you want me to do? Change it to Fordham?"

Frank had stepped out of the courtroom for a smoke break. He was watching me through a small window in the courtroom door. He saw – and probably heard – what was happening, and swooped into the room before a donnybrook could ensue. He excused me to the Colonel on the grounds of youth, all the while signalling to me to stand down. I did. And with Frank's help won my case.

God guards small children and DioGuardis. (In fact, DioGuardi means "guarded by God.")

Thereafter, any time I appeared before Colonel Fordham I took extra care to ensure my preparation was meticulous. He was quite polite afterwards and we got along just fine.

First Assignment

MY FIRST SOLO FIELD ASSIGNMENT drove home the first rule of the crocodile: Never let go.

I was dispatched to the office of a blue chip law firm in Toronto to secure records related to one of their lawyers. The lawyer in question had been unresponsive to repeated requests from National Revenue.

There I was, young and eager, armed with nothing more than my shiny new law degree and my crocodile smile. Remember, I was now inside the jaws looking out. I presented myself at the law firm and asked to speak to the senior partner. His secretary usually rebuffed all unscheduled visitors, but when I told her I was from National Revenue, and that I was a lawyer, she ushered me into the senior partner's office.

For the sake of the story, we'll call him "Simon."

Simon was engaged in a heated telephone conversation with what appeared to be one of his more difficult clients. (I hadn't started private practice yet, so I didn't realize this was probably par for the course.) To me, Simon came across as tough and savvy, and at the top his game, dealing with Mr. Smart Guy client on the phone.

He looked up in annoyance as his secretary ushered me into his office. I sat down in one of two leather chairs and waited for Simon to finish his call. He kept talking. And talking. So I reached into my pocket and quietly took a card out of my wallet and placed it on the desk in front of him.

Simon appeared to be adept at reading upside down – although he probably practiced that art in other people's offices. He took in the card while lobbing a few pungently definitive statements at the testy client on the phone. He saw the unmistakable logo of National Revenue. Then he saw words like "warrant" and "search" and something about entitling the bearer to many things, and suddenly he appeared less confident about ignoring me.

"I'll get back to you," he said into the phone, and quickly hung up. Then he looked at me.

"What do you want?"

I told him I was there to collect the files for one of his lawyers. "I'll need the records of all his files and transactions for the last 24 months, including the files here in your office. And any that are in storage. This should help." I passed Simon a list of requirements typed neatly on National Revenue letterhead.

He scanned the list and snapped back, "I'm not giving you this."

That was a bit of a slap in the face. But I took it in stride. After all, I was the Tax Crocodile and I carried a card that in National Revenue we had laughingly dubbed "the Absolute Power card." That card was already sitting on Simon's desk. I picked it up and handed it to him.

"Perhaps you need to read this more closely," I suggested. "This authorizes me to enter any premises at any time to seize whatever I deem is required. You can cooperate with me now. Or I'll be back in an hour with the RCMP."

First rule of the crocodile: Never let go.

Simon was surprised that a card could give me such far-reaching powers. He knew this was not the time to bite back. Even a tiger's teeth bounce off the skin of a crocodile.

He punched the intercom button on his desk and called for his secretary. "Give him what he wants."

Shortly thereafter the files and records were in my possession and I delivered them up to Crocodile Central.

In Cahoots
with the IRS

I WAS ACTING WITH ANOTHER LAWYER on behalf of the Crown in a case against the International Telephone and Telegraph Company (ITT). At the time it was among the largest of U.S. corporations. The matter before the Federal Court dealt with the taxability of ITT's purchase of information from a large Canadian telecommunications company.

During preparation for the trial, certain disclosures were required from ITT. I travelled with the other Crown lawyer to New York City to meet with senior counsel for ITT. Back then, there were more lawyers in ITT's legal department than in the entire Canadian Department of Justice. They had little respect for two Crown counsels from Ottawa. ITT's general counsel stonewalled us. He had no intention of providing any disclosure.

We returned to Ottawa empty handed, but I was not yet prepared to surrender.

We had contacts at the Internal Revenue Service (IRS). In fact, there were several IRS agents "in residence" at the American Embassy in Ottawa. I made a phone call to one of them, and shared the frustration of my dealings with ITT corporate counsel.

It took less than an hour.

My phone rang, and the voice on the other end was rather stressed. It was the New York attorney at ITT– he who had treated two Crown counsels as unworthy of his time.

"Mr. DioGuardi," said the Chief Legal Counsel for ITT, "our position is changed. How can we help you?"

I reiterated what I had asked for a few days earlier.

"It will go out by courier tonight," the Chief Legal Counsel replied. "Let me know if you need further clarification."

Immediately I shared this surprising development with the other Justice counsel. He agreed that it was a strange turn of events. We both were curious about how the IRS had brought ITT to heel.

I called our IRS contacts at the American Embassy and asked, "What did you say to ITT?"

The IRS agent started to laugh. "We put the fear of God into them. We suggested that maybe they were overdue for an audit. ..."

Subsequently, together with co-counsel, we won a hard-fought case. I made this my public service swan song, and bade adieu to the crocodile.

I had been offered the opportunity of a lifetime to go into private practice and work with one of the best tax lawyers of the day.

So it was on to civvy street.

Anik A and the Men of Manicouagan

ONCE UPON A TIME IN CANADA, television was not available in the northlands.

Anik A would change that. Due to be launched in November 1972, Anik A was the first of three communications satellites that would provide television signals to the Arctic, making Canada the first country in the world to have a domestic communications satellite in geostationary orbit. More important, English and French CBC television signals would now be carried into the far north.

If you're Canadian, you will understand the importance of television in the north. Without television, the only contact with the outside world is by radio. Radio is fine for keeping abreast of the news, but when it comes to hockey, radio is a poor substitute for a television broadcast.

In 1972, hockey was the game on everyone's mind. Canada, as a nation, was eagerly looking forward to the Summit Series against Russia. It would be the series to end all series. Ultimately, the Summit Series broadcasts grabbed the highest viewership ratings in Canadian television history – particularly on September 28th, 1972, when the country as a whole dropped everything to watch breathlessly as Canada beat Russia 6-5 in the final seconds of the game.

The launch of the Anik A satellite would give everyone access to the National Hockey League (NHL) television broadcasts in English and in French. People in the north could hardly wait. The pressure was immense to launch Anik A on time.

Here's how this tax lawyer from Ottawa ended up at the heart of the matter. Note that this all happened before the hockey frenzy of September 1972.

A group of ex-pat engineers, mostly American, had been subcontracted by government communications agencies to work on the Anik project. They were lured by the promises of high pay and the tax benefits of being engaged as independent contractors. In fact, they were told by the bureaucrats who engaged their services that there was too much paperwork involved to hire them as employees.

Revenue Canada, however, had a different take on the matter. The tax agency had made an arbitrary decision that, notwithstanding the subcontractor agreements in place, these engineers were in fact employees of the government department who had hired them to work on the Anik project. The engineers had been reassessed as full-time employees. With penalties and interest, the amounts owing to Revenue Canada were substantial. Far beyond the ability of most of them to pay.

The tax authorities then and now have always used this standard test to determine if contractor agreements genuinely represent independently contracted employment.

- The worker is usually free to work when and for whom he/she chooses and can provide services to different parties.
- He/She does not have to perform the services personally. The worker can hire another to either complete the work or help complete the work.
- He/She can normally choose the time and the manner the work will be performed.
- The worker advertises his/her services to the public.
- He/She does not need to be at the payor's premises to perform the contracted duties.
- The worker can accept or refuse work from the payor.

- The relationship between the client and the worker does not present continuity, loyalty, security, subordination or integration.

These engineers worked out of the government's premises. They were provided with equipment, vehicle transportation, and cell phones. All their business came from one client. They were provided with health and dental benefits. Finally, they could not take on other work during the contract period.

The language as written in their employment contracts had trapped them, and now the crocodile was moving in with his jaws wide open. The engineers came to me as a group. They believed my experience as an ex-Revenue lawyer, now on the other side in private practice, would give them an inside edge. They were right. I took the case with delight.

It was going to be a tough fight, until one of the engineers handed me an ace.

Anik A was on a very tight work schedule. The engineer reminded me that the satellite was scheduled for a NASA launch in early November. If Anik A wasn't ready on time, it would not go into orbit in 1972. If Anik A was not in orbit by November, people in the north would face another long winter without television (read *hockey*) broadcasts. And if Revenue Canada didn't back down, the engineers would discontinue their work on the project. They couldn't afford to continue working as employees with huge tax assessments to be paid.

Which brings us to the men of Manicouagan.

The province of Quebec was building a massive hydro-electric project in the wilds of their north. Thousands of workers had been shipped up to build the dam and the hydro-electric station. Thousands of men who lived and breathed hockey. Knowing that they would be listening to the much heralded Canada-Russia series of 1972 on the radio only, I knew that by the time of the first snow fall (and snow comes early in Manicouagan) they would be ravenous for TV. They had been promised television in time for the coming NHL season. If Anik A didn't launch as planned, there would be riots. Or worse.

I'm not making this up. According to media reports of the day, the men in Manicouagan were bored out of their skulls. There had already been riots, and many had abandoned their work on the project because they couldn't stand the isolation. There was even a popular song that described their loneliness at "la Manic." The opening line of the lyric was: "*Si tu savoir comme on s'ennuie à la Manicouagan.*" English translation: "If only you knew how lonely we are at la Manic."

The future of the Manicouagan project was in jeopardy. The Quebec government was counting on television broadcasts to keep the men calm – or at the very least, keep them in Manicouagan and on the job.

That was my ace. I could pit the Quebec provincial bureaucrats, who desperately needed Anik A to launch on schedule to save the morale of the men in Manicouagan, against the federal communications agency bureaucrats, who, for their own set of reasons, needed Anik A to launch on time, and hope to catch Revenue Canada in the crossfire.

This was a time when the politicians in Quebec would seize on any excuse to rage at the incompetence of the federal authorities, and wave the flag of sovereignty and separation. The federal government in Ottawa would not want a *mêlée* of this proportion. If the government threw Revenue Canada under the wheels of the bus to save face, well ... how could that be bad?

I launched my first warning shot at the communications agency bureaucrats.

I advised them as follows:

1. You engaged my clients as independent contractors.
2. You hired them on the basis that they would not be subject to taxation as employees.
3. You have taken no action on behalf of these contractors to refute the Revenue Canada assessment.
4. The terms of the engineers' contracts have been materially changed without their consent.

5. The engineers cannot continue to work as employees.
6. The engineers demand to renegotiate the terms of their contracts.
7. All work on the Anik project will cease until such time as acceptable terms are renegotiated.

Good luck in meeting the launch date, gentlemen!

And have a nice day.

With that, the proverbial you-know-what hit the fan.

The communications agency mandarins were furious. "You can't do that!" they screamed, in person and in writing. "If the engineers stop work, we will sue."

"Go ahead," I replied, in person and in writing. "The Canadian government broke its agreement to engage my clients as independent contractors. I will countersue."

Meanwhile work on Anik A stopped. But not for long. Too much hung in the balance.

I remind you again that all this was happening at a time when French-speaking politicians and bureaucrats had taken control of the levers of federal power in Ottawa. If Quebec could blame the Feds for catastrophic delay on their massive hydro-electric project, there would be serious political fallout. They would scream at the top of their lungs, "C'est la faute du Fédéral!" In those days anything that went wrong in Quebec was "la faute du Fédéral."

I can only image what went on behind closed doors in the corridors of power. The auditors at Revenue Canada likely didn't know what hit them. There was not an auditor in the land brave enough to wear the blame for delaying the launch of the communications satellite that would bring French-language television broadcasts (read *hockey*) to the men at Manicouagan. At this point nobody cared much about the rest of the Arctic. Manicouagan was the political hot potato, and I kept the potato red hot as it passed from hand to hand.

The Taxman was unaccustomed to having his *cojones* squeezed that hard. To me, the turnabout was fair play.

Presumably the Minister of National Revenue was told, undoubtedly in impeccable French, and perhaps even by the Prime Minister himself, the equivalent of "Turn off your asinine tax auditors."

He, in turn, would have turned on his tax auditors and told them the equivalent of "Make this all go away or there will be hell to pay!" The poor little tax auditors must have peed their pants.

Whatever was said, by whom, and to whom, Revenue Canada vacated the assessments.

Let's hear it for hockey and the men of Manicouagan!

A Tea Party of a Different Flavour

AS MY TAX PRACTICE GREW, it became part of the Ottawa tax establishment. I was the go-to lawyer for many tax matters, including such arcane issues as import tariffs. As such, I assisted a variety of large corporate clients to resolve vexatious situations with the tax authorities. I was often also called on to offer opinions and advice. It made for a colourful practice.

One such matter came to me with a call from the VP of marketing for the largest importer of tea products in Canada. He had a serious problem with tariff classification for his line of herbal tea.

The Director, Industrial and Consumer Goods Classification Tariff Programs of Revenue Canada Customs and Excise, had ruled that herbal tea should be subject to the same customs and excise treatment as regular teas.

Taxation of tea has, historically, been a volatile issue. The Boston Tea Party springs immediately to mind. However, this was shaping up to be a tea party of a very different flavour. My interest was piqued. I wanted to follow this issue as it unfolded.

Apparently the aforementioned Director had based her ruling upon statements received from the Tea and Coffee Association, the majority of whose members did not manufacture or sell herbal teas. Tea was tea, they said, and all tea should be taxed the same way.

The members of the Tea and Coffee Association were direct competitors of my client. It was in the best interest of their collective businesses to ensure that herbal teas were subject to the same tax treatment as imported teas and coffees. Why should herbal teas get a tax break at the expense of the mainstream products?

My client, the purveyor of herbal teas, wanted to challenge the ruling. It was his position that herbal teas should be classified, not as teas, but as "a vegetable material for use as flavourings," under Tariff Item 9050-1. This delightfully obtuse definition would permit this product line of herbal teas to bypass the usual tariffs on imported teas and enter Canada on a duty-free basis.

I was in sympathy with my client's position – if only for the challenge of the battle.

I had discussions with the senior official at Customs and Excise, but she was adamant that herbal teas would be treated as tea. The ruling would stand. A very British position, I thought.

In the spirit of a revolutionary, I recommended to my client that we meet with the Deputy Minister of National Revenue (Customs and Excise) at his offices in the Connaught Building, on MacKenzie Avenue in Ottawa. I did not expect much of the meeting, and was already preparing for court. It was worth a try, however, and my clients were impressed that I could obtain such quick access to the Deputy Minister, who unbeknownst to them, was a long-standing friend. They flew in from Toronto, and we met with the Deputy Minister. Predictably, he stood by the decision of his officials. We would have to appeal the classification.

Our Notice of Appeal sought a declaration that various "herbal teas" imported by the appellant should be classified as "vegetable materials for use as flavourings, n.o.p...." under Tariff Board Item 9050-1 rather than "prepared foods and beverages, including ingredients therefore, for human consumption;...all of the foregoing which otherwise would be classified under Tariff Item 71100-1."

The goods that we described as "herbal teas" were, and presumably still are, available in a variety of flavours that include Gentle Oranges,

Almond Pleasure, Tasty Spice, Cinnamon Apple, Carob Mint, Quietly Chamomile, Tangy Orange, Citrus Sunset and Lemon Soother.

These herbal teas were composed of vegetable material, such as leaves, seeds, peels, flower roots, etc., and in some cases contained flavours that were natural extractives, such as orange oil, fixed in a sucrose matrix. In the manufacture of herbal teas the ingredients are weighed according to the variety batch formula, then dumped into a double coned blender and blended to make a uniform mixture referred to as the indeterminate blend. The indeterminate blend is then fed from hoppers into constanta tea bag machines, at which point it presents the appearance of tea.

It was an uphill battle in court. Tea was tea. What was the difference, for example, between a black tea like orange pekoe, and an herbal tea like Gentle Oranges? Weren't they both leaves that, when brewed in boiling water, created an infusion which we call "tea?"

I had a surprise expert witness in my tea cup. Dr. Alexander B. Morrison, the former Assistant Deputy Minister, Department of National Health and Welfare, had been one of the chief scientists employed by the Government of Canada. He held a doctorate in biochemistry and physiology. After leaving government service, he took a position as a professor of nutrition at the University of Guelph. That is where I located him, and briefed him on my case. Dr. Morrison agreed to appear for us. He believed he could support our position.

Just watching the face of opposing counsel when I called Dr. Morrison to testify was worth all the work I had put into this file. Counsel's jaw almost hit the floor.

Dr. Morrison's testimony was a litigator's dream come true. He said that he had examined the goods in issue from the point of view of their composition and their intended use to determine their nature. In terms of their composition, in his view, they were plant materials, and their intended use was clearly that of "imparting flavouring to water when added in the form of a sachet to a cup of boiling water and allowed to steep."

Calling these flavourings "tea" was simply a marketing label, for the purposes of consumer familiarity, and not a product definition.

The unexpected testimony of one of the Government of Canada's former chief scientists brought our appeal over the top. It was a case of putting a wolf to catch a wolf – or a crocodile against another crocodile.

No one was up to the challenge of challenging this expert.

The other side caved and the Tariff Board allowed our appeal. Herbal teas, despite the misleading marketing label, were not tea, and no duty was applicable.

I believe the ruling stands to this day.

Mon Ami, Jules

ON OCCASION, WHEN FACED WITH a very difficult case, such as the aforementioned "Tea Party," I would discuss it on a no-name basis, with *mon ami*, Jules. He was a Superior Court judge in Quebec, and he was sharp as a tack. Typically, the conversation would go like this.

"Jules, *mon ami*, suppose I was appearing before you, arguing (and I would share a few facts of the matter, to test my theory of the case). ... How would you argue it?"

Jules would consider what I had said, with Bencher-like gravity, and then he might say, "I might put it this way..." and he would sketch out his own line of argument on the matter. Then he would smile and say, "It would be a winning argument – if I were hearing the matter."

Every lawyer needs a helping hand, or an angel on the shoulder. In the tale to come next, my help came from an unexpected silver cloud.

But before we go there, indulge me with a digression. (You were so warned at the outset of our travels together.)

Canadian summers are glorious, but all too short. We squeeze every last moment from them with as many outdoor activities as possible. One my favourite outdoor pastimes is the backyard barbeque. It's a great way to relax with friends on a sultry evening.

One summer night, my wife and I gathered on our patio with a group of good friends: my friend Jules, the wise sage, and his wife Bernadette; Pierre and Lucille; and Bernard and Hugette. *Mon ami* Bernard is small of stature, but large on mirth. We call him *p'tit* Bern.

On this fine summer evening, after our meal, which we ate al fresco, we stayed chatting and sipping our wine until the sun went down and Canada's other summer tradition – the mosquitos – descended. Grabbing the wine and our glasses, we repaired to the screened gazebo at the back of my garden. We lit a hurricane lamp and in the golden light talked and joked. Jules and Pierre serenaded us with song. They were both quite talented, particularly Pierre who had performed on the CBC radio in his younger days. We toasted the singers with more wine as the night grew darker and the candle in the hurricane lamp burned low.

There's a special camaraderie in a soft summer night. We were there together, happy, trusting, sharing stories. Then someone announced they had brought a Ouija board. They wanted to play. So eight grown men and women gathered around the large round table in the centre of the gazebo to join hands and "reach out" to the spirit world.

One of the fellows, I don't remember who, joked about levitating the table. We were all skeptics. Still we joined hands to create a circle and got ready to close our eyes.

"*Un moment!*" cried *p'tit* Bern all of a sudden. "Put out the candle. It works better in the dark." So the candle went out and we joined hands and closed our eyes, and our ring leader lightly rested his fingers on the Ouija board waiting to see if the spirits would talk to us. Of course there was much giggling, and shushing of each other. And nothing happened ... and nothing happened ... until suddenly the table shuddered and slowly started to rise and turn a little to the left.

The ladies screamed and jumped out of their chairs. The men didn't scream, but we were startled enough to grab for the lamp and strike a match to light the candle.

That's when we saw the spirit of the Ouija board. It was *p'tit* Bern, under the table on his hands and knees, grinning ear to ear as he used his back to push the table off the ground.

Such a funny fellow. He gave us a good fright and then a great laugh. Of course to this day he says he was only under the table to catch the ghost.

This tale has nothing to do with sage counsel or the serendipity of the next story, but it reminds me of Jules, who has gone to his well-earned eternal rest. Ouija board notwithstanding, I like to think a bit of his spirit stays with me, when I need it.

To Every Cloud
a Silver Lining

ERNIE WAS A FIGHTER. OVER THE years he worked very hard to build his industrial bearings business. Success gave him the means to buy the car of his dreams – a Silver Cloud Rolls Royce.

Ernie loved his Silver Cloud, and he wasn't too proud to put it to work. Shipments of industrial ball bearings were delivered routinely to clients via Silver Cloud. It greatly impressed clients that the president of the company cared enough to make personal deliveries, in such style. And because the Rolls did double duty as a personal vehicle and delivery car, Ernie always expensed a portion of the car's cost.

The Taxman, alas, challenged the deduction. Ernie was livid and had no intention of letting the crocodile win.

As instructed, I took the case to the Tax Court. The judge there did not accept the evidence and my representations that Ernie truly used the Rolls to deliver ball bearings to his clients. Revenue Canada's assessment was confirmed and our appeal dismissed.

Ernie refused to quit. I knew that in Canada at that time nothing above the expenses of the top of the line Cadillac had ever been allowed as luxury car deductions for business use. Nevertheless, at Ernie's insistence, I filed a notice of appeal to the Federal Court. In those days you could take a case to the Federal Court for a trial *de novo*. If I could win this case, it would set a strong precedent.

Once in court, the judge heard our opening remarks. I called my client to the witness stand and started to question him. The judge heard the first few questions and answers and then, unusually, asked me to sit down while he addressed his own questions to Ernie. I was surprised. But when the judge asks you to sit, you sit.

His Honour, Mr. Justice Cattanac, took over the questioning. He asked Ernie, "What kind of Rolls do you have?"

Ernie beamed. "A Silver Cloud."

"That's what I drive!" said the judge.

"You knew this!" said the Department of Justice lawyer representing the CRA, leaning across the aisle to hiss at me. "You knew this judge drove a Rolls Royce. He shouldn't be hearing this case."

I just shrugged. The judge and his Rolls were news to me, too, but who was I to cry foul?

I couldn't have planned it better.

A lengthy conversation ensued between the judge and Ernie as they compared the merits of their respective Silver Clouds. I waited. The Justice lawyer fumed. Ernie smiled and chatted on. Finally, the judge turned and addressed both counsel as follows:

> I have decided this case. I drive a Rolls Royce. This gentleman drives his Rolls Royce every day. He delivers business materials in it. I see no reason to disallow his deduction for vehicle expenses simply because the vehicle happens to be a Rolls Royce. He is entitled to drive the car of his choice and use it for business deliveries. Therefore, I am allowing the full deduction of his automobile expenses.

Word travels fast. My phone was buzzing with calls from accountants and tax practitioners across the country. "How the hell did you do that?" they kept asking. "A Rolls Royce for deliveries?!!"

The real answer was sheer dumb luck. We hit a judge who drove a Rolls Royce!

Talk about a Silver Cloud lining.

Not Always Tax

I Need a Cheque for a Million Dollars – Yesterday!

EARLY IN MY PRIVATE PRACTICE, I was approached by a group of Italian-Canadians who wanted to form a national congress. They were headed by Alfredo, a very successful Montreal businessman who had founded Canadian Petrofina, which later became part of Petro-Canada.

During our discussions, Alfredo stressed the importance of structuring the congress in such a way that it could be used for both charitable and non-charitable work. He then suggested we get advice from the Canadian Jewish Congress, who, Alfredo believed, had created and successfully managed such a structure for well over half a century. He had some good friends who were senior members.

We were in Ottawa; they were in Montreal. An approach was made and, in due course, Alfredo and I were invited to their Montreal office.

To say that we were cordially received is an understatement. We were fully briefed on how the Canadian Jewish Congress (JC) was organized, and many suggestions were offered in the spirit of helping avoid the lessons the JC had learned by trial and error.

Armed, and forewarned, I incorporated the National Congress of Italian-Canadians as a federal, non-charitable, non-profit corporation, and shortly thereafter incorporated the National Congress of Italian-Canadians Foundation as a federal charitable organization.

Both organizations have been very successful over the ensuing years, and were utilized to come to the aid of Italians in times of great stress.

In 1976, a series of earthquakes struck Friuli in northern Italy. The National Congress collected money to build new housing: a project of single family homes, and two residences for seniors. The endeavour was christened "Borgata Canada," – Residence Canada, as a lasting reminder of the generosity of the Canadians who came to the aid of their Italian "brothers."

Much later, Mother Nature hit Calabria with a series of devastating earthquakes. The situation was much worse than it had been in Friuli, and huge amounts of money were needed to rebuild the towns that had been destroyed.

At that time, the Liberal government was in power in Ottawa, and many of their high officials were from the city of Montreal. Since the president of the National Congress was one of the business leaders of that city, he was well connected to the corridors of power. A meeting between the appropriate government mandarins and the executive of the National Congress was soon arranged on Parliament Hill. As legal counsel to the Congress, I was requested to attend.

During the discussions, the federal Government of Canada agreed to contribute $1 million towards the Calabria reconstruction effort. The funds would come from the Canadian International Development Agency (CIDA). We thanked the feds profusely, and then requested that the money be made available immediately. People in Calabria were living in tents, and the need for housing was dire.

I knew that CIDA had an annual budget of well over a billion dollars, but it had surprised me that money for a *European* relief fund would be coming from an agency set up to assist third world countries. Apparently, CIDA was flush with cash and, more important, was the only agency that could cut through the red tape of bureaucracy to issue a cheque speedily.

I welcomed the decision and, since I was the one tasked with getting the cheque, went immediately to work.

Fortunately for me, the chief legal counsel for CIDA was Jean-Pierre, who happened to be a very good friend of mine. I took advantage of the connection to get some quick action on the delivery of the relief funds.

Herewith is the gist of an amusing telephone conversation between two old friends, both lawyers, both well-versed in the ways of government:

PD: Bonjour, Jean-Pierre. It's Paul. How are you today?

(Pleasantries ensue)

PD: Jean-Pierre, you know that I represent the National Congress of Italian-Canadians. The feds have agreed to give us $1 million to help with the Calabria earthquake, and we need the cheque *tout de suite*. I've been told to get the cheque from CIDA, since it's the only agency that does anything in less than an eternity.

JP: Are you kidding me? CIDA is for international development in the third world. You're talking about Europe.

PD: Trust me, Jean-Pierre. Just take the request up the line. They'll give you the green light on the cheque. A million dollars, they said. And we need it yesterday.

JP: It doesn't make sense to me, Paul, but, since it's you, I will check and get back to you.

(3 hours later)

JP: Paul, seems you are right. I have authorization to make out a cheque for a million dollars to the National Congress of Italian-Canadians for the relief of victims of the Calabria earthquake disaster. But there is one problem. I have to make a contract, which you will require them to sign, before I can disburse the funds.

PD: Make whatever contract you want, Jean-Pierre. You can do it on a scrap of toilet paper if you like, but I want the million dollars *pronto*.

Long story short, in a few days, after a bit of back and forthing, Jean-Pierre and I were able to get the National Congress of Italian-Canadians to sign a *pro forma* contract, and I got a cheque for a million dollars.

It was immediately put to good use, funding the construction of housing for the earthquake victims in Calabria. As with the Fruili relief projects, all the new villages and buildings were named after Canada. It would have been nice if there had been a Casa Jean-Pierre, or a Villa DioGuardi, but that's not how it works. And in any case, I jest.

All the politicians and bigwigs travelled to Calabria to attend the grand opening of the new buildings, and of course they took all the compliments. The people of Calabria were more than grateful for the assistance from their Canadian compatriots.

As far as I know, nobody ever asked a question in the House of Commons about why the Canada International Development Agency wrote the cheque for a relief project in Italy. If ever they do, you have the answer.

Born Under a
Star of David

I CAME INTO THE WORLD AT THE Ottawa Civic Hospital, more years ago than I care to confess. Back then, mothers remained in hospital to recuperate for several days before being allowed to go home with the new baby. My mother, Laura, shared a room with Sarah, a woman of the Jewish faith, who had also given birth to a boy. He would be named Gerome on the occasion of his *bris*.

During their days of "lying-in" as the Victorians had so quaintly called it, the two new mothers talked for hours on end about all things related to motherhood, newborns and baby sons. You know where this is going. The answer is "yes."

My mother was impressed and opted for the *goyim* equivalent of the procedure.

Such was my introduction, essentially at birth, to the Hebrew nation. It has been a very happy association over the years.

Gerome and I reconnected in law school at Queen's University in Kingston. We even lived across the hall from each other, and, through pure chance, we were in the same class throughout. We worked well together, and he helped me to succeed in my law studies. Perhaps the hospital bonding at birth made us feel like kindred spirits.

My wife, Carmen, and I, a young couple living in a small apartment with our own new baby, were embraced by Gerome and his wife, Sarah, almost as family. Gerome, it seemed, was a very finicky eater.

Sarah loved to cook. And she was a very good cook. Given Gerome's pickiness, Sarah turned to me to sample the new dishes she delighted in preparing. After I finished, she would ask: "Will Gerome like this?" If I was very hungry I might suggest I wasn't sure ... and have a second helping. I rarely answered "no."

Thus began my lifelong love of Jewish cooking, and respect on other levels for the "chosen people."

After Gerome and I successfully completed our first year in law school, he and Sarah invited us to synagogue for a service of thanksgiving. Carmen was born and bred in the province of Quebec. I was from an Italian-Canadian family. This was the first time either of us had ever gone to a synagogue. When we arrived, Sarah took Carmen by the arm and led her to the back of the temple to sit with the women. I can't say she liked taking a back seat, but it was their temple and visitors must observe the protocols.

Sitting upfront with Gerome, I was baffled by the prayer book, which was not only in Hebrew, but opened from the back (or at least it was for me), and then was read from right page to left page. Every once in a while the older man sitting beside me kindly pointed to a place in the text to show me where we were in the service.

At one point he turned to his neighbour and muttered, a little too loudly, "What is the world coming to when our young men cannot even follow our book from back to front!?"

Dancing the Horah

WHILE NATHAN AND I WERE STILL in the thick of our Caribbean adventures (if you've skipped ahead without reading "Pirates of the Caribbean," this would be good time to skip back), Carmen and I were invited to Nathan's granddaughter's wedding.

The young lady was to marry the son of an ultra-orthodox rabbi. While Nathan was devout in the profession of his faith, he did not consider himself among the ultra-conservatives. His granddaughter's matrimonial choice would introduce some strict new traditions to the family.

So I discovered, when I accepted the invitation and told Nathan I would be pleased to dance at his granddaughter's wedding.

My old friend laughed. "You'll be dancing with me, then," he chuckled, and then went on to explain that in an ultra-orthodox wedding, the men and women sat separately throughout the ceremony, ate separately and even danced separately.

Fearing a major *faux pas*, I sought guidance from Ken, a lawyer colleague of long-standing acquaintance. He was reform in the practice of his faith, and surprised me by admitting that, in the eyes of the ultra-orthodox, he was not even considered a Jew. He wondered how a Gentile like me – and a Catholic at that – had even been extended an invitation. He had little insight to share, so I gave up on the preparatory work and simply looked forward to the happy event.

The day of the wedding my wife and I gamely arrived at the service. Afterwards, she was escorted to sit behind a curtain with the bride and the other women, while I was with the groom and his male guests behind another curtain. The separations continued during the ensuing celebrations. An orchestra separated the men from the women. The women stayed behind a curtain and the men danced, and drank to the health of the young couple. All supped on a superb dinner.

Soon after the meal, the younger men rose and formed a circle. The music was rollicking and they quickly warmed to the mood. They danced, and clapped, and laughed, and raised the groom high on a chair. They wrapped their arms around the shoulders of the fellow on either side, and danced together in a circle. One by one other men joined in, swelling the circle so that it filled the dance floor. I couldn't resist the fun and the music, and soon I was on my feet, my arms around the shoulders of those on either side of me, dancing and laughing and really having fun.

Nathan, however, had not joined in. He was standing at the side of the dance floor, removed from the frivolity. Not for long. As the ever-growing circle of men twinkled by him, I reached out, grabbed his arm, and pulled him into the dance. He laughed. I laughed more. And we danced and danced until our faces were flushed and we truly were breathless.

I later discovered that they call this dance the horah. It's a wonderful dance. And it's a lot of fun.

When next I met my lawyer friend, he asked how we made out at the big wedding.

"Best wedding ever," I responded. And when a second orthodox wedding invitation was extended, Carmen and I accepted the invitation with delight. It too was most memorable. We are always honoured to be included in these celebrations. Although my wife has suggested that she would prefer to sit with me.

An Unwanted Guest

YOU MAY REMEMBER MY EARLIER tale about the boat people from Nazi Germany who finally found safe harbour in the Dominican Republic after being refused entry by many countries, including our own (see "Hotel Dominican Republic").

Canada, of course, eventually reversed its position, and during and after WWII many Jews found refuge here. The persecutions of the 30s and 40s remained fresh in the hearts and memories of those immigrants and their families. Despite the Canadian attitude of inclusion and accommodation, situations did arise that challenged that delicate balance.

I had one such case in my law practice, wherein my client owned a private event venue that he rented out for weddings and other gatherings. He was an Italian-Canadian, well-established and respected beyond the boundaries of his community. He had signed a contract to rent his premises to a group for a guest speaker event. When he signed the contract, he was unaware that the theme for the event was the Holocaust. Members of the Jewish community came to him and advised that the guest speaker from the U.K. was a well-known Holocaust denier.

My client was confused. "What is a Holocaust denier," he asked. "Should I be concerned?"

When I explained to him that there were indeed people who professed that the Holocaust was a Jewish fabrication, he rightfully concluded that he could not in good conscience permit the event to take place in his premises.

My client had, of course, executed a legally-binding contract with the group hosting the event. Gentlemanly discussions have been known to resolve such situations. In that spirit, I contacted the group and offered to refund in full all monies paid to my client. They refused. Their event had been widely promoted and they were not interested in releasing my client from the contract.

I advised my client that his remaining option was to make an application to the court to permit us to rescind the agreement. And so to court we went.

I first met opposing counsel in the courtroom. I had already been advised that he was Jewish, but "non-practising." I thought it sad that he would take a case to defend the rights of a group hosting a speaker who was a Holocaust denier. Lawyers often do argue cases that are not consistent with their personal values. This lawyer was after a high profile win.

This contest between Gentile and Jew was bizarre, to say the least.

The other lawyer argued that a contract had been signed, and it must be honoured. Furthermore, in his view, the hall was a public place, and any speaker there had the right of free speech. The court could not censor the theme of the speech on the grounds that it was distasteful to the owner of the hall. Therefore, my opponent argued, the court should not abrogate the hall rental agreement.

I fought back with the assistance of legal precedents (and with the kind help of co-counsel, who was a prominent lawyer in the local Jewish community) to argue that the hall, being owned by my client, was private premises. It was, therefore, not a public establishment and the right of free speech was just a red herring. Further, I argued, at the time the contract was entered into, my client was not informed about the topic of the speech, and therefore was not able to exercise his free will to decline to rent to the group. Now that he understood that, effectively, the proposed event in his premises was to preach hatred against members of the Jewish faith, he was entitled to decline to permit his establishment to be used for that purpose.

After a heated battle, to my client's great relief, the court accepted our argument and rescinded the contract.

I don't remember if the event was cancelled, or simply arranged for a different venue. At the end of the day, my only concern was protecting the interests of my client.

Thanks to the court, that day justice was well served.

My client's actions were well appreciated by the community.

The Return of the Ring

THERE WAS A COMMOTION IN THE reception area of my law office. My secretary hurried into my office, clearly flustered, and asked if I would see some people who had not made an appointment, but were insisting that they speak to a tax lawyer.

"They say they're desperate," my secretary said. "Will you see them?" Something about the people had captured her sympathy. So, trusting in her judgement, I agreed to meet them. She ushered in an older man and his daughter, who was weeping uncontrollably, and kept repeating, "They took my ring! They took my ring!"

Between sobs, the young woman's story came out.

Her name was Ruth and she was a bride-to-be. The groom was a doctor in New York City. They were to be married there in 3 weeks' time. She had just returned from New York to finalize wedding plans in Ottawa with her own family. Her re-entry into Canada was the cause of the turmoil.

In New York, her husband-to-be had given her an enormous diamond engagement ring. (Apparently he knew an Orthodox Jewish diamond merchant who had made it affordable for him to purchase a "skating rink" for his bride.) Ruth was delirious with joy. It was a cherished possession. She would show it off with pride to everyone at home, in the final days before she returned to New York to be married.

She had flown from New York to Montreal, and that's when Murphy's Law struck. The customs agent, noticing the large diamond ring on Ruth's finger, asked about it. Ruth was a bride-to-be. She knew her ring was breathtaking. As any young woman would do in the circumstances, she showed the customs agent her ring and explained that it had been purchased for her in New York.

Wrong answer! The customs agent deemed it to be imported goods in excess of the permissible limits, and the ring was confiscated on the spot.

Frankly, I don't know how Ruth left the airport without that ring. I have two daughters and – well, you don't separate a bride-to-be from her engagement ring.

Her poor father was just as distraught.

"The wedding is in 3 weeks!" he exclaimed. "There's not time to go to court to get it back. She can't be married without that ring. Please, what can we do?"

This was a new situation for me. As always, I was ready to suit up and fight.

After some thought, I decided to try some old-fashioned logic. I made an appointment to see a senior tax bureaucrat at Revenue Canada, Customs and Excise head office in Ottawa. They knew me there. I had *entrée*, as it were. So I went to the meeting with a possible solution to put on the table.

"My client has come back on a short family visit to Canada," I explained. "She will be married in 3 weeks, and is going to live in New York. She is therefore not importing the ring into Canada. Why don't we deem her to have left it in bond at the port of Montreal? That way the ring will not have entered Canada. No duty will be due. On her way back to New York for the wedding, the bride can pick up the ring at the bonded warehouse and wear it home."

Maybe I hit a romantic. Maybe it just made sense. In any event, and much to my delight, the excise bureaucrat agreed that this solution would work.

"I'll need a letter instructing the customs officials at the port of Montreal to hold the ring in bond," I told him. "If you can prepare it now, I'll see that it's delivered *tout de suite*." The excise man provided me with the letter, and when delivered, the customs agents complied.

The bride dried her tears and, on her way back to New York for the wedding, stopped at customs to recover her precious ring.

I was not at the wedding, but I believe the cries of *"Mazel Tov!"* for Ruth and her beloved echoed nonetheless in the rooms of my law office.

It was great fun to play cupid.

Keep on Punching

EARLY IN MY DAYS OF PRIVATE PRACTICE I had a call from a man who said he had found my name in the Ottawa lawyer listings, and he knew he had to speak to me. He said his name was Jack, that he was a lawyer from southern Ontario, and that many years ago he had known another Paul DioGuardi. He wondered if there was a family connection.

My curiosity was piqued. I did have an Uncle Paul. I told Jack that there could be a connection, and accepted an invitation to meet him for lunch.

Then I thought back over my family.

I am named Paul after my paternal grandfather. One of my father's brothers was also named Paul, after the same patriarch. I had not seen my Uncle Paul since I was a child, and at that I had only met him once or twice. Uncle Paul, it seemed, had been the black sheep of the DioGuardi family. I never knew why. My father told me this brother was a gold miner in northern Ontario. That's why he didn't visit much. I remember him being small of stature, but looking tough and hard. I can remember thinking, it must be rough work mining gold in northern Ontario.

All in all, I thought Uncle Paul had been a pretty colourful character. Not having seen him since childhood, I had mostly forgotten about him until this phone call.

I met Jack at a restaurant near my office in downtown Ottawa. He was an older man, pleasant and courteous. I was surprised to discover that once upon a time Jack and my Uncle Paul had been close colleagues. During that luncheon, I learned even more surprising things.

Jack told me that when he was a young man, during the depression, money was very tight. Law school had not come into his life until much later. He had gone up to northern Ontario, as did many other young men, to work in the mines and maybe make his fortune. There he met my Uncle Paul, and together, and with the help of some other fine fellows, they discovered a unique way to make money.

Uncle Paul, Jack told me, was a proficient boxer. But he was small of stature and lean as a whip, which made him the perfect "ringer." No one would imagine such a little man could outbox a man more than twice his size.

Hoping to capitalize on this deception, Jack, Uncle Paul, and the other men came up with a scheme they hoped would be financially rewarding for them all.

They would go around to the small towns and Indian reserves in northern Ontario, and one of them would loudly proclaim to all and sundry that "This man," meaning my Uncle Paul, "can beat any man in your town. Here's our money. Put up your bucks and your best man, and winner takes all."

Apparently it was like waving a red flag at a bull. The men in the town would all come running, pushing forward the best flower of their manhood, who was usually some big lug of a lumberjack standing 6 foot 4 in stocking feet. Of course their boy could take Uncle Paul, who was such a runt it would hardly be a contest.

Jack and company would take the bets and hold on to the money while a makeshift boxing ring was set up. Then Uncle Paul and the local champion were pushed into the ring, and the bout began. Jack told me that while the fight was underway, someone was always waiting in the getaway car with the engine running.

Uncle Paul would let the other guy get in a few bruising punches. And then, when the crowd was liquored up and screaming for blood, Uncle Paul would let into his towering rival with a series of punishing blows, finally administering the *coup de grâce*. Before the crowd realized that the local man was on the mat and the match was over, Uncle Paul would be over the ropes and running for the getaway car, where the rest of the gang waited with the money.

Jack said they made a lot of money on these boxing matches. They must have had a lot of fun, too, because Jack couldn't stop laughing as he told me about speeding away in the car with an angry crowd in hot, but fruitless, pursuit. It was a caper worthy of a place in a Mark Twain novel. I laughed, too.

Of course I had to take the tale back to my father, who looked embarrassed by it all. It turned out the family knew something of Uncle Paul's adventures, and they didn't approve. They didn't think it was respectable to dupe people out of their money. Or maybe they didn't approve of boxing. Either way, in their eyes Uncle Paul was not the favoured family son, and his contact with us had been limited.

I may not be a prizefighter, but I do like to land a solid punch between the eyes of the Tax Crocodile. And I keep on punching. Maybe there's a bit of the boxer in the DioGuardi genes.

I do regret that I didn't know about the boxing scheme when I was a boy.

An Honorary Israeli

HELP CAN COME FROM THE MOST UNEXPECTED PLACES.
My wife and I were invited by my friend and client, Abraham, to a celebration in honour of the 25th anniversary of the founding of his business. We found ourselves at a table with a young Toronto lawyer and his spouse, who were also friends of our host. Unsurprisingly, lawyers almost always speak about law, and where they went to law school, etc.

At that time my youngest daughter, Brigitte, who had recently earned her Bachelor of Arts degree, was considering a career in law. She was interested in American law schools. Unfortunately, she had missed all the application deadlines for the academic term starting in September, and, at her age, a year seemed a long time to wait.

The young lawyer was sympathetic, and offered a worthwhile suggestion.

"What about the law programs in England?" he said. I thought that sounded rather complicated, and distant.

"Not at all," he replied. "Abe's nephew is at law school in Sheffield. The university there regularly recruits students from Israel. Perhaps we can find a way to make her an honorary member of the Israeli contingent. We might be able to get her admitted for the next term."

At that point I felt obliged to advise the young lawyer that my daughter was not Jewish.

"No problem," he said. "Just ask Abe to call his nephew in England, and connect him with your daughter. She can ask questions and, if she likes the sound of it, you can take her over to the U.K. to check out the law school in person."

Abe was kind enough to put us in touch with his nephew. Sure enough, he confirmed that he could arrange things to include my daughter in the "Israeli contingent" for the coming term.

"One thing though," he warned. "Steer clear of the male Jewish law students. They're over-sexed and over here."

I laughed, because this was exactly how the British talked about American servicemen during the Second World War.

My daughter took it all in stride. If she decided to go to Britain to study, she would be accompanied by her significant other (now her husband), David, who was then considering studying for a degree in computer science.

Brigitte was interested in the opportunity, so we flew to Britain and visited the law school in Sheffield. It took me back to my first year at Queen's University law school. Sheffield, like Queen's, was an ivy-covered classic university campus, with small classes, good professors and a great law library.

Long story short, Brigitte made her application as part of the Israeli contingent, was admitted for the next term, and in due course successfully completed her law degree. She returned to Canada, did more courses at a Canadian law school and, after articles, was called to the Ontario Bar. Later she was called to the British Columbia Bar and for a time managed the Vancouver office of our firm. She now practices in the Ottawa offices of DioGuardi Tax Law.

She has voluntarily resigned her place in the Israeli contingent.

The Portuguese Schism

SOMETIMES FATE DRAGS YOU INTO something you shouldn't touch with a barge pole.

This is the strange tale of a heated battle over who should own a church.

Many years ago, a group of well-to-do Portuguese businesspeople decided to buy a dilapidated, deconsecrated church in the heart of Ottawa, and restore it for the exclusive use of the Portuguese community. Development was rampant in that part of the city, and whatever happened, the property should be a good investment. So they put their shoulders to the wheel and set about raising capital.

The group acquired the property and, with great care and great expense, turned the old church into a beautiful place of worship. Masses were said. Portuguese festivals were celebrated. The Sacred Church of Best Laid Plans (I don't want to share its true name) was much loved by its congregation.

Then they hit a speed bump.

The Catholic Archdiocese was not pleased with an independent congregation. It exercised its power. It became difficult for the congregation to find priests to say Mass. The community went searching for itinerant priests to assist them, but such priests were few and far between, and were wary of treading on the sacred toe of the Archdiocese. Something had to give or The Sacred Church of Best Laid Plans would wither away.

Two factions formed. One wanted to donate the church to the Archdiocese. The Archbishop had promised to provide priests and the support of Mother Church if the renegade congregation came back into the fold.

The other faction was adamant that the Portuguese community should continue to own the church. They had brought it to life without the help of Mother Church. They weren't about to hand it over.

The first side had already hired legal counsel and was taking the matter to court. The other side, many of whom were my friends, asked me to represent them. This was not a happy case for me to take. I could see all too well that the religious authorities would eventually become involved, and I had no desire to wind up on the wrong side of the Archdiocese.

I advised my friends to find a top-notch, non-Catholic civil litigator. I was a tax lawyer and this definitely was not about tax.

My friends took my refusal personally. "You must act for us," they said. "Or our friendship is over."

I was caught between the devil and the deep blue sea. I knew enough to hedge my bets, though. I agreed to represent their group on the understanding that if the Archbishop became involved for the other side, I would have to cease to act for them. They agreed.

Now engaged, I proposed a civil discussion between the two factions to see if we could come to terms. I arranged for a meeting to take place in the church.

It did not go well. Some people came to the meeting – in the church I remind you – with weapons. Both sides were shouting, and there was much pushing, and ugly threats, and by the time the men were literally at each other's throats, I had to call in the police to restore order. Today I would call it a "Taliban moment."

I had no choice, but to take the matter into the courts. But did we really think a civil judge could cut through the Gordian knot of this spiritual dilemma? Apparently not, because the judge pleaded with the lawyers to find a way to settle it between the parties.

Where was King Solomon when you needed him?

Maybe we didn't have a King Solomon, but we did have an Archbishop. This was really his jurisdiction, not the civil court's. I recommended we meet with the Archbishop to propose some workable solutions.

We were granted an audience, and both lawyers, with the leading representatives of each faction, attended upon this eminent church official.

I didn't expect a miracle. Yet surely, I thought, we could find a reasonable compromise. Perhaps the Archbishop would agree to provide priests on an interim basis, until the Archdiocese could provide the Portuguese community with a church. The Sacred Church of Best Laid Plans, which was on prime city real estate, could be sold to developers and the profit could be donated to help the poor and needy. It was a very biblical solution.

The Archbishop was not open to discussion. He admonished my clients as if they were recalcitrant children, and practically ordered them to donate their property to the church. Of course he had no civil jurisdiction over them. It was a humiliating moment for these proud men who had, with their own funds and hands, created a worship space for their community. Respectfully I say it was not the Archbishop's finest hour.

I advised my friends that, as agreed, now that the Archbishop had ranged against them, I must regretfully resign as their counsel. God does guard DioGuardis because, thankfully, my friends accepted this. They retained fresh counsel, and the Battle of The Sacred Church of Best Laid Plans waged on without me.

Eventually, after years of wrangling, during which the health of the little church grew ever more fragile, my friends put faith ahead of funds and agreed to permit the transfer of the property to the Archdiocese.

Peace was restored again in the Portuguese community. Today the church is thriving and is a spiritual home for the Portuguese in Ottawa within the arms of Mother Church. Recently it celebrated its 25th anniversary. God moves in mysterious ways.

Dinner in High Places

OFTEN OUR FRIENDS WERE KIND ENOUGH to invite us to dine at their home. Aside from being the source of some wonderful culinary adventures, it gave us the opportunity to converse, on an informal basis, with many at the top end of the power pyramid in Ottawa. Some evenings federal and other higher court judges would be among the guests. At other suppers we would be conversing with senior mandarins. Coming from humble backgrounds, neither Carmen nor I had been exposed on a regular basis to such exalted company.

The events were purely social in nature. On one occasion, however, I was able to combine business with pleasure and reunite a family.

We were dining on a Friday evening at the home of a long-time friend of my wife. Our hostess had lately remarried and her new husband, whom we had not yet met, was, as my wife informed me en route to the dinner party, the recently appointed Minister of Immigration in the federal Liberal government. How serendipitous.

A few weeks earlier, a young man had arrived in my Ottawa office with his weeping mother. Speaking for his mother, he explained to me that he was one of her three sons. He and another brother had been able to immigrate to Canada from Turkey with their mother. His last brother remained trapped in Turkey, unable to gain admission to Canada because our government had closed its immigration offices there.

Could I help reunite this family? The poor lady begged me for help through her tears.

To no avail was my explanation that I was not an immigration lawyer. Her obvious distress touched my heart. Not knowing what would happen, I said that I would take her case. I warned that a favourable outcome could not be expected automatically. I was a competent tax lawyer, but this would be my first foray into immigration law.

As it turned out, my words were prophetic. Trying to facilitate immigration from Turkey to Canada was, at that time, like talking to a brick wall. After a few weeks of effort, my results were zero.

This brings us back to the Friday night dinner party. I had decided to enjoy my weekend and then report the bad news to my client on Monday. Now Carmen had informed me that our host was the new Minister of Immigration. Aha, I thought, with the gleam of a good idea. But only if the situation was appropriate. I would have to wait and see.

Upon arriving, we were introduced to the other couple with whom we were to sup. He was the Deputy Minister of Immigration, and a very senior mandarin. Both he and the new Minister were down-to-earth, likeable fellows. I might just have a chance. The jokes and banter went on and on, and the dinner party was delightful in every way.

At long last, while the ladies engaged in conversation amongst themselves, the men began to "talk shop." The Deputy Minister shared how pleased he was that everything was going well at the Department of Immigration. I saw an opening and took it. I told my story of the weeping Turkish mother and the dilemma of her last son, stranded in Turkey because Canada no longer had immigration offices there. Then I mentioned that, despite my best efforts, I could get nothing but the cold shoulder and empty excuses from his bureaucrats.

The reaction was magical. The Minister turned to his second in command and said something to the effect of, "Look into it on Monday. Perhaps we can help this lady."

Long story short. Early the next week, I got a call from a top official in the embassy in whatever country the Department of Immigration had assigned to handle the young man's application. It was like night and day. "Yes, Mr. DioGuardi, we have received a call from the Deputy Minister. Your client's son will be admitted to Canada. You can tell his mother everything will take about 10 days."

And so it happened.

The next time I saw this woman, her tears were gone. She was smiling and carrying an armload of flowers which, after accepting same with as much grace as I could muster, I brought home to adorn our table.

The outcome was truly a Turkish Delight, and far sweeter than the candy.

Another dinner party at the home of these same friends ended with a much different punch line.

On this occasion, Her Excellency, Governor General Jeanne Sauvé, was the guest of honour. One of the other guests was Sarah Jennings, sister of the then wildly popular media personality, Peter Jennings. Peter had grown up near where we lived in Gatineau, and had started his broadcast career in the Ottawa area before going on to greater fame and fortune on the American networks.

At that time, my son, Philippe, then an undergraduate at Carleton University, avidly followed Peter and was one of his greatest fans. Philippe had regularly sung Jennings' praises at our own dinner table.

It was indeed an honour to be asked to dine in company with the Governor General. Madame Sauvé was elegant and gracious, and a delightful dinner companion. At the end of the evening, as we stood at our hosts' door preparing to depart, we said our respectful good-byes to Her Excellency. Then we both turned to Sarah Jennings and expressed to her, several times, how thrilled our son would be when we told him that we had dined with Peter Jennings' sister.

Her Excellency stood there, smiling like the Queen herself, although we made no such comment related to her presence at the dinner. No disrespect was intended. We were, I suppose, dazzled by the star power of an American news network anchorman, reflected in his sister.

It was a bit like that song, "I danced with a man who danced with a girl who danced with the Prince of Wales..."

Carmen and I went home and told Philippe we had dined with Peter Jennings' sister, and thought no more of it.

Early next morning the telephone rang. It was our hosts of the previous evening. They couldn't stop chuckling. We had made such a big deal about meeting Sarah Jennings, they laughed, but had said nothing about how our son, or our two daughters for that matter, would be impressed that we had dined with the Governor General.

"After all, Paul," said my host reprovingly, "Her Excellency is Her Majesty's representative in Canada."

Can you say social *faux pas*? It appears that Her Excellency had taken it all in good jest, which was truly the cause of our host's great mirth.

Guess I would not have been successful as a diplomat.

A Ben-Hur Moment

WITH SKYPE, I AM ABLE TO TAKE ON clients scattered across the globe, and I had one such client in Israel. During one Skype meeting with the client, he raved about the weather and the beauty of his home in Israel, and even held up his computer to show me the view from his windows. I decided it was time I saw the Holy Land first hand.

We decided go at Christmastime. My daughter Brigitte and her husband, David, would join Carmen and me for a tour of some of the prettiest and most historic cities in the region, before we moved on to celebrate Christmas Day in Rome.

That was the winter of a new discontent in the Middle East, and Tel Aviv had been attacked with a rain of missiles. There were traveller alerts about going to Israel that winter. Thus Carmen elected to stay home for Christmas in Canada. Our other children and their families would celebrate the holiday with her, so she would not be alone.

Brigitte, David and I pressed on in the spirit of adventure. A friend suggested we stay north of Tel Aviv, in Herzalia, a small resort city on the sea. It was reportedly a rocket-free zone.

Needless to say, there were few tourists in Israel that year. We were able to see the best of Jaffa, and Jerusalem, and Bethlehem, without the usual crush of Christmas pilgrims. We were brave enough to travel south – the missiles didn't seem a threat by that point – and took the opportunity to cross into Jordan to visit the fabled city of Petra.

The entrance to the ancient city is reached through the Sig, a narrow gorge flanked on either side by towering red rock cliffs. The city is carved into the side of the cliffs, and glows rose-red in the sunlight.

As we walked through the Sig, which is more than 1 kilometre in length, the heat was stifling, and by the time we entered Petra my strength was sapped. I gave cursory attention to the ancient buildings carved out of the rock, and then was ready to leave.

I was too hot and exhausted to face the walk back through the Sig.

Brigitte and David were hot and tired, too, yet weren't as ready to admit defeat. David agreed to find a solution, and quickly spied some young Jordanians with "people-carts" for hire.

These people-carts were little more than wooden crates on rubber tires, harnessed to a horse. I told Brigitte and David that I thought they looked like the chariots in the movie *Ben-Hur*.

That was all David needed. He waved over a couple of the young men and quickly negotiated a fee for two carts – one for me, and one for himself and Brigitte. Then David declared that this would be a chariot race, and that there would be extra "*bakshees*" for the winner.

The young Jordanians grinned, and I barely had time to climb up behind my driver before he whipped his horse into action. David and Brigitte were laughing in the other cart as their driver did the same.

And so we raced through the Sig, scattering tourists in our path and bouncing about in the wooden carts as our drivers pushed their horses into full gallop. It was as exciting as the chariot race scene in *Ben-Hur* – and probably almost as dangerous.

The gorge seemed to grow narrower and narrower as we careened through it, laughing and yelling cries of encouragement to our respective drivers. As we neared the gates of the city, David and Brigitte's chariot pulled ahead and crossed the "finish line" first.

David was elated and counted out a huge bonus to his driver. My driver was disappointed to have lost the race, but still asked me for the same bonus. I gave him a runner up prize. He had earned something for his death-defying efforts.

But to the victor go the spoils.

And the Angels Sing

OVER THE YEARS I HAVE BEEN retained to assist clients in estate matters.

One such client was an elegant elderly woman named Ibolyka. A violinist of some renown, she had performed in the concert halls of Europe until the Nazis invaded her native Czechoslovakia, and she was forced to flee. She eventually found refuge in the U.K., and just before the start of WWII she had purchased, in London, an extraordinary violin. She told me she had paid £38 for it. She had played it ever since. Now that she was old and unwell, she was unable to play with regularity. It was time for her to let the violin change hands. It deserved to be played.

The instrument was made in the 1700s, likely in Venice, by the renowned Italian luthier, Pietro Guarneri. A violin crafted by a member of the Guarneri family is much sought after among collectors and musicians. Some of the world's most famous violinists, including Paganini, Heifetz, and Menuhin, have openly expressed their preference for a Guarneri over a Stradivarius. My elderly client was in possession of a rare treasure. Selling the violin broke her heart, but she needed the proceeds of the sale to fund her retirement.

When she brought the violin to my office, even I, with no musical training, could see the beauty of the instrument. I was told that the Guarneri provenance was clearly established. I told her I had no experience in brokering such a sale, but she insisted that I handle the matter. She looked so much like my grandmother on my father's side, that my resistance crumbled and I agreed.

After consulting several persons knowledgeable in the field, I compiled a list of eligible dealers in fine instruments, and invited them to attend at my office on Sparks Street in Ottawa to view and bid on the Guarneri violin.

On the day of the viewing, to my great surprise, there was quite a line up. I had underestimated the attraction of a Pietro Guarneri violin. My client and I permitted each dealer to view the violin, individually, before submitting their bid. The eventual buyer had come all the way from Florida. After examining the instrument extensively, he asked to play it before making his final offer. As he reached to take the violin out of its case, my quiet, little-old-lady client leapt suddenly to her feet and screeched at him.

Ibolyka would not permit the instrument to be touched without gloves, or a similar protective covering. It was over 250 years old. It was an original Pietro Guarneri. The finish was both delicate and precious.

I was surprised that a dealer in fine instruments was not sensitive to this. Perhaps he was testing us to see if we were selling the genuine article. Who knows? At any rate, he was quite flustered by my client's outburst, but regained his composure and produced a handkerchief, which he placed over the delicate wood before picking up the violin and raising it to his chin. Then he began to play, there in my law chambers over a trust company on the Sparks Street mall in downtown Ottawa.

And in that moment the angels sang. Even I, with my minimal knowledge of music, could feel the true beauty of the sound. The tone was sweet and captivating as it echoed through the law chambers. At once the other lawyers, and all the staff, stopped to listen in awe. Later, I was told that in the trust company below their staff and clients alike looked skyward toward the angelic sounds, and they, too, paused to listen.

The dealer played for several minutes, then quietly and with meticulous care laid the violin back in its case. "I must have this," he said.

We were back in my territory now. I did my stuff and secured a bid that satisfied my client. And so the Guarneri changed hands.

I can't reveal the price paid. But I note that in 2013 an Internet search catalogued the sale of a Pietro Guarneri violin for sum the of $302,000 USD. Ibolyka was sad to part with her beloved violin. However, the money, while something less than $302,000, gave her the means to live out her declining years in dignity and comfort.

When she eventually passed on, I was privileged to be the estate trustee for this remarkable woman. There remained enough money from the sale to endow several music schools in Europe where she had studied. Best of all, in those days before the capital gains tax, the Tax Crocodile could not sink its greedy teeth into any of the funds. Being no big fan of government, she would have been happy.

Flights of angels sing thee to thy rest, dear lady.

An Indulgence

Never Trust a Crocodile or an Offshore Banker

CHUCK HAVERS HAD ENJOYED HIS life in high finance. After a stellar career that took him from Bay Street to Wall Street and even a short stint in The City, riding the wave of the offshore banking frenzy, he had built a well-respected bank in the Cayman Islands.

Physically, the effort had extracted its toll, morphing a once slim, athletic Canadian boy into a florid and slightly paunchy middle-aged businessman. He could carry off a Tommy Bahama shirt with ease, and when he returned to the mainland, he was always impeccably dressed. His ability to "chat up the ladies" overcame his past-my-prime physique.

On boarding Cayman Airways Flight 24 to Miami, Chuck found himself seated beside an attractive blonde. She said her name was Aynsley. She looked about 22. During the short flight they chatted comfortably and, as usual, Chuck did most of the talking. He couldn't resist sharing tidbits about himself and his private, offshore bank. There was just enough of the James Bond in it all to make him feel attractive.

Later, he reflected that he might have been a bit too vocal about the clever ways he knew to help Americans and Canadians hide their money from the Taxman in investments managed by his bank.

It wasn't until Chuck and his seat mate were waiting at Miami Passport Control that he noticed anything unusual. Four men in dark suits had come out of the back rooms and were standing at the counter. They looked like they were waiting for someone.

Chuck didn't pay much attention. The DEA always had narcs assigned to the inbound flights from the islands.

Then Chuck saw the blonde smile ever so slightly at one of the narcs. And he thought she nodded – nothing more than a fast dip of the head – but it made his adrenaline start pumping.

The blonde showed the customs agent her passport, and was waved into the United States. Then it was Chuck's turn. As he held his passport toward to the customs agent, one of the narcs stepped forward and took his elbow.

"Come with me, sir," he said, as the three other men moved in behind Chuck. They herded him out of the lineup and into a small grey room. The door closed and he was left alone with the first narc.

If they thought he was carrying drugs or money, they would have searched him by that point. It had to be something else.

"Take a seat," said the narc, and pulled a grey metal chair out from under a flat grey table.

Chuck sat. His knees were wobbly, and he was sweating profusely. "Is there a problem here?" he asked.

The narc produced his ID. "Agent Chambers. IRS."

Chuck was a Canadian. He was the president of The Bank. The Internal Revenue Service had no direct jurisdiction over him. Unless ...

Chuck knew he had set up accounts for a lot of Americans. Park Avenue doctors. Investment brokers. Even a few bankers, like himself. The IRS could get very nasty with him. His first instinct was to demand his lawyer. But then he decided it might be better to hear Agent Chambers out. At any time he could call a halt and demand his high-powered American attorney.

Chuck pulled himself up in his chair and said, "How can I help you, Agent Chambers?"

Chambers put his hands on the table and leaned in close. "Your bank in the Caymans. I believe some of your clients are American citizens."

"Some are," Chuck agreed. "Americans are permitted to hold accounts offshore."

"I'm talking about the clients who don't report what's in those accounts."

"How is that my problem?" Chuck shot back. "I don't do their taxes."

"But you do give tax advice," Agent Chambers countered. "In fact, we have reason to believe you actually advise your American account holders on how not to report the accounts they have with your bank."

Chuck didn't answer. He knew anything he said could be used against him. He didn't know what evidence the IRS had, but if they had picked him out of the passport line in Miami, they had to have something.

"Cat got your tongue, Mr. Havers?" Agent Chambers was trying to goad him into a response. "More like a crocodile," Chuck thought to himself.

Finally he spoke. "You would have to have evidence."

Chambers held up his cell phone. "Got one of these?"

Of course Chuck had a smartphone. It was his lifeline to everything. Every phone call he made, every contact he did business with, every text and e-mail message...!!!

The light bulb went off in Chuck's head with blinding clarity. The National Security Agency had snooped his cellphone records and scooped his contact list. Chambers likely already had enough to send him to jail for at least 2 years. Chuck thought hard. It was time to demand his lawyer. But before he did ... .

"I'll make you an offer," he said. "I'll provide full disclosure of the names of Americans with accounts at my bank. If you charge them, I will testify to confirm that they are account holders. In return, I want immunity from prosecution. Not just for me, but for all the directors of my bank."

While he was talking, he pulled out his cell phone and called up his contact list. He scrolled through to a name. "This is my secretary's private phone. I can text her now and instruct her to e-mail the account holder list to me here. Then the phone is yours." He smiled. "You've already got everything important off it by now."

Chambers took the phone from Chuck's hand and tapped in a text message. "Call ASAP." He showed the message to Chuck. "Shall I send it?"

"Go head," Chuck said and watched as the Agent tapped send.

They waited for perhaps 40 seconds before the cellphone rang. Chambers gave the phone to Chuck. "You answer."

Chuck took his phone and accepted the call. He chose his words carefully. "We have a situation," he said. "Please do exactly as I ask. I need the ZFiles list. Yes, the ZFiles. PDF it and send it through now."

Chuck ended the call and handed the phone back to Chambers. "Are we done here?" And he stood up to show he was ready to leave.

"Not yet," Chambers motioned him to sit down again. They waited in silence for the tell-tale ping that announced the receipt of a message. When it came both men jumped.

Chambers tapped the message to see the contents. Sure enough, it was a PDF file with a list of account numbers, names, and contact info.

"I've done my part," Chuck says. "It's time I was leaving."

"I'll be back," Chambers said, heading for the door.

"We had a deal," Chuck shouted after him. But Chambers was gone and the door locked behind him.

Chuck sat down to wait. He already knew what came next.

About an hour later Agent Chambers slammed back into the room and practically tossed the smartphone at Chuck, who was still athletic enough to catch it smoothly.

"The files are bogus!" Agent Chambers shouted. "What's your game, Havers?"

Chuck laughed. "They're real enough, if you know the encryption code. Did you think I was stupid enough to trust you? I want full immunity. And immediate release. And I think it's time we call my lawyer. Deal?"

Agent Chambers was cornered. He needed the collar. The real win would be a list of several hundred citizen names. One banker, and a Canadian citizen at that, wasn't important enough to risk the rest.

He looked at the phone, and then at Chuck. "Deal," Chambers said.

Chuck's lawyer in New York had an attorney at the airport within 40 minutes, and Chuck was free.

Several weeks later, the phone rang in the Park Avenue office of a leading orthopedic surgeon. The receptionist frowned into the phone, then put the call on hold and punched the doctor's extension. "Sorry to interrupt, Doctor," she said, "but you probably want to take this call. It's the IRS."

The banker had thrown his clients into the jaws of the Tax Crocodile to save his own skin.

It was later reported by the media that the IRS had secured access to a list of American citizens with accounts in Cayman Island banks. They were all investigated, and some were convicted of tax evasion and severely fined.

Some even served prison time.

As for the banker ... he was back on the island in no time flat.

No Place to Hide

Nowhere Safe

THERE WAS A TIME THAT BANKERS in the islands were jolly and reassuring when helping clients open offshore accounts. But when the tax authorities came snooping, as they inevitably did, bankers often put their own well-being ahead of their duty to protect their clients.

Chuck's experience in "Never Trust a Crocodile or an Offshore Banker," lightly gilded, I confess, for the sake of the tale, but essentially true, shook the island banking community and, in the eyes of many, challenged the integrity of the Caymans as a tax haven.

The Caymans were not the only haven under attack. The secrecy of the offshore bank account has now been eroded to the point of virtual non-existence.

THE WIKILEAKS OF OFFSHORE TAX HAVENS

The deluge may be said to have started in 2010 when a disgruntled bank employee at a bank in Lichtenstein absconded with a list of client names, which he sold to the German authorities, who in turn shared it with their tax treaty partners around the world, including Canada.

Hundreds of Canadians with secret offshore bank accounts were named on that list.

That leak paled in comparison to a 2013 data dump.

In May 2013, the International Consortium of Investigative Journalists in Washington, D.C., released to select media partners around the globe a list of account information delivered anonymously on a hard drive to an Australian journalist in 2011.

The scope and specificity of the personal and account information leaked absolutely exposed Canadians with hidden and legitimate offshore trusts and corporations to the scrutiny of the CRA, and international revenue watchdogs.

The media frenzy surrounding this 2013 massive database leak was expected to shame the Minister of Finance into calling for heads and taking true action against the thousands of Canadians who are hiding money offshore. Nothing would have been easier than to immediately audit the 450 Canadians named in this database leak. It has been reported by the press that little has been accomplished. Who really knows the full truth of it all?

Notwithstanding the Minister's apparently soft treatment of exposed offshore account holders, as a tax lawyer I have an ongoing warning for Canadians who may not be declaring the money they have hidden offshore.

The CRA's Voluntary Disclosures Program (VDP) offers the opportunity to come forward voluntarily to report the offshore income, and revise past tax filings accordingly. In and of itself, a voluntary disclosure is not adequate protection against the potential of such a witch hunt. If accepted, a voluntary disclosure offers protection against prosecution for tax evasion. Before a disclosure is accepted, the CRA can – and generally does – audit everything in your financial records. If you hold back anything, the disclosure can be disqualified, at which point the CRA is already in possession of enough information to launch a criminal investigation and then prosecute. Moreover, the CRA could decide that the disclosure is not voluntary because they were already aware of your tax evasion simply by virtue of the presence of your name in this database.

Any Canadian who believes their name and account details are in the leaked database should, as a cautionary measure, consult with appropriate experienced tax counsel to secure the protection of solicitor-client privilege. Such protection can help shield you from investigation or, at the very least, limit the scope of any investigation

Adding urgency to the need to seek legal protection is the Minister of Finance's commitment to pay a reward for "good clean information" about offshore accounts that leads to the recovery of tax revenues. When greedy vigilantes get involved, you can't trust your employees, your financial advisors, or in some cases even your own family. Your offshore account(s) can become a ticking time bomb.

Whistle-blowers, too, may need the protection of legal counsel. In verifying the calibre of the lead, an investigation might also delve into the whistle-blower's financial affairs. An audit is always an audit. It's not something anyone should engage in unprotected.

It's important to remember the experience of American whistle-blower, Bradley Birkenfeld, the former UBS AG banker who played an instrumental role in the United States' international crackdown on tax evasion. Mr. Birkenfeld, who began cooperating with the U.S. authorities in 2007 to expose his bank's promotion of tax evasion opportunities while still working at UBS, was himself implicated. He eventually plead guilty to one count of conspiracy to defraud, and received a 40-month sentence. He also was paid what is believed to be the highest reward to a whistle-blower – a whopping $104 million USD.

The reward was commensurate with the magnitude of the revenues the IRS recovered thanks to his cooperation. UBS ultimately disclosed the names of some 4,000 account holders and paid a $780 million settlement. More than 33,000 U.S. taxpayers confessed to holding undisclosed accounts offshore, and the IRS collected in excess of $5 billion in taxes and penalties.

The UBS debacle, together with the 2013 leak, has effectively shredded the veil of offshore secrecy, in island paradises and in sophisticated European jurisdictions, including Switzerland, Lichtenstein and Luxembourg, and forced changes in the way G20 countries are expected to share information about tax evasion and "hidden" accounts with their tax treaty partners.

At the G20 meeting in St. Petersburg, Russia, in September 2013, G20 leaders committed to work towards implementing a system of automatic transfer of tax information between governments, in a global attempt to close down tax havens and tax evasion and make the international financial system more transparent.

It may be more talk than action. The international Tax Justice Network has created a Financial Secrecy Index that combines a secrecy score with a weighting for scale of activity to create a ranking of the countries that most actively and aggressively promote secrecy in global finance. Here are the rankings for 2013:

1.	Switzerland	12.	Malaysia
2.	Luxembourg	13.	Bahrain
3.	Hong Kong	14.	Bermuda
4.	Cayman Islands	15.	Guernsey
5.	Singapore	16.	U.A.E. (Dubai)
6.	U.S.A.	17.	CANADA
7.	Lebanon	18.	Austria
8.	Germany	19.	Maritius
9.	Jersey	20.	British Virgin Islands
10.	Japan	21.	U.K.
11.	Panama		

If you're surprised that Canada ranked in the top 20, read "Canada, the U.K. and the U.S.: Tax Havens Close to Home."

Canada, the U.K. and the U.S.: Tax Havens Close to Home

OVER THE YEARS, IN ORDER TO KEEP up to speed, I have researched the benefit and legitimacy of tax havens as a means to shelter income from tax. Numerous clients have needed assistance in repatriating offshore money, with the minimum tax possible. If the crocodile tries to take an unfair bite out of a client, I will use the full extent of the law to refute the assessment.

That said, I confess that the use of tax havens and preferential tax regimes mostly benefits the rich and powerful.

There are two types of havens: no-tax havens and low-tax havens.

As you would expect, no-tax havens have no income, capital gains or wealth taxes.

Low-tax havens, or preferential tax regimes like Barbados, usually have double taxation agreements that reduce withholding tax imposed on income derived from the revenue authority country. Canada Steamship Lines and the T-shirt manufacturer Gildan are legitimately set up here.

No-tax havens, not being party to any tax or information treaties, are not required to furnish tax information to other governments, but even this rule is subject to change as pressure is put on them by western governments.

The U.K. has long been a tax haven. Brits still allow trusts to be secret. There is some movement towards ensuring that there is a level of transparency about the beneficial ownership of trusts, but at the time of writing, and despite continuing commitments from the G20 countries to endorse transparency between countries, no firm decision has been reached. Also, it is accepted that, even if a transaction takes place in London, if it were undertaken by parties not resident in the U.K., it will not be subject to U.K. financial regulation.

Albeit reduced somewhat in scope in 2008, their non-domicile (non-dom) rule states that anyone who immigrates to the U.K., but declares a wish to return to their country of origin in future, is not liable to pay local tax on their worldwide earnings. The person need not actually return to their own country, but only declare that this is his or her intention. Their children, whether born in the U.K. or elsewhere, are also exempt from paying tax on their worldwide earnings. As a result, non-doms flock to London and, of course, declare their intention to return home one day.

Although there is talk of change, at the time of writing it is still possible to form a British company and provide little or no proof of identity. Companies can be bought "off the shelf" with no evidence of identity being required. Apparently, it is quite easy to establish a company there using a false name and information. Nominees can act as directors and shareholders and be recorded as being located at a local U.K. address. It seems that you can set up and run a company there without outsiders having any idea who is behind it.

If this doesn't sound like what you can do in an offshore tax haven with an International Business Corporation (IBC), I miss my guess. An IBC offers secrecy of ownership, no filing requirements and, in certain jurisdictions, bearer share certificates. Doesn't that sound like what you can do in the U.K.?

I must remind you that while the U.K. ranks 21st on the International Tax Justice Network Index of Financial Secrecy, Canada ranks 17th, and the U.S. ranks 6th.

Here's why.

In Canada, we tax on the basis of residency. Persons who are non-residents of Canada do not have to pay tax in this country. Normally, they will, however, pay tax on money if it is earned here, but there are exceptions. These exceptions make Canada a tax haven for some non-residents. The *Income Tax Act* has a number of exceptions that allow people to place their money into special types of investments that have no withholding tax. Some manage to park their family in Canada, become non-residents themselves and earn money tax free here.

I share the following specific example.

I was visiting family in Vancouver some years ago, and I heard my brother-in-law, Albert, refer to some very large new homes as "Hong Kong specials." The locals were selling their older homes to offshore investors, who promptly ripped them down, cut down all the trees and built huge new residences on the properties. Then a family from Hong Kong or Taiwan would move in.

Using an offshore relative living in a low- or no-tax jurisdiction to act as a man of straw is still one of the most popular ways to pay no tax in Canada.

(For the purpose of this example I am using a Hong Kong family, but the offshore family concept cuts across all ethnic lines.)

Typically, a well-to-do family (not including say, the eldest brother) immigrates to Canada. Before the family arrives here, all the family wealth is transferred to this elder sibling. He will continue to reside in Hong Kong, or wherever. Since Canada taxes on the basis of residence and he is not living here, there is no requirement for the family members living in Canada to pay Canadian taxes.

Meanwhile their older brother very generously supports his "Canadian family" with non-taxable gifts such as money, luxury cars and large mortgage-free houses. The only tax the family members in

Canada must pay are the municipal taxes on the house. Likely the older brother, who technically owns the house, pays for that too.

What should concern taxpaying Canadians is this: the family living here receives the benefits of Canadian residency, such as free health care, low- or no-cost education, and social assistance. In some circumstances, sick relatives may be brought to Canada to be treated free of charge.

To add icing to the cake, our tax laws allow the non-resident brother to invest his money in Canada, in a special type of Canadian government bond created for non-residents. Alternatively he could put his money into an investment in foreign currency held by a Canadian bank upon which interest is paid in foreign currency. This gives him two benefits. First, there is the security of having these funds safe in a stable country like Canada. Second, there are no Canadian withholding taxes on the earnings. That is, all returns on the investment can be sent out of Canada to the elder brother tax free.

The non-resident brother can invest all the family's money here and, at the time of writing, never pay a penny of tax. He won't even be taxed in Hong Kong because income from a foreign source is not subject to tax there.

It makes Canada a very attractive tax haven. And there's no need for the secrecy of an offshore bank account.

WHY THE U.S. RANKS 6TH ON THE SECRECY INDEX

The Internal Revenue Service leads the hue and cry for transparency and disclosure of the names of Americans who hold bank accounts abroad. Yet within its own borders, the United States of America harbours a number of robust tax havens.

Delaware permits the anonymous use of registered corporate entities. As long as the majority of a corporation's directors are not American, a Delaware corporation can legally hold its assets in the U.S. at an effective zero tax rate. Thus Delaware reportedly is home to some 945,000 private companies, many of which are simply shells.

Miami is even worse. It is a huge banking centre catering to dodgy money mainly from South America. Once arrived in the U.S., these funds, much of which are the proceeds of criminal activity, are cleansed through real estate deals.

Wyoming and Nevada also have rules that attract international tax evaders.

When American legislators complain about foreign tax havens, there is more than a little hypocrisy at play.

The bottom line is that there are still places where money can be held more or less secretly, but, as time goes by, they are getting to be fewer and much more open to attack.

Words of Warning

IN 2004, PHILIPPE DIOGUARDI and I wrote and published the book *Tax Amnesty – Avoiding the Tax Trap.* In our law firm we pioneered the concept of tax amnesty – a truly *protected disclosure* of unfiled tax years and/or unreported income. The "tax amnesty" label was quickly adopted by lawyers, accountants and anyone else who offers assistance in resolving issues with the CRA, and applied to the CRA's Voluntary Disclosures Program (VDP).

But a voluntary disclosure and a *protected disclosure* are not the same.

In 2008, we published a second book, *The Taxman is Watching* (HarperCollins).

When the UBS scandal became news, Philippe DioGuardi, speaking for the law firm, placed the following open letter in the *Financial Post* national newspaper on October 14, 2010.

Further to my son's specific warning to offshore account holders, here are my own words of warning to non-filers, late-filers, and anyone who made incomplete disclosures of income on their tax returns.

VDP: PERILS AND PITFALLS

The two most common circumstances for making a voluntary disclosure are to file outstanding tax returns or to report previously undisclosed income.

In either case, the returns or amended returns you file under a voluntary disclosure *are likely to be flagged for audit.*

Dangerous Dialogues

A Warning to Canadians with undisclosed Swiss accounts.

On October 7, 2010, Diane Francis, in her *Comment* column in this newspaper, accused Canada of doing nothing about offshore cheating and lack of disclosure, suggesting corruption, incompetence, or both as the root cause of this inaction.

The Minister of National Revenue, the Hon. Keith Ashfield, responded within a day (see *LETTERS, FP19, October 9, 2010*) to rebut Ms Francis' allegations and defend the efficiency of the CRA's soft core approach to tax enforcement, otherwise know as the Voluntary Disclosures Program.

How Canadian. And how dangerous.

The speed and vehemence of the Minister's letter reveals two things:
1. Ms. Francis clearly touched a nerve; and
2. The gloves are off and the Minister is demanding heads in the form of high profile prosecutions to vindicate his mandate.

Both are perilous to any Canadian engaged in tax behaviour as defined by s. 239 of the Income Tax Act, which deems failure to report income for the purpose of evading tax an offense **prosecutable in the criminal courts** and punishable by penalties, fines and jail time.

Notwithstanding the unquestionably legal nature of offenses under s.239, and the threat they pose to the security of the person, the CRA disingenuously presents the off-the-shelf Voluntary Disclosure application as a prophylactic against both prosecution and punishment. Yet the VDP is no more than a policy created from an administrative interpretation of s. 220 (3.1), which permits the Minister the discretion to waive or cancel penalties and interest. Prosecution is not part of the equation, and is not in the purview of the Minister to dismiss. Thus there is a glaring disconnection between the promise of protection from prosecution, which is the most compelling consumer proposition of the VDP, and the section of the law on which it is founded.

A Voluntary Disclosure application does not confer automatic absolution. **Prosecution is an option always preserved** as a sword of Damocles to be wielded at the absolute discretion of the CRA. To protect from prosecution, a legal approach must be established at the outset of the disclosure and maintained throughout. Failure to do so leaves a taxpayer bereft of legal rights, and even undermines solicitor-client privilege, both of which will become essential in the event the disclosure is denied. It is thus surreptitious of the CRA to encourage tax professionals – particularly lawyers – to approach the resolution of such tax delinquency strictly through administrative policy, not law.

It must be remembered that **a Voluntary Disclosure is only viable when the CRA deems it has no prior knowledge of your offense**.

That leaves Canadians whose names are already in the possession of the CRA naked and at the mercy of a Minister, who, while personally calling for heads, will continue to mask his true intentions behind the all-too-Canadian happy face of gentle inquiry.

Beware of any contact from the CRA requesting, among other things, completion of a simple questionnaire presented in the guise of an innocent audit of tax years past. These questionnaires, issued by the Aggressive Tax Planning unit of your local tax office, are in reality an investigative audit of your holdings offshore, onshore, indeed anywhere in the world where you hold accounts. Any information you provide can and will be used against you if the Minister decides he can get your head quickly and with minimal effort.

Protecting your head and your wealth is not a matter of playing the odds. It's a matter of seeking cover and comfort in the law.

The Prime Minster has declared that he will pursue offshore tax evaders with the full extent of the law. The policy-driven VDP and audit questionnaires, for all their friendly demeanour, are in fact means to that end.

Therefore, I exhort the people of Canada to be wary of well-meaning administrative policy and those who re-sell it. Instead, celebrate and avail yourselves of the protection of the law.

Philippe DioGuardi, LL.B, LL.L
October 14, 2010

Follow the dialogue @ dioguardi.ca

It can take months for the CRA to finish their assessment. Along the way the auditors will look into your reported income and expenses with gusto. They'll also consider reviewing the tax filings of any person or business associated with the returns presented under your disclosure. Odds are you, or someone associated with you, will get questions from an auditor before the assessment is completed.

If the disclosure is accepted as filed, you'll be assessed with no penalties and usually with interest at a slightly reduced rate from what CRA normally charges. If it's not accepted as filed, you'll be assessed late filing penalties, and possibly other penalties for misrepresentation or failure to disclosure all income, all with interest at the normal and astronomical rate of 5% compounded *daily*. That adds up to an interest rate comparable to the costliest credit cards.

Either way – disclosure accepted or not – *CRA remains in possession of the information you disclosed or they discovered in their audit(s).* Make no mistake, the auditors will measure your future returns against what they already know about you. In all but the most straightforward of tax situations, the protection offered by an administratively processed voluntary disclosure is simply *inadequate.*

PRIVILEGE = PROTECTION

Understanding that a voluntary disclosure involves a behind-the-scenes audit, it's wise to pre-empt the CRA by reviewing the tax situation as the precursor to an audit. If it is determined that filing the overdue or amended return(s) presents no risk of detrimental exposure, it's likely safe to invoke the opportunity of the voluntary disclosure process, always under the protection of solicitor-client privilege, to reduce interest and eliminate penalties. However, at all times your financial information must be protected from unnecessary scrutiny. Hence the value of legal representation. Thus CRA is provided only what's required for the assessment of the tax years at issue.

If risk is identified, counsel must utilize more effective legal strategies to present tax returns to the CRA and limit the scope of any ensuing audit or investigation.

In this way, the client and his/her financial information remain under the protection of solicitor-client privilege until the tax matter is resolved.

A final word to the wise – before rushing into a voluntary disclosure, consider your exposure.

Interview with a
Tax Lawyer

IN APRIL 2013, THE CBC RELEASED details of an international data dump that shook the world of offshore banking and tax havens to its very core. Characterized as the biggest data dump since Wikileaks, it exposed over 30 years of offshore account records and personal data for more than 100,000 people around the world; 450 of them were identified as Canadians.

The incident raises a number of continuing questions, at least in the minds of the media.

If I were to interview myself on the topic of off-shore accounts and the 2013 data dump of account holder names, here are the key questions I would want answered. And here's how I would answer them.

First, the questions:

- Should the rich be allowed to hide their wealth from the Tax-man while the middle class pays?
- How much tax revenue does Canada lose to secret accounts in Switzerland and other tax havens?
- Do most Canadians really care about the rich and what they do?

And now my answers:
(Author's Note: This text is derived from an interview I prepared for the DioGuardi TaxTV online tax news channel. If you'd like to watch the interview, instead of read it, follow this link to *www.taxtv.ca* and look for the program "Interview with a Tax Lawyer.")

Interviewer: *We're looking at what might be the biggest exposé of offshore account holders in the history of modern tax. How is this info leak dangerous to the Canadians whose offshore accounts have been outed?*

Paul: You have to understand that the scope of the personal information and account details is intimately specific. The hard drive "secretly" sent to the Australian journalist, who ultimately shared its contents with the world press, held over 30 years' worth of information. It's estimated to be 160 times bigger than the volume of information in the Wikileaks scandals. Over 100,000 account holders were identified, with very personal financial details. So the information potentially implicates anyone with any connections to banking offshore.

Interviewer: *How many of those people are Canadians?*

Paul: The CBC reported that about 450 Canadians were on the list, and about 4,000 Americans. Then there were Russian politicians, heads of state in Middle Eastern countries. The daughter of Ferdinand Marcos, and the list goes on.

Interviewer: *Let's look at those 450 now infamous Canadians. What can they expect, now that the world can look into their offshore activities?*

Paul: Now that the Canada Revenue Agency (CRA) has been given access to that list, those 450 Canadians are exposed to scrutiny – audits, net worth analysis, which is something the CRA does without you knowing about it, and then reassessments. Any or all of it can be dangerous.

Interviewer: *Wherein lies the greatest danger?*

Paul: It's no secret that governments around the world are desperate for revenue. One of the biggest sources of new money – or more money – would be to tighten up the tax loopholes and catch the people who are robbing the public treasuries of the world of hundreds of billions of dollars of tax revenue. All of us would pay less tax, and our governments could balance their budgets, if even a fraction of this lost money could be recouped.

The Canadian government has been under fire from business people and taxpayer advocacy groups for its soft track record in seeking out offshore tax cheats. This data leak gives the government the opportunity to look tough.

And if you're going to go after the tax evaders, the easiest targets are the birds in hand.

Interviewer: *We remember the Swiss bank account scandal with the bank in Lichtenstein in 2010. Did the CRA use that list of account holders to find tax cheats?*

Paul: A Canadian television network news investigation suggested that there had been no more than 75 audits and 25 reassessments as a result of that leak. Just a drop in the bucket, really. And Canada has apparently signed an agreement with Lichtenstein that protects anyone who currently has an account there from the CRA's scrutiny.

Interviewer: *What do you suggest these 450 Canadians do?*

Paul: If you're on the list, and you're not reporting the account or the money hidden offshore, you definitely need to protect yourself.

Interviewer: *How does one do that?*

Paul: Without reviewing the facts in detail, it is not wise to just shoot from the hip and rely on the Voluntary Disclosures Program so popular with accountants and less specialized tax helpers.

Remember, by proceeding with a voluntary disclosure, you are voluntarily waiving your *Charter* right against self-incrimination in a situation where potential criminal charges are present.

The Canada Revenue Agency's Voluntary Disclosures Program in and of itself is not adequate protection against the potential of a witch hunt like this. If *accepted*, a voluntary disclosure offers you protection against prosecution for tax evasion. However, before a disclosure is accepted, the CRA can – and often does – audit everything in your financial records. If you hold back anything, the disclosure can be disqualified, at which point the CRA is already in possession of enough information to launch a criminal investigation and then prosecute.

Moreover, the CRA could decide that the disclosure is not voluntary because they were already aware of your tax evasion simply by virtue of the presence of your name in this database.

You need a lawyer, not an accountant or tax preparer, representing your interests. If anything goes wrong, these accounting types can be forced to testify against you. A tax lawyer who is your retained counsel cannot be forced in this situation.

Interviewer: *What protection do you recommend people with off-shore accounts seek?*

Paul: As a tax lawyer, I would advise any Canadian who believes their name and account details are in the leaked database should, as a cautionary measure, consult with legal counsel to secure the protection of solicitor-client privilege.

This protection can help shield you from investigation, or at the very least limit the scope of any investigation. In a situation as volatile and as highly publicized as this, both the honest taxpayer and the Canadian who's been hiding something offshore can be victimized. Especially now that the Canadian government has agreed to reward whistle-blowers for information about offshore tax evaders.

Interviewer: *This was big news in the spring budget of 2013. The finance minister announced rewards for information leading to the recovery of offshore tax revenues. Do you think he knew about this data leak?*

Paul: The CBC apparently had been working on the information for about 7 months before they announced the leak. So most likely he did.

Interviewer: *Then why start a reward system now?*

Paul: Most first world countries pay for information. Canada decided it was time to do the same. But there is always a danger when you pay someone to snitch. Greed can tempt anyone to turn against you – your employees, your financial advisors or, in some cases, even your own family.

As a tax lawyer, I would suggest that if you're going to be a whistle-blower, you should first seek the protection of legal counsel. The

Minister of Finance may be happy to pay a reward for "good clean information" that leads to the recovery of tax revenues, but in verifying the calibre of the lead, the investigation might also delve into the whistle-blower's own financial affairs. That could mean an audit. This is not something you should enter into lightly, or unprotected.

Interviewer: *More than a year has passed and the media story seems all but dead. Are you aware of any related special investigations yet?*

Paul: No, I'm not. Presently I am working for clients who have been approached, but, of course, I cannot comment on their cases.

Interviewer: *Any guess as to why no real investigations?*

Paul: Canada's tax laws place a heavy burden on the shoulders of the middle class – especially the salaried middle class. Unfortunately our tax laws are used against us by offshore investors, who find ways to come here and enjoy the benefits of living here without paying any tax at all.

Interviewer: *Do you think it's fair to the taxpayers of Canada that non-Canadians can use our country as a tax haven?*

Paul: Money is a competitive business. Canada needs to keep up with the other financial nations of the world.

END OF INTERVIEW

As I said at the outset of this book, there is no fairness in tax.

Doubly Taxing Times for Americans "Abroad"

THEY MAY LIVE ONLY A SHORT DRIVE north of the border, but Americans cleave staunchly to their country, and refer to themselves as "Americans Abroad" when they are living outside the border of homeland U.S.A.

It is estimated that there are roughly one million "Americans Abroad" resident in Canada.

From a tax perspective, this was never much of an issue. Then came *The Foreign Account Tax Compliance Act* (FATCA). This American legislation has as its goal the identification of U.S. citizens who have undeclared assets in Canadian bank accounts. It's all part of the Internal Revenue Service's initiatives to count up every last penny held by every American in the world, anywhere in the world, in the hope of taxing as much of the money as possible.

Canada has caved to the pressure from our behemoth neighbour to the south and, effective July 1, 2014, has agreed to collect names, addresses and financial information of U.S. citizens, green-card holders and permanent residents with money in Canada and pass it along to the Canada Revenue Agency who will share, as appropriate, with the IRS.

There is one saving grace in all this. Information about holders of certain types of savings accounts, such as Registered Retirement Savings Plans, Registered Education Savings Plans, and Tax-Free Savings

Accounts, are exempt from the FATCA agreement, permitting a modicum of privacy to Americans who live and work here in Canada.

Why has Canada consented to cooperate with the IRS? The U.S. threatened to impose a 30% withholding tax on cross-border investments.

If you thought the Canadian Tax Crocodile had wide jaws and sharp teeth, peer into the mouth of IRS crocodile.

Regardless of where they reside, the IRS requires American citizens to file a tax return on their worldwide income each year. If taxes have been paid in Canada, the IRS will give a credit for that. Penalties for failure to file an annual U.S. tax return are very steep, regardless of whether there is tax owing.

In addition to the tax and interest accrued on the unreported income, a penalty of 20% of all tax underpayments, plus fines for failure to file proper returns will be levied. Additionally, a fine of between 5% and 25% of the highest total amount in their foreign bank account in the tax period is levied.

The new legislation provides for an additional penalty for failure to file a foreign bank and financial accounts form (FBAR) each year.

The IRS Offshore Voluntary Disclosure Program is usually the best possible solution to what could otherwise turn into a fiscal nightmare.

COMBINED CANADIAN/U.S. TAX DISCLOSURES

As you will read in the next section, Travels for Tax, I have been party to many and ongoing discussions with American tax lawyers to ensure that our firm is at all times current in our understanding of the terms of disclosure and the amnesties for penalties available.

In situations involving a family group who are U.S. citizens, some of whom live in Canada and others in the U.S., it may be necessary to combine a Canadian and U.S. tax disclosure. My practice is that, after successfully completing the Canadian amnesty, I meet directly with IRS criminal investigators to discuss the file on a no-name basis.

The American disclosure process differs from ours and the IRS must be approached with caution. Prior to making a disclosure, there may be an opportunity for tax counsel to discuss the facts of the situation on a no-name basis with IRS officials. After this meeting, tax counsel is in a position to advise the client, who can make the decision whether or not to come forward with a voluntary disclosure.

IRS officials normally start with a caution that when the disclosure is being made, the taxpayer's name must be given upfront and there is no guarantee that a criminal prosecution will not result.

Understand that making a voluntary disclosure does not negate the Justice Department's right to prosecute. Thus it is essential that counsel work towards securing a commitment that, if the disclosure is accepted, Justice will not prosecute.

DIFFERENT DISCLOSURE RULES BETWEEN CANADA AND THE U.S.

In Canada, the disclosure can cover the past 10 calendar years. At the time of this writing, the IRS tax amnesty will cover only the past 6 calendar years.

A comprehensive strategy has to be worked out before negotiations take place so as not to fall into any tax traps.

I am consulted regularly by American citizens concerned about how FATCA and its sister legislation, FBAR, affect them.

Working together with American legal counsel, I have negotiated several U.S. voluntary disclosures.

Many Americans living here wish to hide in the weeds and not come forward at this time. Members of this latter group are worried about whether, if caught, the U.S. authorities can seize their Canadian assets. In my view, it is unlikely. The only possibility of this happening is under the collection provisions of the Canada-U.S. Tax Treaty.

However, dual U.S./Canadian citizens have some protection because Article XXVIA, paragraph 8 of the Treaty appears to shield residents of Canada from enforcement of either FATCA or FBAR. In fact, the existence of this section, when it becomes more commonly known, may well start a mini-stampede of U.S. citizens living here to acquire Canadian nationality. Of course, the problem will remain if a U.S. citizen who has not complied with FBAR or FACTA enters the United States. Tax and regulatory traps could then be sprung.

The best protection is a private consultation with experienced tax counsel. You likely will have some warning before the IRS crocodile comes hunting and fishing in Canada.

Two Sisters/
Double Trouble

SANDRA WAS A DUAL CITIZEN OF Canada and the United States. She had lived in Calgary for many years. Her sister Carol lived in California and was only an American citizen. The sisters shared a tax problem.

Twenty years ago, their father, a well-to-do American businessman, had set up a bank account in Switzerland. He never reported the account to the Internal Revenue Service (IRS). The savings grew and grew and had provided him with a tidy annual income. When he died – and by now he had been gone nearly 10 years – he left the account to his daughters. They had never reported the inheritance to their respective tax authorities. To me that spelled double trouble.

Helping Sandra in Canada was relatively easy. I was able to do an analysis of the unreported income, amend 10 years of personal tax returns, and present them for assessment to the Canada Revenue Agency (CRA) under the Voluntary Disclosures Program. CRA accepted the disclosure and Sandra's Canadian tax problem was solved.

The IRS would not be so easy. As you've read and will read, I have travelled the world and built relationships with tax counsel and tax authorities in many countries, including the United States of America.

I have also maintained cordial relationships with the IRS agents of my acquaintance who were stationed in Ottawa.

I decided to avail myself of these relationships to help Sandra and Carol come clean to the IRS. I invited two senior IRS criminal investigators to my office. When they arrived there were telltale bulges under their jackets. It looked like they were "packing heat." The IRS doesn't take any chances.

On a no-name basis I sketched out the facts of the sisters' dilemma and asked the IRS agents to review my draft submissions to the IRS. They seemed surprised that a Canadian tax lawyer knew so much about the American tax laws, and complimented me on the completeness of the proposed disclosure. They didn't know that I had been ably assisted by a special consultant to the firm, who, before he joined us, had been head of the CRA Voluntary Disclosures Program in Ottawa. The American tax agents graciously offered to help shepherd the disclosure through the IRS if we ran into heavy seas.

I proceeded with disclosures to the IRS for both sisters, and when the IRS international tax office in Philadelphia (where international discolosures are reviewed) raised some troublesome questions, I called upon my IRS colleagues for help.

Apparently their chat with the folks in Philadelphia worked. What had been presented as a roadblock to the disclosure melted into a minor problem that could be worked out, and the disclosures for Sandra and Carol were approved.

Sometimes it's not what you know, but who you know, that makes the difference.

 # Travels for Tax

My Secret Swiss
Bank Account

IN MY EARLY DAYS AT CROCODILE central (inside the Department of National Revenue), the offshore tax havens of Europe were of particular interest to us.

We knew Canadians were stashing wealth in secret offshore accounts. In the aftermath of WWII, Europeans who had immigrated to Canada and established Canadian residency were still holding accounts in Switzerland, Lichtenstein, Luxembourg and Andorra. The Caribbean islands were not yet trusted as safe havens, making these European nations the prime locations for hiding money from the Taxman.

As a young lawyer working inside the Department of National Revenue, I was fascinated by how these tax havens worked, and I wondered how easy it would be to set up a secret account.

An opportunity presented itself on a family ski holiday to Switzerland.

The Civil Service Recreational Association (the R.A., as we called it) offered a family membership through which group travel could be booked at cheap prices. Swiss Air had a very affordable fare from Ottawa to Geneva, and my wife and I decided we could take our three children skiing in the Alps. A condition of the trip was a side-excursion for me to pop over to Zurich, Lichtenstein and Luxembourg to experiment with opening secret bank accounts, and speak to the local tax professionals.

Once arrived in Geneva, my wife and children toured the local environs while I took the train into Zurich. Armed only with a few hundred American dollars in cash and my Canadian passport, I walked into the branch of one of the largest of the Swiss banks.

I went over to the service desk and politely asked for help in opening a numbered account. The young man at the desk didn't blink. The Swiss banking act enshrined the privacy of account holders, and clearly my request was nothing out of the ordinary.

I was conducted into a small office, where one of the bankers completed the paperwork to open a numbered account, took my American cash, and handed me a deposit record. That was it. I was the proud owner of a secret Swiss-numbered account. I confess! But that was the only transaction the account ever saw.

The value of the exercise was that I had demonstrated, at least to myself, that it was easier to open an offshore account than to set one up in Canada. No wonder these accounts were so attractive to wealthy Canadians.

I also spoke to Swiss lawyers, posing as a Canadian who was interested in stashing money here, but concerned that the Canadian tax authorities would sniff it out. Repeatedly, I was assured that there was no requirement for me, as a Canadian, to report the existence of income paid into a Swiss account. Further, I was assured that bank secrecy in Switzerland was absolute, and that a banker could be prosecuted if he/she disclosed to the Canadian, or any other, tax authority the existence of an account.

It was the same in Lichtenstein and Luxembourg where, again, I opened numbered accounts with very modest deposits of American cash.

Emboldened by the success of my Swiss banking adventures, over the years I developed a personal practice of visiting other tax havens as they emerged, in particular such Caribbean island havens as Dominican Republic, Grand Cayman, and Turks and Caicos. I also travelled to Curacao, Hong Kong, Ireland, Argentina and Israel. I didn't open secret accounts in all these places, but I did make a point of meeting with local business people, bankers, and tax professionals to get a first-hand understanding of how their tax systems (or lack thereof) operated and what protections were (and, just as important, weren't) applicable to Canadians with bank accounts in the jurisdiction.

There are book smarts and street smarts. You learn the latter with hands-on experience. Or that was the excuse I used for this tax travelling.

A final note on my first trip into Zurich.

On the train back to Geneva, I was hungry and went into the dining car to order a meal. The food was excellent, and I enjoyed the cuisine. I wondered, however, why everyone else in the dining car wasn't eating. They just kept staring at me.

I finished my meal and went back to my seat. The stares were explained when, shortly thereafter, all the passengers were served with bread and cheese, compliments of the train service.

Those in the know ate for free, while I paid a pretty price. Watch the locals and do what they do. For travellers, these are words to live by. And validation for my practice of learning about tax havens first hand.

Our Lady of the Andes

THE SNOWY PEAKS OF THE ANDES glittered above us in the afternoon sun. Carmen and I were standing before a monastery with pale gray walls whose occupants were sworn to absolute silence and prayer. A relative in Ottawa, who was afflicted with cancer of the liver, was particularly devoted to the Virgin Mary. He requested that, after attending the tax conference in Argentina, I find him a medal of Our Lady of the Andes.

Locating the medal was the easy part. The problem was the afflicted person had also asked me to get it blessed by one of the pious monks at Our Lady of the Andes.

Finding the monastery was a quest worthy of the most devout pilgrim. The sanctuary was in a remote part of a heavily forested area at the foot of the Andes. Of course, there were no signs posted to show us the way, or tell us how much farther it was to the monastery. This was rural Argentina, and the concept of American-style signage is non-existent. We were constantly stopping to ask local farmers about the "*Monasterio.*" We learned the word quickly. We would say it, with a question mark at the end, and the farmers would nod, and smile and point us in the right direction. Or so we hoped.

Each successive farmer pointed us in the same general direction, so we were reasonably confident we would eventually reach our goal. We drove ever onward until, at last, the pale grey walls came into view.

There was a gate, with a bench out front, and a bell hanging from a tree branch. Adjacent to the bench was a small chapel whose doors proved to be locked. The majesty of the mountains, coupled with absolute quiet and a magnificent setting, made it seem to be the perfect place to live a life of contemplation and prayer.

We got out of the car, and waited, hoping someone would see us and come out to help. No one came. Eventually, I pulled on the rope. The little bell pealed quite loudly, and the sound carried far. Still nothing. We sat on the bench and waited. It seemed the right thing to do in a place of such quiet contemplation.

After several more minutes, a young acolyte came out from the gate. He greeted us and asked why we had come. I told him of my mission. I was seeking a blessing for the medal of Our Lady of the Andes, as requested by my ailing relative in Canada. The young man was understanding. The Superior was at prayer, he said, but afterward he would come out to open the chapel and bless the medal. Please, would we wait?

We did. I don't know how long we waited. It was very still there, at the foot of the Andes, sitting on the bench outside the walls of the monastery. At last, the Superior emerged with a key in hand. He opened the chapel, and invited us in. He asked for the name of my relative, and the nature of his condition, before he took the medal from me and blessed it. He told me that he, as the Superior, was the only monk in the monastery allowed to talk, and only on special occasions. In this instance, it appeared that he was very happy to speak and happy to bless the medal. I carefully carried the medal home with me, where it was cherished by my relative. I believe it helped him to bear the affliction that eventually claimed his life.

After the Andes excursion, we returned to Buenos Aires, where I was attending the tax conference. The city is magnificent, with a population in large part descended from European immigrants.

After the sessions at the tax conference were completed, before we returned to Canada, we had a hankering to visit the spectacular Iguazu Falls. If you have seen the feature film, *The Mission*, you will recognize this magnificent location.

We were lucky to have, as our guide, an Argentine friend, Marguerita, who had boarded with us in Ottawa while completing her studies. She was now a history professor in Mendoza and, happily, on her break between semesters.

Marguerita shepherded us out to Iguazu Falls, where we climbed into rubber boats and went behind the massive torrent of water. Then we explored the ruins of the Mission set up by Jesuit priests in the 1750s.

From Iguazu we journeyed to a Dutch-owned wine estate in a valley at the foot of the Andes. It was a state-of-the-art facility. We stayed for the weekend and, of course, we sampled the wines and dined well.

While we were there, a helicopter landed with a camera crew from, of all places, British Columbia. They were scouting for places to build mountain ski resorts. What better way to do this than by helicopter?

They were staying at the winery that night, and we were happy to dine and chat at length with our Canadian compatriots. We were sorry to see the helicopter lift off with them in the morning. But all too soon, we too were on our way back to Canada, the blessed medal safely in my care.

Too Close to Paradise

FOLLOWING MY "VISIT-THE-TAX-haven-personally" policy was a wonderful excuse to travel to some of the most beautiful spots on earth. But even a trip to paradise is not without peril. In this case we literally came too close to eternal paradise.

Carmen and I landed in Mauritius at Sir Seewoosagur Ramgoolam International Airport in a blinding tropical rainstorm.

We'd been on safari in Kenya, travelling cross-country on potholed, ever-shrinking roads built more than 70 years earlier by Italian prisoners of war, and not repaired since. After this wilderness adventure, our next stop, Mauritius, via Air France, sounded like a piece of cake.

The flight from Nairobi to Réunion had started off beautifully. As we flew past the snow-covered summit of Mount Kilimanjaro, the flight crew played *I'm Sitting on Top of Kilimanjaro* on the sound system. I happily sang along – very likely out of tune. The sun shone brightly, and as we circled to land in Réunion, we could see the island gleaming like a jewel in the azure seas. The moment our plane touched down the storm hit.

Waiting on the runway was a small Mauritian Airways plane – our transfer flight. The little plane was rocking violently in the wind. The wind blew the rain into solid sheets of water. Just getting into the plane was a feat equal to climbing Kilimanjaro. We wanted to turn tail and run for shelter in a warm hotel for the night, or longer if need be. But friends, and our eldest daughter, Anne, were waiting for us in Mauritius. We were compelled to travel on that night. In retrospect, perhaps it was not the wisest choice.

We boarded the plane and ascended into the raging storm. It was like being on a roller coaster. Outside, the wind and rain lashed against the plane. Lightning flashed.

We were travelling with a priest, a relative of my wife. Father Reginald was a missionary priest in Kenya. He taught at the Starahe School in Nairobi and had been our guide and companion on our African safari. He had never been to Mauritius, which I explained was arguably the most beautiful tax haven in the world. He was intrigued, so we invited him to come with us. Propitious foresight, as it turned out.

The storm raged on, and we were not exactly the most intrepid of travellers. Death was literally staring us in the face. We asked Father Reginald to intercede with the Almighty on our behalf, and grant us safe arrival at our destination. He led us in prayers, and then all we could do was sit tight and hope. It was touch and go, but after what seemed to be an eternity, the little plane managed to land in one piece, and with all aboard safe and sound. Our welcoming party whisked us off to our hotel to rest and recuperate.

The next day dawned gloriously sunny. It was Sunday so we scouted around for a church where we could hear Mass and give thanks for our safe deliverance.

One of the earliest groups of settlers on Mauritius had come from France. They left a few churches in their wake, and we were lucky enough to find one in a lovely wooded glade. It was a beautiful building, reminiscent of those built in 18th-century France. It was empty when we entered. Reginald spotted an organ near the altar. He was an accomplished musician, and we had come to give thanks. So he sat down at the organ and began to play.

The music was wonderful. So wonderful, that it aroused the parish priest, who came looking for the source of the heavenly song. He greeted us warmly, and called upon his staff to give the ladies a tour of the church and the ancient cemetery beside it while he took Reginald and me aside and invited us to join him in the rectory for breakfast. He thought that I, too, was a priest, hence the invitation to the inner sanctum. As we ate, I realized his mistake, and confessed that I was not only a lay person, but husband and father, respectively, to the lovely ladies who were touring the cemetery. The priest laughed at his mistake, and then asked Reginald to say mass with him. I re-joined my wife and daughter, and together we attended the mass. After our ordeal, the ceremony was quite calming.

In the ensuing days, as we travelled around the island, I was struck by how members of the various religions got along together. We could see for ourselves, and were told, that many stopped to pay their respects at each others' roadside shrines. They also celebrated each others' festivals. There was an easy island informality about the many faiths. You could, for instance, as we did, climb up to a Hindu temple on a high mountain and speak to the priest for hours on end about their pantheon of Gods, and leave with his good wishes and blessing. While all of this could and probably will change, it was beautiful to witness the concept of peace and brotherly love in practice.

We were lucky enough to be the guests of close relatives of the Associate Prime Minister. A grey Mercedes and driver was put at our disposal on an "as needed" basis. This was not often required, since our travel needs were modest. But I had work to do. While the rest of the party stayed at our hotel near the sea, I began my research into how they operated a tax haven in such a paradise.

Since Mauritius is located nearly in the middle of the Indian Ocean, much of its business comes from India. I discovered that a lot of business people from France made use of the banking and other financial services on the island, presumably to reduce their visibility to the tax authorities back home. This often was done in conjunction with their vacations.

The banking and financial services in Mauritius were similar to, and certainly much cheaper than, those offered by Switzerland, Lichtenstein, Luxembourg and other high-end tax havens. However, the distance one needed to travel was simply too great to make the island useful to most North Americans.

As always, the experience enhanced my understanding of this tax haven, and I established a number of good contacts who could be of assistance should the need arise in future.

A Viennese Waltz
for One and
Other Bagatelles

AUSTRIAN AIRLINES HAD JUST called out the boarding announce-
ment and we had almost reached the gangway when Carmen suddenly
exclaimed, "I can't get on the plane."

Given some of our earlier adventures and frightening plane rides
en route to tax conferences and tax havens, perhaps she was unwilling
to roll the dice one more time. In any case, this sudden panic came as
a complete surprise to both of us.

It was our 45th wedding anniversary and I had mapped out an
itinerary worthy of an ideal husband. We were going to Vienna. Yes,
for a tax conference, but for so much more. I had booked a large hotel
suite on the Ringestrasse. We had tickets to the famous Viennese Ball,
where I planned, in my own clumsy way, to whisk my beloved bride
into many a waltz, in the ballroom where the waltz originated. We
were going to experience firsthand the Musikverein, and numerous
other venues that paid homage to a city where many of the composers
we revere today – Mozart, Haydn, Strauss, Bach, Beethoven, Brahms
– had lived and composed their masterpieces.

All that was suddenly in jeopardy if my wife could not board
the plane. Clearly, I could not press the matter. The problem then
switched to the bureaucratic regulations. Once a passenger's luggage

was loaded into the belly of the plane, if that passenger did not board, the cargo hold would have to be unloaded again and the baggage removed. That could take hours. Both the airline and the other passengers would be angered at such a delay. After a hurried conference with a senior Austrian Airlines official, it was agreed that, provided I boarded the plane, the luggage could remain and the flight could depart on schedule.

So I flew to Vienna with an empty seat beside me.

Vienna was all that I had expected. In addition to my attendance at the International Tax Association events, I had scheduled my own meetings with Austrian financiers, lawyers and accountants. It was all part of my ongoing research on trends and best practices for international tax planning and other tax related issues.

It was after the business of tax was managed that the full impact of flying solo to Vienna hit home.

There I was, alone in the Golden Ballroom of the Musikverein, watching the men in white tie and tails whirl ladies in long white gowns across the dance floor. Everyone asked if my wife would be joining me soon, expressed their regret that she was back home in Canada, and then got up to dance, leaving me the odd man out. Afterwards, I made the rounds of the wine festivals in the hills around Vienna, but the wine, for all its flavour, was lacking when enjoyed without the companionship of *ma douce moitié* – my softer half.

I made side trips to Salzburg and Prague, but being a loner lessens one's enjoyment.

From a tax perspective, however, there were some highlights. During the conference I met Harvey, a senior tax attorney from Chicago. He practiced in a very large firm of tax lawyers. We were both stag in Vienna, so we often dined together and enjoyed lengthy discussions about how our Canadian tax amnesty system was different from that in the United States.

In my view, our Canadian tax amnesty rules were way ahead of the Yanks in how we brought forward and rehabilitated tax cheats. In some ways, my American friend did not disagree.

Harvey and I met thereafter in Chicago, at a tax conference hosted by the American Bar. He and some members of his firm very kindly walked me through the inner workings of the Internal Revenue Service (IRS) practices and procedures in dealing with voluntary disclosures. This later stood me in good stead when I had to follow up several Canadian disclosures with companion submissions to American tax officials.

They say that travel broadens one. Well, the tax traveller not only broadens his knowledge, but adds the power of important contacts to his kit bag, ready to deal with future problems in an expeditious and efficient way.

IN THE EMERALD ISLE

That philosophy took me to the (ABA) American Bar Association's tax conference in Dublin. The Irish were hosting the conference in the hopes of attracting more American corporations to take advantage of their revised tax laws. At the time, Ireland was offering huge incentives for foreign businesses to locate there. American businesses were always prime targets, which explained the invitation.

So with our good friends, Jean-Pierre and Agathe, Carmen and I travelled to Dublin. (You will remember Jean-Pierre from the tale of the Calabria Earthquake relief fund, "I Need a Cheque for a Million Dollars – Yesterday!")

The tax conference was tremendously productive. I spoke with several Irish tax professionals who had been working abroad, and had been able to return to their homeland now that there was so much business coming in from overseas.

On the first day of the conference, I heard the speeches of welcome from officials of the Irish Tax Office. What a surprise! They said taxes had been reduced very substantially and regulations cut because they wanted to welcome American business to set up in Ireland. They repeated over and over that they were open for business and would help in every way possible. The benefit for them was that Irish men and women would be employed. The upside for the U.S. companies was low taxes, minimal regulation and, best of all, easy access to the European Economic Community.

The Irish are legendary for the "blarney" that invariably charms their listeners. Here it worked very well indeed. After we discussed in session the nuts and bolts of the tax and corporate legislation, they held a big party for the ABA members in a resort complex near Dublin.

We Canadians were included in the invitation. It was quite a shindig. Our hosts went all out. It all started off quietly, but soon, what with the fun, the music, the Irish dancers and, of course, the liquid refreshment, they had us eating out of the palms of their hands. Maybe in the light of day things would change a bit, but that night everyone was ready to recommend to their clients that Ireland was the place to do business.

Notwithstanding the generous servings of blarney and Irish whiskey, the Irish tax officials were a delight to speak to, and the source of a wealth of information on how we could set up our clients there to obtain maximum tax and other benefits.

I share, as an aside, that the Irish provided a stark contrast to the Canadian tax establishment and the minimal tax incentives provided to do business in Canada. Maybe, even given the present difficulties in the Irish economy, our own government could take some lessons from the Irish experiment and help out Canadian business with a simpler tax system.

After the Dublin tax conference was over, our small company of Canadians embarked on a tour of the Emerald Isle.

We stayed in quaint little towns along the coast, drinking in the atmosphere – and a few other things, too. One morning we got up early and went out to explore the town and enjoy the rare morning sunshine. Agathe stumbled on the cobblestones and broke the heel of her shoe. We asked the shopkeepers if they could direct us to a cobbler, and soon we were standing in the doorway of a very tiny and ancient shop. The shoemaker himself was tiny and ancient. (No, he was not a leprechaun, but he had the look of one.) As he worked at his last, we saw that he was wearing on his feet a pair of very ratty and very old slippers. He took Agathe's shoe in his hands, looked it over, and said he could fix it, but it would take about an hour.

We left him the shoe and went back out into the sunshine. Jean-Pierre and I clearly weren't paying attention to the details, because after a few minutes we noticed that Agathe was shuffling along behind us. We looked down at her feet, and there she was, in the shoemaker's old slippers.

We all laughed and laughed and laughed. This *soignée* woman from Quebec was shuffling along the streets of an Irish town in shoddy slippers several sizes too large for her slender feet. We laughed so hard, in fact, that a pair of local constables came over to see if we needed assistance.

"Yes," I said, still laughing. "I'd like to buy a bottle of Irish whiskey."

No sooner had I said the words than the constables were escorting us down the street, around a corner, and up the lane to the seller of spirits. I expected them to leave us at the door of the shop, but to my surprise they came right in with us and shared their personal opinions on the relevant merits of a number of different whiskies. I followed their advice and chose the one they recommended as "the best."

We weren't about to stop there in the whiskey shop to taste it, so the constables finally tipped their hats to us, wished us well and went on their way.

We shuffled back with Agathe to the shoemaker's shop, where her shoe was waiting, freshly mended and ready for wear. Like the prince finding his Cinderella, Jean-Pierre slipped it on her foot, and we went on our merry way.

Another day, as we drove along the coastline, a Canadian flag came into view. It turned out to be the residence of our Ambassador to Ireland. Well, the little devil had built a private 18-hole golf course on the grounds of the residence. He was living like a prince on the backs of Canadian taxpayers. That was the only downer of the trip.

I understand that the Ambassador's residence has now been sold and more modest premises are presently at the disposal of our representative in that country.

As we journeyed on, we kept to the back roads and went from town to town along the coast. Jean-Pierre and Agathe both had a wonderful sense of humour, and we all enjoyed jolly banter with the locals.

The quirks of human nature make you remember the oddest things. One day, along the coast, we ran into a massive storm. The sea was very angry, the rain was pelting down and the wind howled around us so fiercely that the rain was getting under our raincoats. Nonetheless the feeling of being out in a storm was exhilarating.

Jean-Pierre, who is always fast with the quips, grinned at me and said, "If anyone needs to break wind, now's the time!" It was even funnier in French, "*Ceux qui veulent péter, c'est le temps!*"

Despite the downpour, we were all convulsed with laughter. There remains a bit of juvenile wit in all of us. Later on, we sought the refuge of a local pub to dry out, and had a great and jolly chat with the locals.

At the end of the trip we were all in agreement that the Emerald Isle was certainly a rare jewel in the Irish Sea.

AND IN A JAPANESE GARDEN

As a final bagatelle, I share one last memory from the many international tax conferences I attended.

My brother-in-law, Albert, is a retired Air Canada pilot. He has flown the world and stayed in more places than anyone I know. He recommended that, on my journey to Kyoto for a tax conference, I land at Norita Airport. It was closest to Kyoto, and the ground transportation would be easiest from there.

Following his advice, I landed at Norita and was driven into the former Imperial City and first capital of Japan. The tax conference was scheduled to take place in a Western-style hotel. But Albert had recommended Japanese-style accommodations nearby that catered to local business travellers.

Albert's travel insights were, as always, impeccably accurate.

My rooms looked out onto a beautiful Japanese garden, which could be accessed through sliding doors. The furniture was located at floor level, and one needed to kneel down in order to use it. Futons for sleeping were hidden in cupboards at the edge of the room.

It was excessively hot in Kyoto. When I would come back from a day at the tax conference, my favourite pastime was a Japanese shower/tub soak ritual. You stripped down and stepped into a cool shower. From there you plunged directly into a huge wooden tub filled with very hot water, and soaked for a good half hour. Once out of the tub, I would don the robe and sandals provided in the room and go out to sit in a beautiful garden. In such a hot climate, it was an exquisite pleasure to cool off and power down in this elegant setting. One could sit quietly for hours without being disturbed. I took full advantage of the opportunity during my stay.

At the tax conference meetings, I noticed that few of the representatives from the big Canadian accounting and legal firms bothered to attend the technical sections. They were there to schmooze with their Japanese counterparts and get business. Our tax law practice caters to the little guy who has tax problems and needs resolution. Thus my focus was to learn as much practical information as possible. One does, however, make contacts that may be useful in future. In a Japanese tea house, I met a number of businessmen who gave me the real scoop on how to deal with their tax bureaucrats. It was an eye opener, and I am able to use those insights in assisting my clients.

While in Kyoto I participated in the events organized by the tax conference, which included visits to geisha houses for tea ceremonies, and the like. True to my own practice, as you have already seen in previous tales, I also go beyond the organized tours and travel on my own to see the country and experience the culture first hand. The local food and everyday people one encounters are the window to the soul of any country. So it was in Japan and my personal side trips, as always, paid great dividends.

The Tax Games

Confession of a Tax Evader

IN 1906, SAMUEL CLEMENS, more popularly known as Mark Twain (author of, among others, *The Adventures of Tom Sawyer* (1876) and *A Connecticut Yankee in King Arthur's Court* (1889)), spoke to an affluent audience at Carnegie Hall.

It was the Silver Jubilee of the Tuskegee Institute, and Twain's goal was to raise $1,800,000 for the school. In 1906, that was a very great deal of money.

Twain was up to the challenge. He sought to charm his listeners into opening their wallets by talking on a subject near and dear to the heart of any man with money – tax. In particular *not paying* tax.

The talk began with Twain reminding his listeners that, under New York City law, once a year taxpayers had the perfectly legal right to make an oath that they did not own as much property as the records showed, for the purposes of being assessed at a lower tax rate.

Twain made an amusing confession of his tax evasion (excerpted from his speech "As to Tax Dodgers").

> There are two separate and distinct kinds of morals, so separate, so distinct, so unrelated that they are no more kin to each other than are archangels and politicians. The one kind is private morals, the other is public morals.

The loyal observance of private morals has made this Nation what it is, an upright people in its private domestic life, an honest and honourable people in its private commercial life. During 363 days in the year the American citizen is true to his private morals, and keeps undefiled the Nation's character at its best and highest; then in the other two days of the year he leaves his private morals at home, and carries his public morals to the tax office and does the best he can to damage and undo his whole year's faithful and righteous worth.

Once a year he lays aside his private morals and gets out his public morals and goes to the Tax Office and holds up his hand and swears he hasn't got a cent in the world, so help him! The next day the list appears in the papers a column and a quarter of names in fine print, and every man in the list a billionaire and a member of a couple of churches.

I know all those people. I have friendly, social, and criminal intercourse with the whole of them. They never miss a sermon when they are around and they never miss tax swearing-off day, whether they are around or not. The innocent cannot remain innocent in the disintegrating atmosphere of this thing. I used to be an honest man. I am crumbling. No, I have crumbled. When they assessed me at $75,000 a fortnight ago I went out and tried to borrow the money, and couldn't; then when I found they were letting a whole crop of millionaires live in New York at a third of the price they were charging me I was hurt. I was indignant, and said: 'This is the last feather! I am not going to run this town all by myself." In that moment, in that memorable moment, I began to crumble.

In fifteen minutes the disintegration was complete. In fifteen minutes I became just a mere moral sandpile, and I lifted up my hand along with those seasoned and experienced deacons and swore off every item of personal property I've got in the world, clear down to cork leg, glass eye, and what is left of my wig.

Those tax officers were moved, they were profoundly moved; they had long been accustomed to seeing hardened old grafters act like that, and they could endure the spectacle; but they were expecting better things of me, a chartered professional moralist, and they were saddened. I fell visibly in their respect and esteem, and I should have fallen in my own, except that I had already struck bottom and there wasn't any place to fall to.

At least Mr. Twain made an honest, albeit tongue-in-cheek, confession.

In my experience, active tax dodgers have little or no shame. When exposed by the tax authorities they become victims of bad advice, naivety, ignorance, and a host of other attributes that, in their opinion, should excuse the failure to report their income, or their involvement in a scheme to avoid payment of tax.

Here follow anthropological insights, tales and confessions of some of the more colourful tax avoidance attitudes and efforts of my experience.

Taxpayer Demographics: A Behavioural Study

PAYING MONEY UNDER THE TABLE in order to avoid tax is endemic across Canada. Either people think nothing is wrong with the practice, or they do so believing that the chances of getting caught are very slim.

EVEN JUDGES DO IT

Many people, including those who really should know better, treat tax evasion as a mere social *faux pas*. Here is a recap of a *National Post* article about someone who really should have known better (January 19, 2013):

> A Quebec Judge was so upset when the granite countertop in her kitchen cracked that she sued the contractor in Small Claims Court to get a refund of her money. At trial, the evidence revealed that there was an agreement between the parties to do the work for cash under the table. The judge who heard the case remarked, "This contract was made for cash payments in contravention of tax law, with an ultimate

goal of depriving the community of taxes. Just as surprisingly, the parties do not even seem to want to hide it."

He was astonished that a judge was unconcerned about actively assisting in tax evasion. A spokesperson for the Chief Judge of Quebec stated that all judges are expected to respect the law. It is required for their code of ethics.

The Canada Revenue Agency (CRA) has studied the problem and come up with its own answer.

Based on their analysis of the 25 million-plus tax returns filed each year, with additional insight from the non-compliance team in the field, who chase down all the other taxpayers who *don't* file, Canadian taxpayers, according to the CRA analysts, fall into six behavioural categories:

1. *The Law Abiders – 31%:* This group exhibits the lowest risk of cheating on taxes. They think it is risky to cheat on taxes and that people who do so will get caught – and should get caught. They often think Canada's tax rates are too high, but follow the law because they are afraid to risk getting caught.

2. *Altruistic Compliers – 18%:* This group exhibits similar behaviours to law abiders, but they are less likely to believe that people who cheat on their taxes will get caught. They view tax cheating as serious, and might be tempted to do it, but don't because they are afraid they will be caught. If times got tough, they might change behaviours and become part of another group.

3. *Rationalizers – 12%:* This group is most likely to think that cheating on taxes is "not a big deal," and believe that it's not really a crime. They are likely to accept services without tax when offered. This group believes there's no risk to them, because they pay their taxes. They shrug their shoulders at the tax cheats. If cheaters can get away with it, they think, lucky them.

4. *Underground Economists – 12%:* What, me a tax evader? This group is most likely to have some income on the side that they never declare. They pay enough tax, they say, and there's nothing wrong with keeping some money from the Taxman. They don't think they will ever be caught. If the Taxman catches up with them, it's still no big deal. They'll just pay the tax then.

5. *Over-Taxed Opportunists – 14%:* These people believe that taxes are too high and seek out opportunities to avoid taxes, or to get refunds on their at-source deductions. These people were, and are, prime targets for the various tax refund schemes that I'll discuss in the following pages. They see "everyone else" paying less tax and want in on it. They still profess to be honest taxpayers.

6. *Outlaws – 13%:* This group flatly refuse to follow the rule book. They won't report all their income, or won't file for several years, or will overstate business expenses. Everyone else is doing it, and if their tax preparer says it okay to try this, they see nothing wrong in playing the odds. Outlaws are likely to use serial bankruptcies to wash away tax arrears. Like the "rationalizers," it's no big deal, because it's just tax.

Based on the foregoing, the CRA suggests that at least 40% of taxpayers will – or do – practice a form of tax avoidance that is really tax evasion. Even more would participate if they thought they could get away with it.

As part of the DioGuardi TAXTV® online tax news programs, I have sent editorial teams out to the street armed with videocams and questions for passersby.

Here's a sampling of the questions we asked, and the spontaneous answers.

(If you want to watch the program in its entirely, follow the link to *www.taxtv.ca* and look for the title "TaxTV Talks Back.")

As you read the questions and answers, choose which of the above six groups you think each of the respondents fits into. (I'll share my own assessments at the end of the quiz.)

Question: Do you think we pay too much tax?
Answer 1: It's a privilege to pay taxes.
Answer 2: Taxes? Who pays those?
Answer 3: The more you get, the more you give away.
Answer 4: I think it was Bismarck who said, "There are two things no sensible person should ever know about. How sausages are made, and taxes are calculated."

Question: Have you ever cheated on your taxes?
Answer 1: I'm basically a tax avoider. I do my best to not pay taxes.
Answer 2: No. I don't want to go to jail.
Answer 3: I haven't filed for 3 years. When they finally come after me, then I'll just pay what I owe.

Question: Have you ever *thought* about cheating on your taxes?
Answer 1: Every year, but I'm afraid I'd get caught.
Answer 2: If people don't get to keep 2 out of every 3 dollars they make, they start thinking about cheating, or at least finagling.
Answer 3: It's the biggest mafia in the world. They do what they want and you do what they tell you.

Given the "person on the street" answers above, I suggest that 40% is much too low.

WHICH BEHAVIOUR GROUP DID YOU ASSIGN TO EACH ANSWER?

Here are my assessments:

Question: Do you think we pay too much tax?
Answer 1: Law Abider
Answer 2: Underground Economist
Answer 3: Rationalizer
Answer 4: Altruistic Complier

Question: Have you ever cheated on your taxes?
Answer 1: Outlaw
Answer 2: Rationalizer
Answer 3: Underground Opportunist

Question: Have you ever thought about cheating on your taxes?
Answer 1: Altruistic Complier
Answer 2: Rationalizer
Answer 3: Overtaxed Opportunist

And the judge I referenced at the start of the chapter? Definitely a Rationalizer.

Tax Credits and Crocodile Traps

COME TAX TIME, CANADIANS and their media are obsessed with tax refunds. Getting money back when you file your return seems to be the greatest good, and the standard by which all accountants and financial advisors are measured. All this is in pursuit of the candy trail carefully laid by politicians to buy your vote.

While there is merit in organizing one's financial affairs to pay the least amount of tax possible under the law, the unmitigated quest for a *tax refund* creates dangers for both the tax filer and anyone with whom they have had financial dealings. And to what end?

Here's a short list of four write-offs and tax credits that, while worthy of consideration, may expose you or others to the scrutiny of the Taxman.

Remember, the crocodile lies patiently in wait, jaws wide open, to snap at every morsel offered by your disclosures. That tax credit may cost you a finger – if not an arm and a leg.

1. CHILDREN'S ARTS TAX CREDIT

You can claim up to $500 per child for fees paid for dance/piano/arts classes your kids take. But before you go after the maximum of $75 (per child) that you might get back, consider this. In order to get the credit, you'll need receipts from the school or the nice woman down the street who teaches Jimmie the do-re-mi's of the keyboard. When you're assessed, the CRA might ask to see your receipts, and your proof of payment (cancelled cheques, or bank or credit card statements – something you really don't want to be showing the CRA for a $75 credit).

The CRA might also request more information from you about the teacher, such as her name, address, SIN and whether she charged you HST on the lessons. When the CRA asks, you have to answer. The piano teacher will not thank you when the CRA comes to audit her and requests the names and addresses of all her students. After all that, you still might not get the credit. See this cautionary note reproduced from the CRA website: "**Note:** A receipt does not guarantee the eligibility of a program."

2. CHILDREN'S FITNESS TAX CREDIT

For soccer/hockey/baseball/gymnastics and other kids "fitness" programs, the same principles apply as above.

3. ONTARIO HEALTHY HOMES RENOVATION TAX CREDIT

This renovation credit, designed to buy the votes of the elderly and the aging baby boomers who are now themselves so often caring for aged parents, succeeds the home renovation credit from a couple of years ago. (That one had a hidden catch. To get the credit for your new furnace or the window retrofit, you had to pay $500 for an energy audit from a government-accredited energy audit company, who reported on the energy efficiency of your home. Speculatively, this was likely so your energy audit could be held against you if and when the government found a way to introduce a "green" tax, like a carbon tax, to be levied against everyone whose home wasn't up to the standard determined by the government. Sounds like pre-revolutionary France where you were taxed on the size of each window. ... But I digress.)

This healthy homes renovation tax credit reimburses Ontario residents over age 65 for up to 15% of the cost of eligible home renovations (to a maximum credit of about $1500) for the purpose of making the home safer for seniors. Eligible expenses are things like ramps, stair lifts, handrails and other home safety aids for seniors. Before you go to grab the credit, make sure your renovator or handyman gave you accurate invoices and charged HST, etc., because the CRA will want your receipts so they can make sure the renovator reported everything.

4. PUBLIC TRANSIT TAX CREDIT

If you took public transit to get to work or school, you deserve a break. Just make sure you're not trying to write-off parking, gas and mileage at the same time. If the Taxman thinks you're double-dipping, he'll look closer.

At the end of the day, there's no such thing as free money. Every write-off has strings attached to someone else, somewhere else in the system. But, if you're still hell-bent on squeezing every dollar you can from the public treasury, remember the rules of tax refunds.

You'll only get a tax refund if:

- you file a tax return,
- you identify and qualify for the tax credits you're after,
- your return is assessed as having no tax owing, meaning that you've already paid throughout the year, and you have no balance owing from earlier years and
- your return is assessed as filed, meaning that CRA accepts everything you've reported.

A FINAL CAVEAT

After you receive your refund, *the CRA can still go back and review any of your write-offs and expenses for up to 3 past tax years*, ask to audit what you claimed, and then may deny the write-off(s) and ask for the refund back with interest. So just because it worked last year doesn't guarantee you're safe.

The Bigger the Refund, the Better the Accountant

THE PRECEDING CAVEAT AGAINST the overzealous pursuit of tax credits, in "Tax Credits and Crocodile Traps," pales in the face of the ingenious tax rebate schemes conceived by some of the most unscrupulous accountants, financial advisors and tax planners I have ever come across. (And in nearly 50 years of tax practice I have seen more than my fair share of scamsters.)

Over the past 10 years, thousands of ordinary people across Canada – people just like you – were invited by friends, co-workers, even family members, to attend a seminar that would help them get back all the taxes deducted at source on their salaried income.

They were told that it was all perfectly legal. The folks running the seminar, we'll call them M.T. and O.P., said they knew all the inside tricks at the Canada Revenue Agency (CRA), and how CRA policies "trapped" you into paying tax.

M.T. had written a book about how the CRA was tricking Canadians into paying tax which, legally, was not collectible. The book was available for sale online.

O.P. claimed to have been a senior auditor for the CRA. So you believed him when he said you were entitled to refile your tax returns and secure the recovery of all the tax collected from you at source. O.P. did not mention that this tax recovery was achieved by reporting fabricated business income and much larger business losses, in amounts precisely calculated to essentially secure, through loss carry-back provisions, the rebate of all tax deducted each year at source as per your T4 summary.

The cost: $500 upfront to M.T. and company, and then 20% of the tax rebate once you received it.

You could refile from 3 to 10 years of past tax returns to receive the tax rebate. Or you could start with your present year's tax return. Or you could do both. M.T. and O.P. found tax preparers to prepare and submit your returns. Usually you were sent the signature page only, which you signed and returned to the tax preparer. And presto, each year you got a big fat cheque back from the CRA. It was as good as magic!

Year after year you continued to get the big payback. Until, one day a letter arrived from the CRA, "reviewing" your business expenses and losses as reported on your tax returns. You were asked to provide details of your business, your employees and all the other expenses you wrote off over the years.

You wondered what was going on. You don't have a business. You don't have employees. What was the CRA thinking?

By this time – roughly sometime in 2008 or 2009, M.T. realized that the jig was up.

He contacted all his clients, with reassuring messages. "Don't worry." said M.T. "The CRA's position is illegal. You don't have to answer them. Or if you do, here's a guide on how to create dummy T4 slips for your dummy employees."

Eventually, the CRA reassessed your returns, and demanded repayment of the rebates received, along with arrears interest and, in many cases, heavy penalties for making false claims on your tax return.

"Don't worry," said M.T. again. "We'll object. Here's a sample objection letter. Print it, sign it and send it to the CRA."

By 2010 he had added a new twist to the scheme. He introduced you to a tax lawyer who would file a variation of a boilerplate objection for you. Just send him $500 and he'll file a Notice of Objection on your behalf. He'll make it all go away. You haven't done anything wrong. The CRA can't collect any of this money from you while you are under Objection.

You didn't hear anything for almost a year. Then you got a fresh e-mail from the tax lawyer, or M.T., or both, advising that your Objection was not going to be successful, and that your reassessments from the CRA had been, or would be, confirmed.

Now the tax arrears were due, and the CRA was demanding payment. The amounts at issue were typically huge. In some cases the tax bills were over $100,000, or even twice that. It was enough to make bankruptcy a serious consideration.

Once again M.T. e-mailed to say he could advise you on how to appeal to the tax court. He could do it even better than the tax lawyer, he said, so you should really pay him $500 and forget about the lawyer. M.T. would provide you with a template Notice of Appeal and you just had to send it to the Tax Court. This would delay the CRA from being able to collect on the tax arrears.

And the court, M.T. was certain, would agree that the CRA's assessments were bogus. You would never have to pay back the tax rebates.

Unfortunately, M.T. and O.P. and certain of their tax preparer accomplices were already under criminal investigation by the CRA, who raided their residences in November 2012 and then charged both with defrauding Her Majesty and the public treasury by filing false income tax returns for clients and, of course, for themselves.

Now you were really on your own or left looking for a different tax lawyer to help you deal with the CRA.

M.T. had his first court appearance in March 2013. I have not yet been able to determine if O.P. has been located, or has appeared in court to face charges.

Other agents and tax preparers of this ilk are still at large or, in the case of one promoter from the Vancouver area, have escaped to foreign tax havens.

Conservatively, this scheme has likely defrauded Her Majesty's treasury – your tax treasury – of hundreds of millions of tax dollars. Conservatively. (Now you have another reason for why your taxes are so high.)

Many participants in this scheme will be forced to file consumer proposals or personal bankruptcies to discharge the arrears. Most of those hundreds of millions of tax rebates paid out will never be recovered in principal, let alone the interest and penalties assessed as punishment.

Leaving people like you to foot the tax bills.

An unhappy ending to an unhappy tale.

Another Chapter in the Book of "Get Your Tax Back"

IN THE EARLY 2000S (IRREVERENTLY dubbed the "naughty aughties"), many thousands of well-to-do taxpayers were duped by financial advisors and friends into participation in leveraged charitable donation schemes that stripped the public treasury of hundreds of millions of dollars.

Around 2003, the Canada Revenue Agency (CRA) began noticing that an unusually high number of taxpayers were receiving very large tax refunds under the provisions of subsection 118(1) of the *Income Tax Act*. Cursory reviews of these tax returns confirmed that receipts were provided for large cash donations to a number of ostensibly legitimate charitable foundations. Some of the foundations used the donations to purchase artwork. Some purchased educational computer software, pharmaceuticals or comic books, the value of which was "donated" to humanitarian organizations, children burn victims or homeless shelters. The list of supposed beneficiaries across the various charitable foundations was wide and varied. Participants in these charities believed they were making a philanthropic contribution to "a good cause," even though the beneficiary on the receiving end of the donation was often vague.

The participants also knew that their philanthropy would net them a substantial financial return. They had connected with the promoters, or attended seminars at which they were introduced to the promoters, on the understanding this was a sophisticated tax planning strategy. It would seriously reduce their tax payable and, when combined with various other strategies, could result in the rebate of much of the income tax they had paid over the years. Most of them did not consider it tax avoidance.

Besides, they thought they were doing good, so they did not believe that their leveraged donations were anything but legitimate.

As mentioned above, sometime around 2003 the CRA started to scrutinize the first of the art-flip donation charities. Soon they were reviewing the educational software, the pharmaceutical donations (often presented as medicines for AIDS victims in Africa) and the comic book donations. Investigators followed the money and found that most of these charitable foundations were actually complicated financial structures, often with offshore participants that flowed money into the promoters' hands outside of Canada, and offered the participants large, long–term, interest-free loans to enable the taxpayer to make a very large cash donation to the charity. In return, the charity would provide the taxpayer with a "legitimate" tax receipt for the full amount of the donation. Come tax time, the taxpayer would receive a large tax refund.

Slowly, and on a charity-by-charity basis, the CRA began to single out the tax returns of participants in the various charities. It was difficult because some of the charities and donation plans were indeed legitimate.

One by one, these taxpayers, who often had participated in the scheme for several years in a row, and had thus received several very large cash refunds, were reassessed, with the deductions for the charitable donation denied in part or in full.

Most taxpayers were stunned at the magnitude of the reassessments. Not only were they required to repay in full the amount of their tax refund(s), the assessment included arrears interest calculated back to the taxation year for which the refund was issued. Additionally, having determined that the donations were disingenuous from the outset, gross negligence penalties were often also assessed.

The promoters of the various schemes retained big muscle legal counsel, who advised them on how taxpayers could object to the reassessments. When the objections were unsuccessful, the lawyers appealed to the Tax Court of Canada.

A significant appeal, considered a benchmark decision for these charitable foundations, is *Maréchaux v. R.* (2010 FCA 287, affirming 2009 TCC 587).

Mr. Maréchaux had, in December 2001, agreed to make a $100,000 donation to an art-flip charitable foundation. He put up $20,000 of his own funds, and received another $80,000 from a non-interest bearing 20-year loan from the promoters of the scheme. He spent a further $10,000 of his own funds on a "security deposit," together with an insurance policy to ensure against the risk that the security deposit would not accrete to $80,000 in 20 years' time. In January 2002, the taxpayer assigned the security deposit and the insurance policy to the lender (who was owned by the tax shelter promoter) in complete satisfaction of the $80,000 loan.

When his 2001 tax return was assessed, he received a large refund. When he was reassessed a few years later, CRA alleged that his donation did not meet the test of a gift, the *animus donandi* (the spirit of the gift). His refund was clawed back with interest and penalties. He objected, and eventually appealed.

The Tax Court determined that his $100,000 donation was not a gift, on the basis that the $80,000 interest-free loan was a significant benefit that the taxpayer obtained only by making the donation. Furthermore, the Tax Court found Mr. Maréchaux had a reasonable expectation, at the time of making the donation, that he would be able to assign the security deposit and the insurance policy to the lender in satisfaction of the loan, which represented a further benefit to him. It was irrelevant that the benefits came from a third party.

The Court's finding was devastating for all participants in these leveraged donation programs. However, with assistance of legal counsel, another case went to Tax Court to challenge the Maréchaux decision

In *Kossow v. R.* (2013 FCA 283), Kathryn Kossow had participated in a leveraged art-flip donation program similar to the one in *Maréchaux*. She made substantial donations over several years, financed 80% by a non-interest-bearing loan with a term of 25 years received from one of the promoters. When assessed, she received tax credits greater than her cash outlay (20% of her reported gift amount), which resulted in substantial cash refunds each year. The evidence indicated that virtually all of the cash portion of her donation was indirectly used to pay fees, and that the 80% financing received from the promoter was used, through a series of transactions, to finance the promoter. There was no evidence that the artwork, which supposedly was to be purchased for a charity with the donated funds, actually existed.

Ms. Kossow appealed the decision of the Tax Court of Canada, but was ultimately unsuccessful in defending her position.

For those of you interested in the "technical" details of the decision from the Federal Court of Appeal, here is a key excerpt:

> In finding no "gift," as the taxpayer had received a significant financial benefit as the recipient of long-term, interest-free loans as part of the same transactions, Near JA stated (at para. 25):
>
> In my view, Maréchaux stands for two propositions, as follows:
>
> (a) a long-term interest-free loan is a significant financial benefit to the lender; and
> (b) a benefit received in return for making a gift will vitiate the gift, whether the benefit comes from the donee or another person.

This decision in December 2013 delivered a death blow to the believers in the legitimacy of leveraged donation programs.

The CRA now posts on its website warnings about this type of tax avoidance scheme.

It is, alas, too little too late. Emboldened by the apparent success of the art-flip, software, and pharmaceutical schemes, one promoter in southern Ontario had already launched a very high profile charitable donation that snared thousands of affluent participants. Most had the foundation recommended to them by financial planners, who themselves were either participating in the program, or were endorsing it by including it in their annual tax filing strategies for these well-heeled clients.

As the Jenga tower began to fall apart, the promoter, when interviewed by the CBC, simply stated, "I am turning human greed into philanthropic work."

Participants in this program, which I will not name as a courtesy to all who were involved in it, are estimated to be each facing CRA reassessments in the order of $100,000. The CRA suggested it paid out some $208 million to taxpayers claiming tax credits related to this foundation.

Being well-heeled, this group of participants were also well-connected, and a class action was commenced against the promoter and the large law firm whose letter of endorsement had figured in the program's promotional materials. A settlement was reached before the matter went to trial, and the participants received dividends in proportion to their "investment" in the foundation.

Most, however, are still grappling with the aftermath of their reassessments.

DioGuardi Tax Law has represented participants in most of these donation programs. The remedies available are specific to the individual taxpayer, and we are working with each one to assist them to put this devastating experience behind them. The work is slow, and the CRA even slower in responding to the legal submissions. Eventually, the tax nightmare will end.

By that time, I expect even more cunning financial folks will have dreamed up some new way to help honest taxpayers organize their affairs to pay less tax.

I can only suggest that you approach with great caution any program that promises the return of all the tax you paid at source, or a zero tax liability at the end of the year. If you earn income, in all but the rarest of cases, you should be paying some tax.

Perhaps that's not the answer anyone wants to hear, but it is one of the ultimate truths.

Disturbingly, when clients come to DioGuardi Tax Law as victims of these and other schemes, there is evidence in their files of real dishonesty by financial advisors and tax preparers. Some clients are telling me that they paid their "accountant" money to get them the tax savings. They didn't even realize that these advisors were then filing false charitable donation claims, or false business revenue and expenses, and then pocketing a large percentage of the "tax savings."

In one case, the "accountant" claimed a tax credit for a donation to a church. The problem was that the church didn't even exist. By the time the CRA discovered the fraud and reassessed the taxpayer, the advisor had skipped town. My poor client was left alone to take the fall. Not a pretty picture! We were able to help him deal with the CRA and get some reduction on the amount owed. As for the donation – you can't give money to a church that doesn't exist.

IN SOME CASES, JUSTICE DOES PREVAIL

In 2010, an Alberta lawyer pleaded guilty to tax evasion for his role in a software tax write-off program.

The court found that he was the directing mind in a well-orchestrated scheme to defraud both the public purse and unsuspecting Canadian taxpayers. He issued false capital cost allowance documentation for computer software that was, through a series of complex transactions, sold to a partnership at highly inflated prices. Participants in the program, who were deemed members of the partnership, were given receipts for tax-write offs.

The lawyer had backdated documents to facilitate his plans, and used offshore companies to mask his involvement.

At sentencing, the court stated that he had involved innocent people in his scheme, and throughout had traded on the trust placed in members of the legal profession. The lawyer was sentenced to a fine of over $704,000, and given 3 years' jail time.

However, the real punishment was visited on his victims, whose tax refunds were clawed back with interest.

An Ever-More
Tangled Web of Deceit

IT IS FASCINATING TO SEE THE intricacy of the tax planning involved in creating a tax avoidance vehicle that dances a fine line between savvy strategy and out-and-out fraud.

Having distilled a few of the simpler schemes into reader-friendly terms in "Another Chapter in the Book of 'Get Your Tax Back'," I present this more technical overview of some of the more convoluted of the tax schemes that thrived in the naughty aughties. It's not for the faint of heart. Readers with a bent for financial analysis may be impressed by the precision in which the following financial planning concepts leveraged the arcane, dare I say, sometimes inane, provisions of the *Income Tax Act*.

VARIATIONS ON THE THEME

The Back-to-Back Loans Scheme

A "back-to-back" loan uses the provisions of the *Income Tax Act* in section 212(1)(b)(vii), which allows for the non-application of withholding tax on payments of interest when a Canadian company borrows money from a foreign lender.

The requirements to qualify for the exemption are: interest must be payable to an arm's length non-resident lender by a Canadian corporation; and no more than 25% of the principal amount of the debt must be paid within 5 years of the date of issue.

Assume a resident of Canada is able to "park" money in what appears to be an offshore mortgage company that he or she appears not to, but, in reality, does own or control. He or she can then have the Canadian corporation take out a mortgage with the foreign lender for 5 years. If the money is used for business purposes in Canada, it is deductible against Canadian taxes and not taxable to the offshore entity.

This scheme allows the resident access to previously unreported funds sitting in offshore bank accounts. The borrowing company gets a tax deduction in Canada and no tax is payable on the mortgage interest.

The structure is highly sophisticated, and, I suspect, has been used only by an elite group of business people with access to banking and financial advisors. It's high return, but very high risk.

If the CRA catches on, if the amount of money parked offshore is large, the punishment could include confiscation of assets and jail time. You might want to consider a voluntary disclosure before CRA catches on.

The Offshore RRSP Strip Ploy

This scheme offered participants the opportunity to transfer the assets of their Canadian-based Registered Retirement Savings Plans (RRSPs) to an offshore structure. The promoters claimed the funds could be withdrawn from the Canadian accounts on a tax-free basis, because they were being deposited into an RRSP-qualifying account offshore. Going forward, legally the earnings outside Canada were, themselves, not taxable.

To the best of my understanding, the game plan went something along this line.

- The Canadian resident RRSP owner opened a new self-directed RRSP account with a Canadian financial institution (the "RRSP Trustee").

- Funds were transferred from the owner's existing RRSP account to the new RRSP Trustee.
- This new RRSP account then loaned the money to a qualified Canadian company (hereinafter called "QCC").
- The Canadian resident RRSP owner was never a shareholder of the QCC.
- QCC then made an investment in preference shares of a financial services company (hereinafter called "FSC").

Are you confused yet? Wait, it gets even worse!

- An offshore trust was created in which both the settlor and the trustee were non-residents of Canada; and the beneficiary of the trust was an offshore corporation.
- An offshore corporation was formed and it issued bearer shares to the trustee.
- The FSC and the offshore corporation then entered into a joint venture to invest the client's RRSP money. This was placed in an active business structured in such a way that any active business income would be excluded, under the *Income Tax Act*, from the foreign accrual property income rules.

The promoters of this scheme said they were "tax experts." They told their clients that these transactions – in particular the withdrawal and reinvestment of the RRSP funds – were proper and conformed with Canada's tax laws. This may prove to be an academic point for those who used it.

There was a problem with all this. Most, if not all of the clients, lost their money when the offshore investment providers went bankrupt or absconded with the money. To add insult to injury, the CRA reassessed the funds withdrawn from the RRSPs as taxable income in the year of the withdrawal.

Many taxpayers have been defrauded in this way. They are, for the most part, older, at the end of their employment years or already retired. Some were dependent entirely on their RRSP funds for their retirement. Others were lucky enough to have pensions in addition to the RRSP funds. All have enormous tax assessments, plus arrears interest, related to the withdrawals. In some cases the CRA has registered a lien against their home, and is garnishing private pension incomes and social security benefits such CPP and OAS.

We are working to secure some tax relief on their behalf, but the RRSP funds that were stolen away are lost forever.

Natural Persons and a Bizarre Tax Cult

There is a unique group of tax protestors who believe that you can legally set yourself up outside the law, and in particular the tax laws of the land, and thus never pay tax again. There are many labels for these believers – "detaxer" or "natural person" being the most common.

This tax cult has been evident for years in both Canada and the United States.

Movie actor Wesley Snipes refused to pay taxes, taking the "untax yourself" position that they are illegal. He also instructed his employees to stop paying their own taxes and sought a refund of $11 million that he had already paid the Internal Revenue Service (IRS). As a result of this and other tax infractions, Snipes was sentenced to 3 years in prison.

In Canada, the detaxer's argument usually starts off from the proposition that the CRA "tricks" people into paying taxes. According to them, paying tax is not a legal requirement.

There are several spins on how they say you can go about "untaxing" yourself.

One argument is that only legal persons are required to pay tax, while it is a principle of common law that natural persons, acting in their private capacity for their own benefit, are free to carry on their business outside the scope of any tax statute. Typically the *Canadian Bill of Rights* is cited as the authority that the *Income Tax Act* cannot infringe on any of a "natural person's" rights and freedoms. They state that the *Income Tax Act* must be construed and applied so as not to deprive natural persons of their private property without due process of law. They refuse to file tax returns and present what they say is a "legal argument" against the income tax legislation. Some go so far as to set up trusts to hold their assets and receive income in this manner.

The natural persons argument was woven into a tax credit scam discussed at the outset of "The Bigger the Refund, the Better the Accountant." In this instance the participants offset their income with enormous business expenses that they claimed were "payment of wages for the labour of the free agent, or natural person, who is exempt from payment of tax on these wages." Canadian courts have rejected this type of argument. The originator of the "natural persons" theory in Canada, who set up seminars and ran videos that are still available on YouTube, was convicted in 2012 of failing to report $1.1 million in income, and was also charged with counselling people who attended his school to evade taxes. He was sentenced to 4.5 years of jail time and ordered to pay almost $275,000. His wife was also convicted and sentenced.

It is estimated the proponents of the natural person's theory, many of whom have also been convicted and sentenced to jail time, collectively evaded at least $11.5 million in taxes between 2004 and 2008.

Some of those adherents include an Ontario dentist and her husband, who were sentenced to jail time of 2.5 years and 4 years respectively. In addition to the prison time, this dentist was assessed with a civil tax bill of almost $900,000. When sentencing the couple, the judge shook his head at the thought that, otherwise intelligent people, could be caught up in such a ridiculous scheme.

In another case, involving a different dentist and his wife, the headline in the *Ottawa Citizen* on November 21, 2012, read, "Dentist, Wife Face Ruin Over Tax Dodge."

In court, both admitted to failing to declare income over a 6-year period, he from his dental practice and she from her position as his office manager.

The dentist and his wife were required to pay a fine of $273,811 and $78,596 respectively. He received a conditional sentence of 1 year and she was given a conditional sentence of 6 months. Half of their sentences were to be spent under house arrest. At sentencing the Superior Court Judge stated that their behaviour was an out and out fraud and was motivated solely by greed.

Another spin on the detaxer concept is to declare the taxpayer a fictitious entity created by the natural person. The fictitious entity, who is usually T4 salaried, files a tax return, but pays himself, as a "free agent," an enormous wage for his labour, which is deducted against a carefully calculated amount of business revenue from a business that does not exist. The net effect is to create a huge loss carry-back that essentially equals, with frightening accuracy, the sum of income tax deducted at source by the taxpayer's employer on his salaried wages.

Extracted from one of the law firm's many cases files, Figure 1 provides the typical, and boilerplate language that is distributed to these detaxers by the promoters to send as a response to the CRA.

Figure 1: Detaxer Letter to CRA

The certified facts are that [NAME OF TAXPAYER] and the Social Insurance Number attached to [NAME OF TAXPAYER] and identified as the taxpayer are a trust created by the Crown in right of CANADA or a province thereof. Therefore as the taxpayer is a fictional entity as stated above, it cannot misrepresent or make any false statement or have interest and therefore any penalty or action under subsection 163(2) of the ITA is a nullity.

Notwithstanding the *Income Tax Act* of Canada, and in particular subsection 152(7), the facts are that all information provided on and with the original income tax return filed, has been certified to be correct, complete and true by the Homo Ingenus principal of the fictional entity styled as the name of [NAME OF TAXPAYER], and accordingly, the principal of the fictional entity is entitled to be compensated for labour in providing the means through which [NAME OF TAXPAYER] conducts all manner of commerce to the benefit of its creator, the Crown in right of CANADA, or any province thereof, pursuant to the principal's fee schedule

Notwithstanding a Notice of Assessment to [NAME OF TAXPAYER] accepting the return as originally filed, any attempt to contact the principal, other than through REGISTERED MAIL for the sole purpose of refuting the information contained herein, shall constitute immediate acceptance of the information contained herein as the facts in truth and accordingly, shall bind the Minster of Revenue and Canada Revenue Agency and any and all of its agents **privately and individually** as parties to the contract and become immediately liable for payment of the principal's fee, pursuant to the principal's fee schedule.

It is interesting to note that in this specific instance, in addition to the legitimate T4 supplied to this taxpayer by his real-world employer, the taxpayer had been instructed also to submit a T4 for the labour of the free agent (the taxpayer known as the fictional entity, etc.) in amount of several hundreds of thousands of dollars. This amount was then offset as an expense against a fabricated figure representing business revenue. The calculations were precisely calibrated to net the taxpayer a return of essentially all tax deducted at source on his income.

Some months later, when the CRA had rejected the foregoing response as providing no explanation for the claims on the tax return(s) and had reassessed the taxpayer, the following were stated in the again boilerplate objection provided by the fraudulent tax preparers:

> The above noted (Re-Assessment) is hereby objected to and the Minister of Revenue, The Canada Revenue Agency, and all of its Agents including the Chief of Appeals and the Commissioner of Revenue, collectively and individually in their public and private capacity, are hereby appointed as trustees for the above mentioned cestui que trust and are directed to act in its best interests in their trustee capacity. Please use the items below as required and any and all other information to which you may be privy in order to fulfill your trustee duties.

Among a number of bullet points presented in apparently random order are these gems.

- All amounts claimed are allowed expenses under a partnership under the *Income War Tax Act, 1917.*
- Subsections 152(4) and 152(7) of the *Income Tax Act* are not compliant with the *Canadian Charter of Rights and Freedoms* and as such are nullities and void *ab initio.*
- Assessment amount is not consistent with section 4 of the *Income War Tax Act, 1917.*

- CRA, without knowledge or reason, denied income which had been declared and the related expenses to generate that income.

There were several more specious points in the objection. For purposes of illustration I have showcased the more colourful of them.

As you can imagine, the CRA in the normal course reviewed this objection and confirmed their reassessment. I can only wonder at the arcane thought processes and calculations that went into the development of this most elaborate, and deliberately fraudulent, scheme.

This thought, adapted from a quote attributed to the writer Herman Wouk, sums it all up rather well, "Income tax returns are the most imaginative fiction being written today."

How Could this Happen to Me?

IT'S FAIR TO SUGGEST THAT participants in any of the foregoing tax credit/rebate scams in this Part demonstrate the behaviour of our over-taxed opportunists from "Taxpayer Demographics: A Study."

We must blame their attitude and their seeming insatiable quest for tax refunds on the accounting industry, who promote their services and their value on a platform of getting you a bigger tax refund. I'm not sure when taking a bite out of the Taxman became a noble objective.

I have seen far too many respectable, responsible, middle-class persons whose lives have been ruined by years of big tax refunds, the repayment of which, with the addition of arrears interest plus, in some cases, gross negligence penalties for participating in the false claims for refunds, will push them to bankruptcy.

Surely they knew that these refunds were too big to be true. Surely they must have felt some responsibility to be paying some amount of tax each year.

Nine-tenths of wisdom is to be wise in time and at the right time. These people, alas, were neither.

I can only surmise that even the solid, honest, hard-working, middle-class Canadian eventually hits a point of terminal tax fatigue, making him or her vulnerable to the allure of an opportunity to get back "some of his own."

WHERE WAS THE CANADA REVENUE AGENCY IN ALL THIS?

Year after year, the CRA pumped out huge rebate cheques to these taxpayers – cheques the magnitude of which returned all monies paid on behalf of the taxpayer as source deductions by their employer.

Surely the CRA's computer matching system should have red-flagged all these T4 salaried taxpayers who, apparently, paid no tax on their salaried income.

Surely the matching system should have identified that these taxpayers were reporting T4 salaries to "employees" on the order of hundreds of thousands of dollars – yet $0 was ever paid as source deductions for these employees.

Surely the CRA computers should have identified some serious anomalies – and withheld the issuing of a cheque in each and every one of these circumstances, until such time as human eyes verified the legitimacy of the rebates.

I have seen many victims of the scheme.

In every case, had the CRA not blithely spit out the rebate cheques without human verification, the taxpayer would owe no tax today.

This suggests that some tax officials were themselves grossly negligent in not identifying the anomalies and reviewing the refunds. We likely will never know the truth of it. It would be too embarrassing for the CRA to admit.

Be that as it may, somewhere between 2009 and 2012, someone at the CRA finally figured out what was going on, and bureaucratic policy suddenly changed. The CRA now advises that payment of such rebates will not be executed until such time as the CRA verifies the validity of the tax returns.

Equally on point, the CRA has posted on its website the following fraud alert for taxpayers. (See next page.)

INFORM YOURSELF: TOP 5 TAX SCAMS

1. Natural person vs. Legal person – In this scam, promoters convince you to treat yourself as two separate people for income tax purposes: a "natural person," who is the flesh and blood individual, and the "legal person," who is a legal entity created by the Government. They argue that the income a person earns belongs to the natural person who is not subject to Canadian income tax law. As part of this scam, the promoters might suggest that you:
    *   prepare your T1 return and claim fictitious losses;
    *   apply for a CRA business number in your name and create false information slips to report losses on securities;
    *   not file a return at all, based on the argument that you are not taxable and, therefore, not required to do so.

    Reality: The courts have repeatedly and consistently rejected this scheme and have confirmed the legality of the *Income Tax Act*. For more information, see Tax Alert – Don't buy into illegal tax protester schemes.

2. Tax-free Registered Retirement Savings Plan (RRSP) and Registered Retirement Income Fund (RRIF) withdrawals – In this scam, promoters promise to return part of your investment by offshore debit or credit cards, offshore bank accounts, or loan back arrangements. They also promise you immediate access to assets in "locked-in" RRSPs or RRIFs, as well as income tax receipts providing deductions of three or more times the amount invested in an RRSP, plus unrealistic returns on investments. Typically, they ask the owner of a self-directed RRSP or RRIF to purchase a particular investment through a specific trustee. The investment could be shares in a company, units of participation in a co-operative, a mortgage, or other types of investments, all of which are owned/controlled directly or indirectly by the promoters.

    Reality: You can lose your entire retirement savings. Under these schemes, the amount you withdraw from your RRSPs or RRIFs counts as additional income and will be taxed in the year the investment was made or when the withdrawal occurred, even when your savings have disappeared with the promoters. For more information, see RRSP Tax-free Withdrawal Schemes.

3. **False losses or expenses** – In this scam, promoters convince you that you can claim large losses or expenses equal to your personal expenses. These might include payments for mortgages, personal loans, vehicle loans, and common everyday expenses. You are provided with a CRA business number and an "RZ account" (an information account) used to submit information slips for amounts related to your personal debts and expenses. These slips include the T5008 *Statement of Securities Transactions*, the T5 *Statement of Investment Income*, and the T4A *Statement of Pension, Retirement, Annuity and Other Income*. The amounts from the slips are reported on T1 tax returns as business losses, professional income losses, capital losses, or as expenses.
   Reality: Under the *Income Tax Act*, you cannot make deductions for personal expenses. If you do not operate a business, you cannot claim personal expenses as deductions from other income. For more information, see our tax alert. Warning: If you claim false losses or expenses on your tax return, you can be fined, penalized, or even convicted.

4. **False charitable donation receipts** – In this scam, individuals preparing tax returns for you will offer to *sell you* a large charitable donation receipt for a fraction of the value of the receipt. The receipts are false, and the donations are never made to actual or fictitious charities.
   Reality: The fee you pay goes directly to the preparer of your return and there is no donation involved. Under the law, you cannot purchase a receipt for tax purposes, so your tax return will be reassessed.

5. **Purchase of precious gems or other high-value collectibles** – In this scam, individuals convince business owners to buy expensive goods such as gems as an investment, claim the GST/HST input tax credits, and then sell the stones to a buyer in another country that the individual provides. The business owner never retains possession of the gems as the individual offers to "hold on to" the items in a secure location and save the business owner the cost of transporting and insuring the high-value item. Since the proposed "buyer" is out of the country, the individual tells you that there is no GST/HST charged on the sale.

   Reality: You are out of pocket for the cost of the items since there is no actual transfer of the goods, and, therefore, no actual sale for GST/HST purposes. If there are actual goods, they may not be worth as much as the individual tells you they are, and a buyer may never materialize. The CRA will reassess your GST/HST return to reverse the credits claimed.

It's all very nice. But, in the opinion of this tax lawyer, it's too little too late

Crocodile Tactics

Crocodile Dundee Meets his Match

"Come forth alive from the crocodile's mouth..."
- *The Taiheiki*, 14th-century Japanese historical epic

WHEN I WAS A STUDENT AT St. Patrick's College, a boy's school in Ottawa run by the Irish oblates of the Catholic Church, some of the lads had a hard time with my name. Sometimes "DioGuardi" came out as "Mick Garty." Maybe Mick "Crocodile" Dundee should have called on "Mick Garty" to pry him out of the crocodile's jaws. He didn't, and now he has the scars to prove it.

In August of 2010, Paul Hogan ("Mick Dundee") went home to Sydney for the funeral of his mother. When he arrived in Sydney, the Australian Taxation Office (ATO) had a surprise waiting. They accused him of hiding millions of dollars earned from his film royalties in an offshore tax haven, and presented him with a super-crocodile sized civil tax assessment.

To add teeth to the bite, the ATO also secured a court order preventing Hogan from leaving the country until his tax bill was paid.

The battle was fierce, and Mick Dundee came out bloodied and battered. In the end, after numerous court applications to set aside the order, he was allowed to post a bond so that he could leave the country and rejoin his family in Los Angeles.

Score one for the crocodile. It seems that crocodiles in the movies are but pale shadows of the very real tax crocs.

Lying in Wait

AT THE EDGE OF THE LAGOON, the crocodile awaits his prey. He lies under the water, with only his eyes above. He is still, quiet and lethal, jaws at the ready to snap closed the instant his victim is within reach.

So, too, behaves the Canada Revenue Agency (CRA) when it senses a kill in the offing.

In this tale, a restaurant owner walked smiling into the waiting jaws.

John owned a successful restaurant in a large Canadian city. After many years in business, he decided to retire and advertised that his business was for sale. As is customary in such circumstances, his ad made general reference to the annual income that could be expected from the business.

Apparently, the CRA smelled an easy kill.

John had no bites on his ad for a few weeks, then Bill called. He was looking to buy a restaurant, and asked to meet John to check out the property. John happily agreed and gave him a tour of the premises the next day. Bill said he was interested and would come back to look at the revenue statements.

At the second meeting, John opened up the corporate books and records, and showed Bill the restaurant's tax returns. Bill then revealed his real agenda. He had a partner and, together, they were looking for an operation with large cash revenues that could be – on the QT, of course – "skimmed" out before the tax reporting.

"Are you a CRA agent?" John joked. Bill laughed. "No problem," John went on. "You could work it that way. I do."

At the next meeting, Bill came with his partner Sam, who spoke up quickly and expressed his doubts about the restaurant taking in enough cash revenue to support a skimming strategy.

John offered to prove it. He drove them to his home and got out the second set of books. He showed them the actual cash intake versus what was reported on the "official" books and his tax returns.

Sam was still in doubt. Books could be fiddled. Where was real proof?

John reached into his private filing cabinet and pulled out a collection of customer chits. He singled out a particular month and gave the books and chits to Sam. It was pretty easy for Sam to reconcile the skimmed income reflected in the books for May 2003.

Sam was happy. John smiled, and the men shook hands on a deal.

Snap went the crocodile jaws.

Bill and Sam went back to their office at the CRA, and referred the matter to tax enforcement, who obtained search warrants and, a few days later, sent seven tax agents, accompanied by the police, simultaneously to the restaurant, John's house and his accountant's office to serve warrants and seize records.

John was charged with tax evasion, and eventually was convicted.

I read about this case in court files. It was relevant to the situation of a client who found himself in similar circumstances. The details are revealed in the next chapter and the tale of "Thin Crust Pizza with Crocodile Tears and Cheese."

Thin Crust Pizza with Crocodile Tears and Cheese

FROM THE CASE FILES OF PAUL DIOGUARDI

PIZZA PROSCIUTTO (not the real name) was arguably the best privately owned pizzeria in the city. People came from miles around to sample the crispy, thin crust and savoury toppings, and visitors were often directed there by the local hotels. So the manager wasn't surprised when two men he had never seen walked in one afternoon and stood just inside the doorway, looking around. They were wearing suits. Must be visiting businessmen, he thought.

He put down his cup of espresso and went over to greet the newcomers. "Would you like a table, gentlemen?" he asked, about to lead them to a small round table at the side of the restaurant.

"We're not here to eat, thank you," said one of the suits. "Are you the owner?"

"No," said the manager. "But I can certainly help you."

"We need to speak to the owner," the suit insisted. "Is he here?"

The manager wasn't comfortable with these men. Something didn't smell right. He started to explain that the owner, Mansour M., was only at the restaurant in the evenings. Perhaps the gentlemen could come back after 6 PM?

"This can't wait," said the suit. "We need to speak to him now. Do you have a phone number?"

A group of regular customers came in the door, and the manager didn't want a scene. "Sure," he said, and scribbled a number down on a paper napkin. "Try this."

The suits took the napkin and pushed past the incoming customers on their way out the door. The manager hurried over to show his customers to a table. Then he forgot about the men as he carried on with business.

A few hours later, Mansour was still at home, sipping his own cup of espresso in the kitchen while watching his favourite TV program. The phone rang and, not taking his eyes off the TV screen, he answered. This was in the days before telephones had call answer screens, so he had no idea who was calling.

"Mansour here."

"Am I speaking with Mansour M.?" asked a friendly, but no-nonsense voice.

"Yes," Mansour answered cautiously. Another telemarketer, he thought.

"This is Mr. Smith from the Canada Revenue Agency," said the caller.

"How may I help you?" Mansour was on his guard now, but still polite. His years in the food service industry had trained him to take a proactive approach to most situations.

"I'm calling about the 2004 tax return for the business Pizza Prosciutto," said CRA Agent Smith. "You are the owner?"

"I am," Mansour responded. "Is there a problem with the return? I already paid the tax."

"Yes, I see that," said Agent Smith. "We have only a few questions." Famous last words, coming from a tax auditor, but how was Mansour to know?

"Can we meet at your restaurant on ..." the Agent paused and rifled through some paper on his desk. "How about next Tuesday at 10 AM?"

The request was unusual, but Mr. Smith didn't sound threatening. Mansour did not yet know about the earlier visit to his restaurant, so he agreed to the meeting, jotting down notes about what he should bring with him to review with the CRA.

He went into his study, where he kept a filing cabinet, and pulled out copies of his tax returns and some other relevant documents.

ROUND ONE

Tuesday morning, he was in the restaurant early, much to the surprise of his manager. Right at 10 AM, two men in suits walked in. Mansour came forward, always the good host, and shook hands with them and pointed to a table where they could sit.

He offered them coffee, which both declined, and then the meeting began in earnest.

At first the questions were general in nature. Mr. Smith just wanted to understand a bit more about Mansour's business operation. How long had he been in business? Did he have more than one location? When did he open his second, and then third locations?

Mansour was proud of his success, so he answered the questions openly. Then the conversation took a more specific turn. How much cash was kept in the registers? Did any of his family work in the restaurants? His wife? His two sons? Did they have access to the cash registers? Did he have family back home in Lebanon? Did he ever send them money? Was it by way of bank draft or money order? How much did he spend on decorating his restaurants? What equipment did he buy? How did he pay for it? Did he have supplier invoices?

As the questions became more invasive, Mansour began to feel uncomfortable answering on his own.

"I'm a simple man," he said. "I came to Canada 12 years ago with no education. I've worked hard. With these two hands and the help of my wife and sons, we built a good business. I file my tax returns. I pay my taxes. Why are you asking me all these questions? Am I in trouble?"

Mr. Smith assured him that they were simply verifying a number of items on his tax return, and that there would be no trouble if he co-operated with them. Mansour was now very nervous.

"You will have to speak to my accountant and my lawyer," he said. "I will ask them to help answer your questions."

He gave the agents the names and telephone numbers of his business lawyer and his accountant, and the meeting was over.

As soon as the agents had left, Mansour went to the phone and called Bill, the chartered accountant who had done his taxes for many years.

"Two men from the CRA were just at my restaurant," he said. "They were asking a lot of funny questions."

Bill asked about the questions, and then thought for a moment. "Sounds like a routine field audit," he said. "It happens a lot to restaurants. I guess it's just your turn. I'll call this Smith guy and see what's up."

Mansour said fine, but he was also going to speak to his business lawyer. So he hung up and dialed Chuck at the law firm who had helped him negotiate his leases and incorporate his business. Chuck said the same thing; it sounded like a routine audit and not to worry. He agreed to speak to Bill and then the CRA agents, and said he would let Mansour know if there was anything out of the ordinary.

But Mansour did worry. His business was all he had to support himself and his family. If there was no trouble, why was the CRA asking such specific questions? Why didn't this all just go away?

Mansour had no idea that someone had called the CRA snitch line and told them he was not reporting all his income. The CRA agents were auditors from Special Investigations, and they were looking for evidence of tax evasion.

Bill, the CA, and Chuck, the lawyer, spoke to the CRA, and realized that this "audit" was more than routine. As Mansour's representatives, they met with Agent Smith and his team several times over the following weeks, co-operating by providing copies of bank statements and business records, expense receipts and anything else they thought would answer the auditors' questions.

But the CRA was insatiable, asking for more and more until, one day, Bill was surprised by a visit from the police and the CRA auditor, who arrived at his office with a warrant to conduct a search and seizure. Similar visits were made to Mansour's home, and all three of his restaurants.

As soon as Bill saw the warrant, he knew the matter was serious, and he called Chuck, the lawyer. Chuck advised that he co-operate, because there was nothing to hide. He could see no harm in the CRA taking away Mansour's accounting records. Mansour's tax returns were clean. Bill agreed. Thus Mansour was advised to co-operate with the authorities, and the CRA took possession of all the records they could find.

After the seizures, Bill and Chuck requested a meeting with Agent Smith and company. The meeting was arranged, and this time there was a surprise. Agent Smith's colleague, who had not said much during previous meetings, introduced himself as a Criminal Investigator from CRA Enforcement.

Chuck and Bill were stunned. Chuck asked why a Criminal Investigator was involved in a routine field audit.

"You told me that the purpose of your audit was to review the assessment for Pizza Prosciutto," Chuck said. "We've been talking about a civil assessment here. This is the first time you've mentioned anything that could result in prosecution."

Later, both Chuck and Bill testified that they had co-operated with Agent Smith on the understanding that, if any irregularities were found, Mansour would, at worst, only face a revised civil assessment, with any applicable interest and civil penalties. Unfortunately, neither the accountant nor the lawyer had been cautious enough to request this assurance in writing.

Even if they had thought to ask, the CRA would not have provided such assurance. Once the CRA has built a case for criminal prosecution, they won't agree to drop the case for a civil settlement. In other words, you can't buy your way out of a criminal prosecution by agreeing to pay tax, penalties and interest on the civil side.

At this point, Chuck and Bill realized the matter was beyond their ability to manage, and they warned Mansour to prepare for the worst.

In due course, Mansour was served with a criminal subpoena. The CRA had reviewed his tax returns, investigated his business, and used all the information they had gleaned from their conversations with Mansour and his professional advisors, and their search and seizures, to prepare a net worth (lifestyle) assessment of Mansour's income. According to CRA, over a 4-year period Mansour had not reported over $275,000 in taxable income. Mansour was charged with tax evasion and, if convicted, not only would he be branded a criminal, but the civil and criminal penalties would be huge. He could easily lose his business and end up in jail.

Mansour was surprised and frightened.

He had no idea how the tax authorities could believe he had ever made that much money. To him, their figures were absolutely crazy.

To make matters worse, his lawyer and his accountant now said they could no longer represent him. By inadvertently providing the Taxman with evidence against Mansour, they were both in a possible conflict of interest situation. Bill the CA was especially fearful of being called as a witness against his client.

The CRA had trapped Mansour and his advisors into co-operating with them, and then turned the admissions into the basis for a criminal prosecution.

The crocodile had won round one. Mansour was caught in its jaws.

ROUND TWO

Mansour was wise enough to seek criminal tax counsel to defend him, and thus he retained me.

I opened Round Two with a plea of *not guilty*, and then focused on obtaining full disclosure of the prosecution's case. The auditors' working papers showed the methodology used in the net worth assessment, and how the CRA had come up with a figure of $275,000 in unreported income.

The disclosure also showed that the criminal investigator had, very early on, posed as a simple auditor. Gotcha! I had the basis for my defense.

In court, my first argument was to allege entrapment and to move to exclude all documents and information obtained through the search and seizure at the accountant's office, and at Mansour's home and business locations. The submission was that my client's right against self-incrimination under the Canadian *Charter of Rights and Freedoms* had been breached.

During argument, I provided to the criminal court judge a precedent-setting case, still awaiting decision by the Federal Court, that dealt with a similar set of facts. In that case, the tax agents had also misled a taxpayer into believing he was dealing only with civil tax agents, rather than a criminal investigation. Since it was being heard in a higher court, the decision, when eventually handed down, would be binding on the judge hearing our case.

The criminal court judge reserved her judgment on the possible *Charter* breach until the decision of the Federal Court was rendered. I was then instructed by Her Honour to proceed with the rest of the case dealing with the net worth audit.

In a net worth audit, an investigator/auditor adds up all of your assets and deducts all of your liabilities at the start and end of the tax years under audit. If there was an increase in your net worth, that is, what you own minus what you owe, without an increase in income from the previous tax year, you may be suspected of tax fraud.

There may, however, be legitimate explanations for how your net worth increased that don't involve taxable, and therefore unreported, income.

As part of Mansour's defense, we needed our own net worth audit of Mansour, using the same records as analyzed by the CRA. Our analysis showed that the CRA had used a series of dubious assumptions to reach a figure of $275,000 in unreported income. It became obvious that they were highballing. They didn't know that the other side – me – knew how to calculate a net worth audit.

The CRA was gunning for a guilty plea on a lesser amount. But I knew that a lower tax assessment wouldn't necessarily mean a softer sentence for Mansour. The conviction was the prize the CRA had in sight.

This CRA tactic often is successful with criminal lawyers, many of whom have little or no tax law experience and get uncomfortable when the case turns into a fight over proper accounting. While it may, at first blush, sound like a good deal to plead guilty to a reduced charge, the problem is that the client is then a convicted criminal.

For me, forewarned was forearmed. Knowing the crocodile and his trick, I flatly turned down their deal. The other side was more than surprised.

My net worth analysis clearly showed that the income that the CRA had deemed taxable, and unreported, largely came from capital, gifts, insurance claims or loans and, as such, were non-taxable and therefore were not required to be reported on income tax returns.

A DIVINE INTERVENTION

Mansour had told me that his grandfather, before his decease, had given him over $95,000 in cash. Unfortunately, there was no paper trail to confirm his statement. Only the family knew the facts, and they would be suspect in court as self-serving witnesses. It then came to light that the grandfather's spiritual confessor was still alive and living in the United States. He remembered being told by the grandfather that he had given almost $100,000 in a cash gift to Mansour because he was his favourite grandson.

I contacted the old priest, and he agreed to travel to court to testify on Mansour's behalf.

It was a rare moment in court. On the stand Father John was a magnificent witness and corroborated that Mansour's grandfather had indeed gifted a large amount of money to Mansour. The prosecutor was caught flatfooted. This, together with provable insurance payouts, cash on hand and loans, shot a massive hole into the CRA's income figures.

Thereafter, over a period of several days, a battle of numbers was waged in court. My attack on the CRA's net worth assessment was making them sweat. It got quite complicated, and the tax bureaucrats were squirming. At one point, the judge called both counsel into her chambers.

"Mr. DioGuardi," she begged. "You need to go easy. At law school I only got a D in tax."

"I'm sorry, Your Honour," I replied, "but we are well on our way to proving that the tax department's figures are pure speculation. Moreover," I added with a smile, "we still have our outstanding *Charter* challenge."

The defense's net worth analysis showed that Mansour had reported 100% of his income from taxable sources. Therefore, I argued, no tax had been evaded. Given that this was a criminal case, the onus of proof was on the prosecution.

Then I moved to my evidence in support of the *Charter* challenge. I called both Chuck, Mansour's lawyer, and Bill, his chartered accountant, as our witnesses. They were asked why they had co-operated with the tax authorities even after knowing that one of them was from the tax police and criminal charges could possibly be laid.

Chuck was a senior litigator, but he did not do any tax work. This was his first, and probably last, foray into the tax world, and he was very believable.

"I'm not stupid," he testified. "I was never specifically told that there would be no criminal charges laid against my client, but the criminal investigator acted in such a way as to lead me to believe that, if we gave him the information, no charges would be laid."

Bill, the chartered accountant, said essentially the same thing.

Then came the *coup de grâce* for the prosecution's case.

The Federal Court ruling I was waiting for was finally issued. It confirmed that the seizure in that case, under circumstances where the taxpayers didn't know they were dealing with Criminal Investigations, had been contrary to the *Charter of Rights and Freedoms*. We were, therefore, able to press our argument that the seizure in Mansour's case had been illegal, and that the evidence gained from the seizure must be excluded. Further, the figures the government had used to calculate $275,000 in unreported income were based on incorrect assumptions. Our calculations, supported by evidence and testimony, showed zero unreported taxable income were correct.

This was a criminal proceeding, and the prosecution was required to prove its case against Mansour *beyond a reasonable doubt*. They had not done so, therefore, I argued, Mansour must be found not guilty of all charges of tax evasion.

In the face of the foregoing, the judge agreed. All charges against Mansour were dismissed.

Mansour was freed from the jaws of the crocodile. He was delighted.

For all that, he managed to take a bite out of me. He declined to pay the balance of his legal fees to me, which, given the scope of the trial, were quite modest.

I elected not to pursue him for collection, and took comfort instead in the real victory – in particular, the success of the *Charter* challenge.

In such instances – and mercifully they are few and far between – I usually pull out the graph below and sigh a little. Then I move on to pull the next victim out of the crocodile's jaws.

Figure 2:
It's a Thankless Job

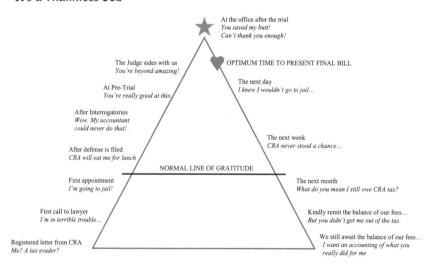

The One and Only True Set of Books

IT WAS A BEAUTIFUL FALL DAY AND Maurice was at his cottage in western Quebec. Early in the morning, a car pulled into the driveway and two casually dressed men got out. Maurice was surprised to see unexpected visitors. But he was in relax mode, so he watched as the men got out of the car and by the time they got to the door, he was waiting there.

"*Bonjour. Comment ça va?*" Maurice offered by way of greeting.

"*Bonjour,*" one of the men replied. "I'd like to speak with Maurice M."

"And how may I help you?" asked Maurice, his curiosity piqued.

One of the men reached into his pocket and pulled out a leather wallet with a police badge. He showed it to Maurice and asked if they could come inside and talk to him.

Maurice opened the door and invited them in. His first mistake.

Once in the cottage, the police officer showed Maurice a search warrant. Then the second man pulled out his identification. He and his colleague were from the Canada Revenue Agency. They had come, he explained, to search the cottage for records related to Maurice's business.

They had a warrant. There wasn't much Maurice could do except let them go about their business. He even offered to help show them where to look. He thought they were just aggressive auditors. At no time did they advise Maurice that he was under criminal investigation for tax evasion, and that anything they found, or that he said, could be used to prosecute him. Specifically, he was not advised of his right to counsel.

Hold on to that thought. It will be important later.

So the search began, with Maurice helpfully pointing out where he kept various files.

In short order the first two men were joined by members of the local police force and other CRA agents.

Maurice didn't call a lawyer. He didn't call anyone, so he was unaware that searches were underway at his place of work and his daughter's home.

The searchers asked Maurice if he had a safe. He showed them where it was, unlocked it and watched as the tax agents took everything out. He was anxious to get the men out of the cottage, and he thought the more he helped the faster it would be over.

So he showed the searchers where he kept his bank statements and other accounting records. He even opened up the bottom drawer of the dresser in the guest bedroom and retrieved some notebooks that had fallen underneath.

Perhaps you've enjoyed the Mel Brooks film of his musical comedy, *The Producers*. You will remember that the Broadway producer and the accountant had kept two sets of books. One was labelled "Show to the IRS." The other was labelled "NEVER Show to the IRS."

Maurice had a set of notebooks labelled "The One and Only True Set of Books." These are the ones he rescued from under the bottom of the drawer and handed to the CRA.

Yes, this is a true story.

You can guess what happened when the crocodile got its teeth into those books.

Eventually they became the star piece of evidence in Maurice's criminal trial for tax evasion.

Maurice still had no clue that his "audit" was turning into a criminal investigation. He watched the tax agents take their evidence away. Later, Maurice, still thinking it was just a civil matter, agreed to meet the "auditors" at his local tax office, without legal counsel, to discuss "what was going on."

At this meeting, Maurice was still not advised that he was under criminal investigation. He was not advised that what he said could be used against him. He was not advised that the "auditors" were Special Investigators. He was simply given a copy of a CRA-created net worth statement and presented with a civil tax assessment.

Incredibly, he still continued to provide the CRA with information about his sources of revenue and his tax reporting.

Then the jaws snapped shut.

Maurice received a registered letter from the CRA suggesting that he could be criminally prosecuted for keeping false records – the two sets of books. Only then did he realize that he could be charged.

That's when he consulted me.

By that time, with so much evidence in hand, the CRA were not willing to negotiate a stay of prosecution. Maurice was charged under s. 239 of the *Income Tax Act* with criminal tax evasion.

TAX EVASION – DEFINITIONS AND IMPLICATIONS

Tax evasion is intentional conduct designed to defeat the income tax laws. Any sort of tax scheme to cheat the government can fall into this broad category. Tax evasion is a serious crime. For example, failure to file a tax return, if tax is due, can lead to a substantial fine or both the fine plus imprisonment for a term not exceeding 12 months. Under s. 239 of the *Income Tax Act*, the fine will be not less than 50% and not more than 200% of the amount of tax that was sought to be evaded, or both the fine and imprisonment for a term not exceeding 2 years.

It is also possible to prosecute by indictment. In this case, if convicted, the fine is not less than 100% and not more than 200% of the tax or net tax that was sought to be evaded, and imprisonment for a term not exceeding 5 years.

More people are charged with filing a false return than with tax evasion, because to gain a conviction the CRA need only prove an intent to file a false return, which is easier than proving an intent to evade the income tax laws.

HAND IN THE COOKIE JAR: MAURICE'S DEFENSE

Maurice was in a tough spot. He had helped the CRA catch him with his hand in the cookie jar.

The case was still winnable – with the right strategy. I had two aces up my sleeve. One was the landmark ruling on *Charter* rights that had saved Mansour (see "Thin Crust Pizza with Crocodile Tears and Cheese"). The other was my law associate, Hamilton. You met him at the start of these tales, when we were up against "Dread Pirate Vince."

Hamilton was a lawyer, a chartered accountant and an actuary. He had a mind like a steel trap. Together, he and I made a formidable adversary. We intended to pull Maurice alive from the jaws of the crocodile and make the CRA hurt.

My defense was that Canadians would not respect a system that permits a "bureaucratic police force" wider latitude than that given to the RCMP and other police forces.

CRA investigators are "secret" in the sense of being much less visible to ordinary people than are the police. If the court allowed the prosecution against Maurice to proceed, it would be seen as approval that tax bureaucrats have greater power than the regular police. If a murder or rapist were ever treated this way, criminal rights activists would be yelling to high heaven.

Was Maurice to be denied the protection of the law because this was a tax evasion charge?

Even a taxpayer with a legitimate defense to a tax assessment is sorely tempted to co-operate in the face of a search warrant and a phalanx of tax agents. Implicit in the Taxman's procedures is a thinly veiled suggestion that if a taxpayer surrenders meekly and pays in full, he has a chance to avoid some horribly large penalties.

In Maurice's case, the CRA agents did not disclose their status as criminal investigators. Thus Maurice was denied his *Charter* right against self-incrimination.

I quoted the court, in *R. v. Baron*, which stated that a physical search of a private premise is the greatest intrusion of privacy short of a violation of bodily integrity. It found that there is a need to protect individuals against unreasonable searches in the form of "fishing expeditions" by the state.

I submitted that the purpose of the CRA raids was clearly a fishing expedition, and one that was undertaken without appropriate disclosure to the subject of the true nature of the raid.

I argued that Maurice had been confused by the blending and merging of a civil investigation, which obliges him to co-operate in the assessment of his civil tax liability, with a criminal examination, wherein the burden of proof is on the CRA and the defendant is entitled to protect himself from self-incrimination.

Where does the taxpayer draw the line, I argued. How does he know what is "criminal" and what is "civil?"

Tax authorities, before using any of their police powers and before interviewing a taxpayer, must choose whether their authority to force compliance is to be used for civil purposes or to gather evidence for criminal prosecution.

In the event of criminal prosecution, the taxpayer must be warned by tax officials immediately of his right to legal counsel, that he has the right to remain completely silent and unco-operative and, most importantly, that no leniency of any kind will be given him if he co-operates. He must be made aware of the potential criminal charge. If this hinders the investigation, then, so be it. Only after the criminal charge is fully dealt with should the CRA's right to proceed civilly be exercised. Any other procedure simply allows the threat of blackmail to be used.

The second choice is to irrevocably waive the laying of a criminal charge. If this alternative is chosen, the CRA would retain all of its powers to force information from the citizen, who then must respond fully since there is no danger of a criminal prosecution. "Police powers" should not be used to collect money, civil fines and penalties.

The tax authorities should not be allowed to mix the two remedies. If they do, it can result in bludgeoning citizens into submission.

My argument quoted the statement of Lamer J. in *Collins v. R.*, "If the admission of evidence in some way affects the fairness of the trial, then the admission of that evidence would tend to bring the administration of justice into disrepute."

I asked for the exclusion of the evidence that Maurice had provided to CRA under "false pretences," and a stay of proceedings or a dismissal of the charge.

The prosecution was dumbfounded. They were still processing that the accused was not going to just roll over and plead guilty. Meanwhile I was running down the home stretch with a *Charter of Rights* argument that might force the CRA to change both its policy and its tactics. Were the judge to recommend "checks" on the way the CRA could deploy the tax police, their strongest weapon could be seriously weakened. It was in their interest to hammer out a deal. Fast.

The judge could see that this would be a difficult case for him to decide, and it would be easier if opposing counsel simply came to terms. He suggested that legal counsel try to work out an acceptable plea bargain.

Opposing counsel must have sensed that the judge was in sympathy with my position. Or perhaps they just didn't want to get dirty in this fight. In any case, and despite the fact that Maurice had been caught with his hand in the cookie jar, we worked out a deal where charges were reduced to a slap on the wrist, and only a relatively small fine was payable. On the civil side, again because of my *Charter* argument, much of the evidence was excluded, and Maurice's tax assessment was substantially reduced.

Maurice was able to pay both the fine and the tax assessment, and come forth whole from the jaws of the crocodile.

Highballing –
A Crocodile Trick

THE CANADA REVENUE AGENCY (CRA) uses many tactics to trap the taxpayer – and his or her unwary counsel – into paying as much tax as possible.

Highballing is a favourite trick in prosecution or threat of prosecution cases. Understandably, in such circumstances the accused will want to reach a settlement before the matter goes to trial, or sentencing. The CRA, knowing that their assessments may not stand up to a rigorous analysis before the courts, often tries to highball the amount of the fine, and then agrees to "settle" for a lesser amount. This permits the crocodile to go home with a kill, but lets the taxpayer escape with some of his or her finances intact.

I'm always wary of highballing, and in my practice make a concerted attempt to get the assessments down to the actual number before I even consider negotiating a settlement. It usually pays off in spades.

In one particular case, by doing a proper analysis, we were able to reduce the taxpayer's alleged unreported income by $415,000, and that of his corporations by $191,000 and $205,000 respectively. Any penalties applicable to amounts not reported were proportionately reduced.

Some criminal lawyers, lacking knowledge of tax law, do not properly analyse the client's true tax position. They jump at the CRA's offer to reduce the fines, thinking it is a good deal for the client. Usually this is not the case. No taxpayer should settle for a tax assessment that is based upon a highballed income level.

Even more dangerous, if the supposed income level is inaccurately high, the tax assessment will also be inaccurately high, with the result that the amount of tax the taxpayer is charged with evading is also inaccurately high. Since judges base sentencing on the amount of tax evaded, accepting a highballed assessment exposes the taxpayer to a greater likelihood of a sentence of jail time.

After the criminal penalties and jail time, the taxpayer still has to pay the civil tax assessment, with its own set of penalties, plus accrued interest. Thus if the amount of taxable income is unchallenged in court, the taxpayer will also pay much more tax than perhaps is required.

Crocodile Chess

From Audit
to Incarceration in
Seven Easy Steps

WHAT STARTS OUT AS A SIMPLE verification exercise – an audit – can quickly escalate into a very serious matter requiring experienced legal tax counsel and, in the worst scenario, criminal defence counsel. (Witness the cautionary tales of Mansour in "Thin Crust Pizza with Crocodile Tears and Cheese" and Maurice in "The One and Only True Set of Books.")

To visualize the Canada Revenue Agency's methodology for catching tax scofflaws, I offer the Audit Escalation Scale in Figure 3 (next page). The further along the scale, the greater the likelihood the matter will go criminal and result in a conviction.

1. AUDIT

At the CRA's first request for a review of books or records, an audit interview or a tour of your home or business premises, retain legal tax counsel to manage all communications with the CRA.

During the course of an audit, the CRA will communicate with you by letter and by telephone. The auditor(s) will request specific books and records, and in some cases may wish to interview you at your place of business. In retail operations they may ask to see cash register tapes or even send an Information Technology (IT) person to download files from your computer.

When requests for information progress beyond books and records to a tour of your premises, to cash register tapes, or to giving a CRA IT person access to your computers, you have moved up the scale to a preliminary investigation.

This is where you need to stop co-operating with a smile, and retain experienced tax counsel, preferably legal counsel. Legal protection at this time may prevent further escalation. At the very least it will give you a better chance of presenting a credible defence.

When CRA auditors believe they have discovered tax fraud, investigation en route to prosecution is *not* an automatic next step. Other considerations come into play first.

Figure 3:
Audit Escalation Scale

1 AUDIT

2 INVESTIGATION

3 CRIMINAL INVESTIGATION

4 PROSECUTION

5 DEFENCE

6 CONVICTION

7 SENTENCING

- If the amount is small, an auditor could simply overlook it in order to close the file.
- If the tax fraud is, arguably, a "small mistake," the auditor can assess with a civil penalty for gross negligence.
- If the auditor finds more serious misdeeds, however, particularly if your omission or over-deduction was deliberately fraudulent, a 50% civil gross negligence penalty plus interest can be added to the tax bill.

The auditor may do none of the above, and instead could push your matter further up the the Audit Escalation Scale to ...

2. INVESTIGATION

As we saw with Maurice and Mansour, investigators do not immediately identify themselves as being more than just auditors. Investigators are the agents who will secure records of your bank accounts, talk to your friends and co-workers, and perhaps even procure a warrant for a search and seizure.

Where Do Investigators Get their Leads?

Usually there's a breadcrumb trail that leads to you. Finding the first breadcrumb, however, is often a combination of serendipity, sleuthing and stooling. Here's a list of the usual sources.

- *Referrals from Other CRA Divisions.* Often auditors will discover undisclosed income or assets during another examination.
- *Tip-offs from Other Enforcement Agencies, such as the Police, Customs Agents, etc.* The crocodile isn't interested in the alleged criminal behaviour itself, only the proceeds of the activity, and whether it was reported on a tax return.

  An example: When Jeremy was arrested for suspected drug trafficking, $150,000 in cash was found in the trunk of his car. The police reported the cash find to the CRA. Enforcement looked at his tax returns where he reported only $35,000 of income per year and then the CRA began a formal investigation.
- *Snitch Tips.* Ex-spouses or disgruntled employees and business associates often whisper into the ear of the CRA. Enforcement usually follows up only on tips that are well-documented and provable. Allegations that appear motivated purely by spite are rarely considered reasonable grounds for investigation. But you never know.
- *Undercover or Sting Operations.* Enforcement agents have been known to pose as buyers of a business to sniff out off-the-books income. (Remember the tale of John and his restaurant deal in "Lying in Wait.") Unwary sellers who brag about a second set of books and how much (more) cash the business takes in can get snapped up in the twinkling of a crocodile blink.

When Investigators Contact Third Parties

Investigators often try to speak to your friends, neighbours, relatives and co-workers. If you're contacted by the CRA about another person, be wary. Don't answer any questions if there is a possibility you could be connected to the individual being probed. Read the words "connected to" broadly. Keep quiet until you speak to a tax lawyer. Anyone can be drawn into the net of an investigation.

Never lie to the CRA. The law does not allow you to protect others by withholding information or lying. It is legal, however, to tell someone that the CRA was asking you about them.

If someone tells you that they have been contacted by a CRA investigator and asks you what to say, don't offer any suggestions. It is a crime to ask someone to lie or to mislead them. Resist the urge to call the CRA and ask what's going on. Instead, call a tax lawyer who handles criminal tax evasion cases, and then let your legal counsel do all the talking.

When Investigators Contact You

If investigations truly is building a case against you, you may be the last person interviewed. You may have already been warned by your bank, or by colleagues, who share that they have been contacted. If they do share that information, and you have still not been interviewed or received correspondence, things aren't looking good.

In an investigation, the CRA usually will speak to you last, in an attempt to get a confession or damaging admissions before they recommend your case for prosecution.

Once you are contacted as the target of an investigation, the CRA is required to advise you of this before asking any questions. You must be advised of your right to remain silent, and the right to have a lawyer, and then must be warned that anything you say can be used against you.

If you are so advised, simply state that you want to contact your tax lawyer and clam up. Trying to talk enforcement agents out of pursuing a case against you is a mistake. It makes no difference to them if your mother is dying, you have money problems or your marriage is falling apart. Mentioning your problems only strengthens their position; giving an excuse often shows that you knew what you did was wrong. Similarly, don't lie. Lying will only compound the crime.

Questions typically asked include:

- Did you report all of your income?
- Where are your bank accounts and safety deposit boxes?
- Can you tell us about the cars, boats, planes and real estate you own?
- Do you gamble?
- What is the procedure for reporting sales in your business?
- Do you keep a lot of cash on hand?
- Who are your business associates?
- Have you recently travelled out of the country?
- Have you or any of your businesses been audited?

Faced with a barrage of questions from a couple of trained agents who show up unannounced at the door, some people just fall apart. They either make a confession or lie. This gives the prosecutor additional rope to hang them with.

At this stage, or during the interview, you may also be served with a warrant for search and seizure.

If You Are Served with a Warrant for Search and Seizure

Ask to see the warrant and read it carefully. Look at the specific premises to be searched and what they are entitled to seize.

Review the identification of each tax agent participating in the search. If possible, make photocopies of their identification cards. Take a photo on your cellphone and e-mail it immediately to your lawyer. Then try to get your lawyer on the phone.

I suggest you ask the agents and the police, who are probably there with the agents, to wait a moment on your doorstep while you call your lawyer. Then go inside, close the door and telephone your lawyer. Tell the receptionist it's urgent, and why. You will get through.

I have been known to ask my client to take the cellphone out to the agents so that I can speak to them directly. Sometimes I can convince them to go away and/or meet with me in my offices.

A search warrant, if all is in order, must not be obstructed. You will have to let the agents into the premises. You will have to watch while they search, and you will have to let them take away whatever they find and deem relevant to their search. This may include your computer(s) and even your cellphone. Hopefully your phone is password protected.

A search warrant does not entitle the agents to ask you or anyone else questions. Do not answer anything but very routine questions such as your name. If they ask you to show them your office, or where you keep your records, point them in the right direction. You don't have to take them to your sock drawer with the false bottom. It's up to them to find that on their own. (Remember Maurice.)

If your accountant's office is also being searched, tell him or her to call your lawyer. The lawyer may be able to have your accountant claim privilege over some or all of the documents found in the office. If privilege can be claimed, the documents in question must be placed in a sealed envelope or box and surrendered to the Sheriff of the county where the seizure is made.

At this point, it's a pretty sure bet the investigators are getting ready to move your matter up the Scale to ...

3. CRIMINAL INVESTIGATION

Evidence of any of the following behaviours is an open invitation to CRA auditor/investigators to escalate your case to a criminal investigation.

- Deliberate understatement of income or overstatement of deduction.
- Using two sets of books – for any reason, but particularly to mask income.
- Lying to tax agents during an audit or investigation.
- Falsifying documents to obtain or sustain deductions.

- Doing business in cash to avoid records of income.
- Using trusts, shell corporations or offshore entities to conceal income.
- Making false or misleading statements on tax returns or other forms.
- Placing assets in the hands of third parties or so-called "nominees" to conceal them from the CRA.
- Using fictitious names or social insurance numbers to open bank accounts.

Now it's appropriate for your tax lawyer to try to convince the criminal investigators that despite what they think they see in your records, there has been no tax fraud.

Credible Defenses Against Allegations of Tax Fraud

Here's an overview of the explanations I believe are reasonable when the CRA alleges an intentional failure to report taxable income. Of course, these defenses should be presented by your legal counsel. This is not a do-it-yourself guide!

Don't expect the CRA to accept any of these defenses at face value.

- *"I lived off my cash on hand."* This defense can be raised if ever the CRA uses the bank deposit, expenditures or net worth methods of proving evasion. There is no law against having cash on hand. The only legitimate concern is whether or not the cash is from unreported taxable income.
- *"My income is from a non-taxable source."* You may indeed have acquired tax-free money by gift, loans, inheritances and other ways, but you will have to prove it.
- *"I made an honest mistake."* Because intent to cheat is required for evasion, your mistaken belief may be a valid defense to a tax evasion charge.

Never Try to Lie Your Way Out of a Fraud Charge

If in doubt, keep your mouth shut. Say nothing to the CRA until you have spoken to your lawyer, and thereafter only speak to the CRA with your lawyer present. You have the right to remain silent whenever there is a possibility you may be charged with a crime.

The CRA and the prosecution also analyze the personal traits of the individual target, including age, physical and mental health and any previous criminal record. They also look at the amount you allegedly cheated the government out of. The larger it is, the more likely they will recommend prosecution.

If enforcement recommends prosecution, it will turn its evidence over to the prosecution service to decide the charges. Individuals are typically charged with one or more counts of tax evasion, filing a false return or not filing a tax return.

When Investigations recommends prosecution, and the Public Prosecution Service of Canada accepts the case, the chances of conviction are relatively high.

4. PROSECUTION

For any crime, including a tax crime, the government must prove your guilt beyond a reasonable doubt. If you remain silent, an experienced tax lawyer may be able to mount an effective defence.

The CRA and the prosecutors look at the case's publicity value – local or national. For them a prominent local person caught in their net is a bonus. They firmly believe that front-page headlines make other would-be tax cheaters think twice.

5. DEFENSE

The same defense arguments that are used to convince investigators not to proceed may be raised by your defense lawyer. To secure a conviction the Crown must overcome a number of hurdles.

What the Prosecutor Must Prove

If you don't plead guilty to the charges, you will eventually have a trial. At the trial, the prosecutor and the CRA must prove you are guilty of the crimes with which you have been charged. Essentially, they must show you acted intentionally and that you are guilty beyond a reasonable doubt.

Proving Intent

The primary element of any tax crime is intent. You can't be convicted of a tax crime if you only made a mistake, unless it was a grossly negligent mistake. For example, a recent immigrant who did not report his or her income from investments made back home, which he or she wrongly thought were tax-exempt, may have made a justifiable mistake and thus might not be guilty of a tax crime.

Reasonable Doubt

All crimes must be proven beyond a reasonable doubt. If a judge or jury has any reasonable degree of doubt about your guilt, the CRA's case will fail. For example, without additional evidence showing his or her intent to cheat, a judge may not believe beyond a reasonable doubt that the immigrant who omitted his or her foreign investment income was filing a false tax return. Another situation could be where a taxpayer suffered severe psychological problems and could not deal with tax matters. In that event, it could be argued that the non-filing was not intentional. Of course, testimony from a psychiatrist or psychologist would be required.

6. CONVICTION

When the prosecution's case is strong enough to secure a conviction, a good defence lawyer will, hopefully, reach a plea bargain before going to trial. There is still a conviction, but the chances are better that your sentence will be restricted to fines, with home confinement. Or you may be sent to a halfway house rather than to jail.

If a plea bargain is not possible, or you reject a plea bargain because you believe the Crown cannot prove intent or overcome reasonable doubt, your trial will proceed.

There it becomes a battle of the lawyers. I will share with you that if the Crown has chosen to proceed with a trial, conviction is a likely outcome. Seriously consider the plea bargain option. It can be the lesser of the two evils. Before you go there, rip the prosecution's case apart to expose any weaknesses. This can give you leverage in a settlement negotiation

7. SENTENCING

Once you are convicted of a tax crime – fraud, evasion or even failure to file – you will inevitably be required to pay criminal penalties, which can be up to 200% of the amount of tax evaded. This is in addition to the tax you are assessed as owing.

You could also receive a jail sentence.

Really, you don't want to be here.

Licensed professionals, such as lawyers, medical doctors, stockbrokers, chartered accountants, CGAs and CMAs can, depending on the decision of their professional body, lose their license or face a period of suspension after conviction for tax evasion, which may be the harshest sentence of all. However, given that their professional accreditations place them in positions of trust, perhaps it is only fitting that tax transgressions, if they are indeed guilty as charged, cost them their privileges.

A Bullet-Proof Case

THE MAN ON THE PHONE SOUNDED QUITE DESPERATE.

"Please, Mr. DioGuardi, I must have your help. Can we meet soon?"

The call came to my office on Sparks Street. It was a few years after I had left my job with the Tax Litigation Section of the Department of Justice and gone into private practice.

I asked the man to tell me the nature of his problem. He said was a research professor and had a doctorate in textile engineering. He said that people from the Department of National Revenue had brought the RCMP to his home, produced a search warrant, and taken away his banking and business records.

"My accountant told me this could never happen," the man said, sounding quite shaken. Then he told me that he had fled Eastern Europe after the Second World War when the Russians invaded his homeland. This invasion of his home by the tax police had shaken to the core his faith in Canada as a safe harbour.

After a few more questions it became apparent that this man had bank accounts in Europe that had never been reported on his tax returns. He was hesitant to tell me more over the phone. Could we meet in person soon? At his home.

I was intrigued by the man and the story that was clearly behind the Department of National Revenue search and seizure, and so

I agreed. He gave me his address and we set a time for an evening meeting the next day.

"The Doctor," as I chose to call him, lived in a rambling old house in an upscale part of Ottawa, near the Governor General's residence. (As the tale goes on, that fact actually becomes quite scary.) I arrived at the appointed time and he invited me into the living room. We sat down and I asked him to tell me about himself. How long had he been in Canada? What did he do for a living? What was the source of the money in the accounts outside of Canada?

The Doctor's story was fascinating. He had been trained in Eastern Europe as a textile engineer and there obtained his doctorate. His family had owned several textile mills in Czechoslovakia, which were confiscated when the Russians took over the country after the Second World War. He wisely sought refuge in Canada, and soon found work developing textiles for new industrial applications. He had an enquiring mind, and a keen sense of innovation. One day while testing for strength he had discovered that certain fabrics, when woven together in a particular manner, reacted to force with a twisting action that could provide protection from knives, and even bullets.

Today, we take it for granted that bullet-proof vests have always been available to protect the police and the military. Even hockey equipment and industrial protection for loggers now use this type of material. However, in the early 70s, a woven cloth that could deflect bullets and sharp projectiles was space-age technology, and still in the test phase.

The Doctor could see how interested I was in his invention. "Come with me," he said, and led me downstairs to his basement. He stopped along the way to get a Mauser pistol, a Colt 45 and bullets.

The introduction of firearms was a bit of a jolt, but I was in it this far, and he had retained me as his legal counsel. I figured it was too late to back out.

We went down the stairs to the basement. He showed me a piece of his ballistic cloth, as he called it. It was heavy, and very dense, although not as heavy as I had imagined. The Doctor wrapped the piece of cloth over a light aluminum backing, and set it at the far end of the long unfinished room. Then he returned to where I stood, raised the Mauser pistol and aimed at the ballistic cloth.

The Doctor was a small, elderly gentleman, and as I stood beside him I could see how much his hand was shaking. Conflicting thoughts crossed my mind. What if the bullet missed the target, ricocheted off the cement walls, and killed either, or both of us? It was not my happiest moment, but turning tail and running back upstairs was not an option. So I held my breath until he squeezed off a shot. His aim was true. The bullet hit the ballistic cloth square on. We went forward to examine the result. Remarkably, as The Doctor had promised, the cloth, with the light aluminum backing behind it, had actually stopped the projectile. The bullet was embedded in the fabric, but had not penetrated it

I expressed my admiration, and made haste to move toward the cellar stairs.

"Wait," said The Doctor. "Now let's try the Colt 45!" I reluctantly returned to his side. Once again, he raised his gun hand, which shook as much or more than before, fired and, thankfully, again hit the ballistic cloth. On examination, the same cloth had stopped the second bullet. By then I was more than ready to leave the basement. The Doctor set down his guns and led me back upstairs.

Back in the living room, the discussion resumed over tea and cookies.

Yes, he was the inventor of an unusual new fabric with amazing military and industrial applications and a huge potential market. However, that wasn't what he wanted to talk to me about.

I had to let him tell me his story, in his own way. Eventually the tale of his tax trouble was revealed.

Having invented this ballistic cloth, he was travelling around the world demonstrating its properties and taking orders for purchases of the cloth in quantity. I don't remember where he manufactured it. Over several hours, I was regaled by interesting stories about the military leaders who were interested in his ballistic cloth, and how he had met them. Many had placed orders. He recounted that on one trip to Taiwan, he outfitted one of the machine gun covers on a patrol boat with the ballistic cloth, and then went with the military on a raid to some islands near mainland China. Live fire was exchanged. Apparently, the ballistic cloth passed the test and the result was a large order from his new found friends.

Here's where the tax trouble came in. Being originally from Europe, and following the customs of that time for businessmen involved in international transactions, The Doctor had opened a bank account in Lichtenstein. Payments for sales of his ballistic cloth were put in his Lichtenstein bank account, and the income was never reported to the Canadian tax authorities on his tax returns.

Before the tax trouble began, and certainly long before I was retained to represent him, The Doctor's accounting advisor had told him he need not worry about the unreported income in the Lichtenstein account. National Revenue would never come to his home without calling him first. This inaccurate advice made The Doctor drop his guard, and the records of his business transactions, including his Lichtenstein bank account, were kept at his residence.

Imagine how he felt when he answered the doorbell one day and was confronted by the RCMP and agents from National Revenue who had come to conduct a search and seizure.

They were armed with a search warrant – and likely armed as well. They entered his premises, grabbed all the transaction documents and bank information they could find, and took them away for review.

I knew immediately that the Revenue agents had been from Special Investigations. They had come to investigate The Doctor. If warranted, they would recommend criminal prosecution for tax evasion.

The search and seizure had unsettled The Doctor. He did not know what would happen next. The events of his past led him to believe the worst. On a certain level, he had reason to be frightened.

I had cut my teeth inside the jaws of the crocodile. I knew exactly where this would go, and how to handle it. I was optimistic that The Doctor could, indeed, come forth alive from the jaws of the beast, but it would take some doing.

All the evidence the tax authorities needed to prove their case had been gathered up during the search and seizure. His accounting advisor's assurance that records could be kept safely in his home was dangerously wrong.

Special Investigations reviewed the seized documents, and raised a civil assessment for tax payable on the unreported income, seriously inflated by the application of gross negligence penalties and arrears interest. Criminal charges for tax evasion followed.

We had anticipated the likelihood of these charges, and before the matter came to trial undertook some precautionary measures. The Doctor asked me to go with him to Europe to review the status of his banking arrangements. We needed to know how much National Revenue could track.

By now you know that I am an eager tax traveller. So off we went to Zurich where we stayed, to my great comfort and delight, in the Grand Dolder – regarded by many as Zurich's finest hotel.

Next morning we met with The Doctor's financial advisors. Then a chauffeur-driven Mercedes arrived at our hotel and took us to Lichtenstein. We stayed the night and next morning met with The Doctor's bankers and a local lawyer. I spent a few days with them, reviewing The Doctor's business plans and banking records.

I now had a very clear picture of The Doctor's income and cash positions. Fortunately for him, National Revenue had not been able to track most of it. Given the levels of secrecy surrounding accounts in Swiss and Lichtenstein banks at that time, the details of the accounts might never come to light.

I recommended that we suggest a deal to the Department of National Revenue to forestall further investigation. We returned to Canada with a plan.

We engaged in lengthy negotiations with senior tax officials and, with the assistance of criminal counsel, an acceptable plea bargain was reached. The income figures from the plea bargain were utilized to settle his civil assessment, and arrangements were negotiated for the payment of the tax owing.

The Doctor did not go to jail, and we were able to settle his fine on a reasonable basis.

The experience unsettled The Doctor to the extent that he no longer felt secure in Canada. Given that his business was focused on military sales around the world, he was advised on a tax planning strategy that contemplated his becoming a non-resident of this country.

Although the Canadian Tax Crocodile got their pound of flesh from him, he had been pulled alive from the jaws of the beast, and his future revenues were protected from Canada's fiscal authorities.

Many years later, after his death, The Doctor's widow consulted me about new tax issues in his estate, and I was happy to assist her.

Every time I notice police on duty, or see hockey players padded up, I think back to the good Doctor and his basement demonstration.

The Crocodile
Misses the Bite

YOU NEVER KNOW WHAT WILL CATCH the crocodile's eye. Sometimes, even after a trial, you don't know how it really started. This case demonstrates how a taxpayer can suddenly find himself at #3 on the Audit Escalation Scale without warning. It's also relevant to my earlier comments on Canada and its tax haven opportunities. (See "Canada, the U.K. and the U.S.: Tax Havens Close to Home.")

The crocodile had his eye on a well-to-do businessman whose family was originally from China. In Hong Kong, the man's father had been a successful and therefore wealthy doctor. Both father and mother, now elderly, were living in Montreal in a long-term care home. A younger brother was a chartered accountant, living in Montreal and practicing his profession there.

The CRA had elected to audit the older brother. Looking at the amount of money he was spending to support a luxurious lifestyle, they suspected that he was not declaring all his income. Perhaps his tax returns had consistently shown low amounts of taxable income and the CRA got curious. Perhaps a disgruntled business colleague had suggested to the CRA that this gentleman was spending more than he reported.

Who knows where or how the breadcrumb trail started? By the time the man became my client, the CRA were already at #2 on our Audit Escalation Scale and pushing hard toward #3.

I asked if there were any issues that might have red flagged his tax returns.

My client explained that, as was the custom of many Chinese families, when the wealthy Hong Kong doctor retired, he put his fortune in the hands of his eldest son (my client), who was then honour-bound to provide for his parents and his sibling. In this way, my client had been gifted almost $2 million. He was spending this money to support a luxurious lifestyle.

This had caught the attention of the CRA, who initiated a net worth audit and then assessed my client with a taxable income commensurate with his spending. The tax payable, with penalties and interest, added up to a very large number.

"I explained that my money all came from my father," my client told me. "But the auditors don't believe me."

Apparently, when he had challenged the assessment, the auditors had glibly said, "See you in Tax Court."

And to Tax Court we would go. I began to build my case.

My client and his younger brother were not on good terms. Likely the younger son resented the elder son's good fortune and irresponsibility. I asked my client for permission to speak privately to his younger brother. What the younger brother shared was eye opening.

He was, I remind you, a chartered account, and a very responsible man. Quite naturally angry at his brother for living the high life, running around with women and running through all their parents' money, it was his great concern that there would not be anything left to pay for the care his mother and father needed in their sunset years.

I asked this younger brother to tell me about his father's investments and how the $2 million had come into Canada. He advised that, while still resident in Hong Kong, his father had invested in special bonds issued by the Province of Manitoba. If the bond holder was non-resident, no tax was assessed on the growth of the investment.

The money gifted to his elder brother had come entirely from the sale of these bonds.

I asked if this brother had proof that the bonds had belonged to his father. He said he did. I believed that he would make a credible witness during the trial, as would his aged father. I asked that the elderly doctor also appear as a witness. I knew that he was, by this time, very ill, but the family fortune was at stake and it was essential that we do everything we could to protect it. Just having the father in court would show that he supported his son's testimony.

On the day of the trial, I had both brothers there, and the father was brought into the courtroom in a wheelchair.

Part of being successful in any trial is to hit a sympathetic judge. They don't tell you in advance who is going to sit and it's all the luck of the draw. In this case, we got a winner. He was an elderly judge who, from all appearances, was not in very good health himself. I felt there might be some sympathy for the sick father from this jurist.

The elder brother was duly called to the stand and recounted his position that he had received the money from his parents and it did not come from his business. Since it was a gift, there was no tax payable on the funds. Alas, he was not a very credible witness, and we would have surely lost the case if I didn't have more to throw into the fight.

I did, of course. I called the younger brother to testify. First, I questioned him about his credentials as a chartered accountant. He worked for a very large and respected educational organization. Certainly, this brother was credible.

As the questioning progressed, I asked if he had accompanied his parents when they immigrated to Canada, and if they had been in possession of a large sum of money at that time. He answered yes to both questions, and described in detail the conversation his father had with the customs agent. His father, he said, had asked if he was to declare money he was bringing with him into Canada. The agent had said it was not necessary, and had waived the elderly couple into the country without further question.

Then I moved on to my clincher argument. I asked my witness, "When your parents were still living in Hong Kong, did they invest funds in Canada?"

The judge quickly looked up and I could tell he was all ears.

"Yes," said the chartered accountant brother. "When my father was in Hong Kong, he made a lot of money from his medical practice. At that time, Canada seemed the safest place to invest his money. He purchased about $1.75 million in tax-free Government of Manitoba bonds."

"Do you have a copy of the bonds, or any documents that would confirm this purchase of bonds?" I asked my witness.

"I do," said the accountant. He produced photocopies of Government of Manitoba bond documents in his father's name, which I then entered into evidence.

I might as well have smacked the Department of Justice lawyer between the eyes with a pole axe. He didn't know what to do.

"I would like to see the documents," the judge said from the bench.

I asked the court if the father could speak from his wheelchair, and the judge graciously allowed it.

The elderly doctor said, in a very low and halting voice that, indeed, this was his money. He had bought the bonds while still living in Hong Kong and after he came to Canada had gifted his wealth to his eldest son, as was the custom of some Chinese families.

That clinched the case, and the judge ruled in our favour from the bench.

The family's wealth was saved from the jaws of the crocodile. My mandate was ended.

To this day I do not know if the elder brother mended his ways and used the money to provide fairly for his parents and his brother.

I like to think he did.

Checkmate – With a Little Help from the *Charter of Rights*

EVA WAS JUST A YOUNG WOMAN when she was investigated by the police for a matter not related to tax. Police had executed *Criminal Code* search warrants on the other matter, entered her residence and seized books and records. They also searched and seized documents in other locations.

In the course of their searches, the police found financial journals. That's not what they were looking for. When they reviewed the journals they found no evidence to support their criminal case. They also thought they smelled tax fraud, and so handed the seized journals to the Canada Revenue Agency (CRA).

Armed with the seized materials, CRA investigations served Eva's banks with requirements to provide information and documents, including her banking records. The journals found during the seizure, plus the banking records, painted a clear picture of tax fraud. The matter shot up the Audit Escalation Scale, and Eva was charged with criminal tax evasion.

At that point Eva retained me to defend her.

None of the defenses I suggested earlier in this section would stand a chance in court. Yet I still had an ace up my sleeve. With criminal co-counsel, I argued that the CRA had violated our client's *Charter* rights by using information gained from an illegal search and seizure.

Section 24 of the *Charter of Rights and Freedoms* provides:

> 24. (1) Anyone whose rights or freedoms, as guaranteed by this Charter, have been infringed or denied may apply to a court of competent jurisdiction to obtain such remedy as the court considers appropriate and just in the circumstances.

> (2) Where, in proceedings under subsection (1), a court concludes that evidence was obtained in a manner than infringed or denied any rights or freedoms guaranteed by this Charter, the evidence shall be excluded if it is established that, having regard to all the circumstances, the admission of it in the proceedings would bring the administration of justice into disrepute.

During argument, we cited the Supreme Court of Canada precedent of *R. v. Law* (2002 SCC 10), which dealt with a taxpayer's *Charter* rights when evidence is discovered during the course of an investigation for some other crime.

Here is the gist of that case.

> The taxpayer, Mr. Law, had owned a restaurant. After a break and enter, he reported a stolen safe. The police subsequently found the safe and when they opened it discovered documents, including cheque books and ledgers. A police officer, who suspected there was tax evasion afoot, gave photocopies of the documents to a CRA investigator. No steps were ever taken to obtain a warrant for search and seizure.

> Notwithstanding, investigators visited the restaurant, reviewed records and laid charges under the *Excise Tax Act* for contravening tax reporting requirements, based upon the information in the photocopied documents handed to the investigators by the police from the recovery of the stolen safe.

At trial, the issue was whether or not section 8 of the *Charter* had been breached in a manner that warranted the exclusion of the photocopied evidence.

After lengthy argument, the judge determined that evidence from the recovered safe was inadmissible.

The CRA was not happy, and appealed the decision under subsection 24(2) of the *Charter*.

The Court of Appeal decided that there had been no *Charter* breach since there was no reasonable expectation of privacy once documents had fallen into the hands of others. It was also held that the police were entitled to photocopy and examine the documents since they were legally in police custody.

The restaurant owner appealed this decision to the Supreme Court of Canada.

The Supreme Court found that the examination of documents in police custody constituted a search and seizure that breached the *Charter*, as the taxpayer had a reasonable expectation of privacy in the contents of the safe. The safe may have been in plain view when recovered, but the contents of the safe were not. The police officers' taking of the safe was restricted to the purpose of investigation of the theft, and did not extend to the pursuit of unrelated matters, including the contents of the safe and the information revealed by the contents. The court concluded that the admission of this evidence would bring the administration of justice into disrepute and refused to allow it to be used.

R. v. Law set a powerful precedent for Eva's case. We presented it with great confidence.

The judge, depending on the Supreme Court decision, decided that Eva's *Charter* rights had indeed been infringed by the issuance and execution of the search warrants at her home and her place of business. The judge found that "the information to obtain in support of these warrants relied on seriously outdated facts that completely undermined the conclusion that reasonable grounds existed to believe that documents would be found at either of these locations."

Moreover, in the circumstances, the issuance of requirements in the course of an investigation for offences under the *Income Tax Act* and *Excise Tax Act* had infringed Eva's rights under sections 7 and 8 of the *Charter*.

Considering the facts of her case, the judge concluded that all of the evidence obtained by these breaches must be excluded under subsection 24(2) of the *Charter*.

Having no evidence available for its use, all tax evasion charges against Eva were dropped.

I was also able to make the CRA completely vacate the civil tax assessments that had been raised on the income uncovered in the seized documents.

Eva walked away, acquitted, and paying not one cent in tax or penalties.

Eva: 2 Crocodile: 0

In this case, the checkmate went to the taxpayer.

The Godfather of Beirut

I MAY NOT HAVE RIDDEN OVER SAND dunes on the back of a camel, but my mission in the Middle East was nonetheless an adventure.

In late 1972 I was retained by a client who had recently moved to Canada from Lebanon. He was the subject of a net worth audit that, according to the tax authorities, showed some very serious discrepancies from his reported income.

Large, unexplained deposits had shown up in his bank accounts, and expensive cars and real estate were registered in his name. There was, however, no clear source of income, capital on hand, or gifts that could explain how he could afford his upscale lifestyle.

The matter had already been escalated up the Scale to special investigators, and everything pointed to a very ugly trial. The investigators had yet to say anything aloud, but it was clear they suspected his income came from the drug trade.

My challenge, as his tax counsel, who might soon also become his criminal tax defense counsel, was to gather evidence that my own forensic auditor could use to construct a net worth favourable to our client.

My client, who we'll call Mr. F, explained that some of his wealth (he never denied that he was possessed of wealth) came from an inheritance from a relative who had lived in a town just outside of Beirut. The rest came, for the most part, from the sale of land in Lebanon and cash gifts.

Our dilemma was that he had no documents or proof to support any of this.

"If we travel to Lebanon I can get these records," Mr. F. said. "But you must come with me, Mr. DioGuardi, so that you can advise my contacts in Beirut. They will not know what will be acceptable as evidence in a Canadian court. We do things very differently in Lebanon."

So I was about to discover.

I agreed to travel with him to Lebanon, and had the inspired idea that, while we were there, we could go to the Canadian Embassy in Beirut where commission evidence could be given under oath by local witnesses. We would likely need this when the case went to Tax Court.

Unlike the fabled Lawrence of Arabia, we arrived in our destination by commercial airline. Less heroic than camel, but by far more efficient – or so I thought at the outset. As the journey progressed I began to feel increasingly like I was a character in a "B" movie.

As we approached Immigration and Customs, Mr. F. produced a roll of cash, and several bills passed into the hand of the customs guard. We were waived through without questions. Those in the line behind us had their bags ransacked and apparently waited a very long time before they were allowed into the country.

In Lebanon money talks.

Two men in dark suits and expensive sunglasses met us on the other side of customs and escorted us to a large, top-of-the-line, black Mercedes. We were whisked to a fine hotel overlooking the sea – one of the two best in the city, I was told. The one next door, the St. George, was owned by the Shah of Iran.

Here we would stay in the lap of luxury until an interview could be arranged with the local powerbroker Mr. F. called his "connection."

We did the rounds of nightlife, which was pretty lively, and went to the Casino du Liban, a world-class gambling establishment frequented by ultra-wealthy visitors from Saudi Arabia and other oil-rich countries. Not being a gambler, it was, for me, an interesting glimpse of how the rich lived in this part of the world.

Many years later I compared the glitzy gambling resorts in Macau and Las Vegas to the Casino du Liban. The Lebanese casino was, in my opinion, far more sophisticated and entertaining. James Bond would have felt right at home.

We waited for several days, which afforded us the opportunity to explore what was still, in the days before the Lebanese began their internecine war in earnest, a delightful and exciting city.

One day, my client wanted to do some banking. The black Mercedes arrived and took us into a section of the city called "The Hamra." We drove up to the front door of the bank and I started to get out of the car. "No," my client said. "Not here." We drove around to the back door, where we were escorted inside.

That's when I started to get suspicious. To an Ottawa Valley born and raised boy, going into the bank through the back door was not what I considered above board.

What the hell had I gotten myself into?

There I was, in Beirut, with my client as my only companion. My best bet was to shut up and play along as if nothing was wrong. Their mentality was not North American, and to them everything was normal.

After my client got his cash from the bank, we were driven to the office of a local lawyer to see about getting the paperwork for the real estate bequest that was part of Mr. F.'s source of capital.

It turned out that Lebanon did not have a formal land registry system, and no papers were available to prove he had received the bequest. The lawyer suggested we go to the deceased's village and speak to the Muktar who, I was told, was the equivalent of the mayor or headman. He would be able to attest to the facts.

We got into the big black Mercedes again and headed out of Beirut. In the countryside, every major intersection was guarded by a tank with guns pointing directly at us as we passed. I felt like the duck in a shooting gallery. Nonetheless, whenever we were stopped, we showed our passports and everyone was friendly. Apparently half of Lebanon had relatives in Canada.

The village and the Muktar was a half-day's drive away. Late in the day, we reached the Muktar's home, with our driver and guards. We were ushered into a large room with seats along the walls. People came and went, had tea and, when it was their turn, asked the Muktar to help them solve their problems. One of the visitors had a relative charged with a serious crime. He asked the Muktar to intercede with the Minister of Justice to see that his relative got leniency. Money changed hands. I never discovered the result. I assume the Minister was merciful.

In due course, the Muktar was ready to receive us, and we were escorted into his presence. My client and the Muktar spoke at length, and then my client turned to me and explained that help and the documents I needed would be forthcoming. (Surprisingly, they were eventually produced.) Part of the puzzle seemed to be solved.

It was now the end of the day and, as the weekend was beginning, I was invited to stay overnight in my client's village, which was nearby. His relatives welcomed us most cordially and we enjoyed a great feast. During the meal I conversed with one of his relatives, who suggested that I join him in the morning to hunt birds. It seemed like a good idea at the time.

Early the next morning it did not appear as wise. However, a promise is a promise. We trudged down from the hill on which the village was built and into the valley in search of birds. My companion handed me a shotgun and some shells, and we started our hunt. I got in a couple of shots, all of which missed the birds. Suddenly there was a loud roaring overhead, and much bigger birds – jet planes – started circling above us.

A look of fear crossed my fellow hunter's face, and he pulled me into the shelter of some giant rocks. They were Israeli jets, he explained. We had to stay out of their line of sight in case they decided that, because we were carrying guns, we looked hostile. It was wise advice.

We waited until the jets flew on, and began the trek homewards. At one point a huge black snake slithered out of the rocks a few feet ahead of us. To him it was a non-event, but I found the snake more frightening than the jets.

That afternoon we drove back to Beirut and it was announced to me that the next morning we would visit the great man in his big house in the hills above the city. Morning came, but still we waited. Early in the afternoon the summons came that we were now welcome to visit.

Again the big black Mercedes with its contingent arrived at our door, and we were duly escorted to a huge residence. The premises was walled and there was an electric gate, patrolled by two guards.

Inside the compound, we were escorted into a huge living room. In Middle Eastern fashion, sofas lined the walls and supplicants sat on them waiting their turn. At the end of the room was a large desk. There sat the Great Man who would help us. It was like that scene in *The Godfather,* when Don Corleone sits in his private study holding audience and granting favours to those who ask, while in the garden the family celebrates his daughter's wedding. In my head, I later dubbed this man "The Godfather of Beirut."

After a time, Mr. F. was invited to approach the Great Man at the desk. Deferentially, we both approached and sat in the chairs across from him. Mr. F. spoke to this man. He did not speak in English, but later my client explained to me that he had asked for assistance in gathering witnesses and documents for his forthcoming tax case in Canada.

The Great Man turned to me and asked, in his own language, what was needed. Mr. F. translated. The questions were thorough.

Was I the lawyer from Canada?

Did I need proof of the inheritance?

Did I need a written will?

What would a Canadian court need to prove the sale of the property?

Why did it all have to be in writing?

I answered the questions as best I could, with Mr. F. translating my responses to the Great Man. At length, His Beneficence nodded and said that it could be done. Orders were given to one of the many men dancing attendance on the Great Man. And then we were dismissed.

As we left the audience room, Mr. F. was smiling. He seemed satisfied that all had gone well. He told me we would have to wait a few days more for the documents to be prepared for us.

What does one do in Beirut with 3 days to kill? I decided to pay a visit to the Canadian Embassy. At a time before we knew anything about terrorism in Canada, it was a great surprise to see doors of bullet-proof glass and a guard with a machine gun at the door. Once inside I learned that my errand was a wild goose chase. It would not be possible to take commission evidence in Lebanon. Perhaps testimony could be given in one of our embassies in another country. If memory serves me right, Jordan was suggested. As it turned out, we did not elect to take any testimony.

Having got all his ducks in a row, Mr. F. had more exciting ideas about how to kill time. He wanted to have some fun. He suggested we find out if any tax or police officials from Canada were in town. By now, I was becoming accustomed to the bizarre way things were done in Lebanon, so I agreed.

We set out to meet with the Chief of Detectives, in a place that reminded me of Rick's American Bar in the film *Casablanca*. At least I was now a player in an "A" list Hollywood feature.

Men in mostly dark suits, some wearing dark glasses, were lolling around the perimeter of a large, smoky room. In a commanding position sat a large, bald man smoking a cigarette. He was the spitting image of the actor Telly Savalas in his TV detective role of Kojak. Could this country get any crazier?

After my client paid the requisite bribe, we approached Kojak and told him our mission. He smiled, and took a long puff on his cigarette.

Then he told us there were two tax agents in town with the RCMP. He told us their names and that they were investigating Mr. F. They were staying at the St. George hotel and would be there for another week.

I knew one of the tax agents, John Spence, from my days working with Special Investigations in the Department of National Revenue. What a joke it would be to surprise John here in Beirut. Now I was having fun! I also wondered if it might give me the edge to negotiate a deal that would solve Mr. F.'s tax trouble.

Mr. F. gave his permission for me to speak to the agents, and the next morning at breakfast I strolled into the dining room of their hotel and said hello to John and his companions. To say they were surprised is an understatement. They asked how the hell I knew they were there.

I didn't answer that, but they invited me to join for them for coffee, so I sat down at their table and ordered. We talked about Mr. F., and without either side revealing its hand, we agreed that perhaps a deal could be worked out – but not here in Beirut. We would have to sit down again in Canada.

I went back to Mr. F. to report. He seemed pleased. The Beirut adventure had been worth the effort after all.

After we returned to Canada, however, he changed his mind. On the evidence we had, it was my opinion that he did not have a winning case. The amount of unexplained money in his bank account did not look good. The judge, like the CRA investigators and the RCMP, was likely to suspect the money came from drug trafficking. A deal with the CRA would be his safest option.

Mr. F. wanted a second opinion. He consulted another lawyer, who said he would take the case to court and win.

I advised Mr. F. that you can always find a lawyer who will say, "No problem – give me money and I will win." Win or lose, they get paid their fee. It's only the client who loses.

Kenny Rogers said it best in his song *The Gambler*, "... know when to walk away."

My tax litigation experience, playing both sides of the game, told me it was time to walk away from the courtroom and sit at the negotiation table. In Beirut the tax enforcement agents had been anxious to talk settlement. Now it was time to cut a good deal.

Mr. F. didn't believe me. He hired the new lawyer, paid him a big fee upfront and lost all.

Mr. F. had all my sympathies, but as they say on Wall Street, "Pigs get slaughtered."

Hafiz Allah!
– A Side Trip

I'LL SKIP BACK TO BEIRUT FOR A moment to share this side trip.

As you'll remember in "The Godfather of Beirut," we had gathered all the evidence we could to support Mr. F. in refuting his net worth audit. As I was preparing to return to Canada, there was an opportunity to visit Egypt.

These were turbulent times in the Middle East. There was heavy fighting in the Sinai, and Egypt had been tossed like a marble from the control of the Russians to the protection of the Americans. It was tough to know who was on which side, the lines were changing so often.

At the time I booked my flight to Cairo, I thought Egypt was allied with Russia. So I prepared to journey behind the equivalent of the Iron Curtain in the Middle East.

I flew Egyptian Airlines on a Comet. Students of history, or old men like me, will remember that the Comet was the first passenger jet to go into commercial service. This Comet looked like it had been in service that long, and it was definitely the worse for wear, but it got me from Beirut to Cairo in one piece.

That's when things got rather surreal. When the Russians moved in they had constructed huge concrete bunkers around the Cairo airport to protect the Egyptian Air force fighter jets from Israeli attack. The bunkers were still standing, and jets were still housed in many of them. As I was driven into Cairo, we passed under huge signs across the roadway welcoming President Nixon. Apparently the Russians had been expelled and the Americans were back running the game. Who could keep up?

Although Cairo itself was in shambles, I found the people very warm and friendly. Samir, an elderly Egyptian who had worked for Aramco (Saudi oil company), identified me as a tourist and kindly offered to be my driver and guide.

By now you will know that I love to get out and see the sights and mix with the locals wherever I travel. I readily accepted Samir's offer and he took me under his wing. We roamed the city. First we drove out into the desert to Sahara City, which was really just a series of large tents, and partook of the local entertainment. To this day I enjoy an evening of Egyptian food, music and, of course, belly dancing.

One day Samir and I drove to the Blue Mosque, an impressive building near the Citadel. Built in 1346, during the heyday of the Ottoman Empire, it derives its name from its interior walls that are covered in blue and turquoise tiles and outlined with plant and flower designs. The view from the top of the minaret is spectacular.

On our way home from the Blue Mosque, Samir asked if he could stop off at a nearby military base. He had a matter of importance to discuss with the General. It was regarding his younger son. On a previous evening, Samir had invited me to his home, and I had met his family. They were lovely people, welcoming and genuine. I had learned that Samir's elder son was in the Egyptian Army fighting in the Sinai against the Israelis. Samir was worried that now his younger son, who was of military age, would be put on the list for active service in the same area.

Samir had a plan to keep his son safe, but he needed to go to the military base to speak to the General in person. He didn't actually tell me that the conversation was about delivering a bribe, but I suspected as much.

I had no objection to the side trip, and was intrigued at the thought of getting a glimpse of the inside of a Middle East military base. We drove into the military enclave and parked near a guardhouse.

Samir told me to stay in the car while he went into a large house to speak to the General. It wasn't safe for me to be there, he said. I promised to stay put.

It was very hot in the car and eventually I just couldn't stand the heat. The compound was filled with all kinds of military equipment including cannons and tanks. I confess that curiosity and the heat got the better of me, and I got out of the car.

I had a good look at the cannons and was just moving over to the tanks when an officer erupted from a nearby guardhouse and ran towards me yelling and pointing his finger. I couldn't understand a word, but I knew I was in trouble. Suddenly I was surrounded by soldiers with rifles, all pointed straight at me.

I put my hands up and let them herd me into the guardhouse. At times like this you shut up and do as you're told.

Poor Samir. I take it the General was not happy that his "guest" had gotten into trouble.

After what seemed like an eternity, Samir appeared, red faced and flustered. "I told you not to leave the car," he said, as nicely as he could. "They think you are an Israeli spy. They want to shoot you."

It was hard to hear him because the guards were shouting and waving their rifles around.

"What do we do?" I asked. Samir motioned me to be quiet and turned to talk to the officer and the guards. They were screaming. Samir was yelling, too. I kept thinking to myself "DioGuardi you've done it now."

I don't know what Samir said. Probably he told them I was just some stupid tourist. Whatever it was, it worked.

The yelling stopped. The officer shook his head and waved us away. He looked disgusted.

We took our cue and left – quietly and quickly.

Samir drove me back to my hotel and I asked him to have tea with me. By then we could chuckle over my escape.

He said, "You told me that in your language DioGuardi means 'God protects me.' In my language your name would be '*Hafiz Allah.*' Today you surely were protected by God. *Hafiz Allah!*"

We laughed and laughed. Nevertheless I think Samir was happy when it was time to take me out to the airport and put me on a plane to Canada.

A Gull, a Getaway, and a Good Laugh at the End

FROM THE CASE FILES
OF PAUL DIOGUARDI

MICHAEL WAS A SUCCESSFUL SALESMAN who had sold in excess of $2 million in securities to his clients. Through no fault of his own, instead of getting a promised annual return of 15%, they lost all their money.

To say the least, Michael was not viewed with much favour in his local community. People who had trusted his financial advice for many years, abruptly deserted him. With his business in tatters, Michael declared bankruptcy. There were no assets to come after. Disgruntled, disappointed and, in their eyes, defrauded, Michael's former clients were left to recover from their losses on their own.

He started a new small business after his bankruptcy discharge. Several years later, the Canada Revenue Agency (CRA) came to audit him. Michael thought this was routine. Maybe the bankruptcy made him a target. Whatever the reason, he thought his tax filings and reporting were accurate and up to date and so he provided the auditor with everything as requested.

The auditor reviewed the books and records, and went away without comment.

Then came a letter from the Enforcement Division advising that he was under investigation for criminal tax evasion. He was advised to seek legal counsel.

Michael's business lawyer suggested my name, and thus I was retained.

After reviewing the CRA's letter, I requested a meeting with the CRA auditor to discuss the matter. When we met, it immediately became clear that she was adamant that a recommendation for criminal prosecution would be forwarded to the Prosecution Service. It did not matter what I told her by way of explanation.

She made a point of telling me that Michael's previous sales activities had caused a lot of local people to lose their money. Although not provable, it was clear that this tax agent was determined to treat him more harshly because of his past conduct.

Before recommending prosecution, it is a standard CRA practice to send to the taxpayer what is called a 30-day letter, setting out their findings and permitting the taxpayer an opportunity to respond. Inexplicably, in Michael's case this had not been done.

I requested such a letter so that I could get more details of the CRA's position.

CRA complied. In the letter, the investigator alleged that Michael had made unreported personal appropriations from his incorporated business bank accounts over a period of 2 taxation years. She adamantly refused to consider any of my explanations for these withdrawals, such as business related disbursements, cash used for business purposes, business travel, phone costs, etc.

It looked like Michael would have a fight on his hands.

I advised Michael that there were two possible ways to handle his situation.

1. Because Enforcement had decided to recommend criminal prosecution, normally we would not say anything or give any information to the tax authorities. In such a situation, the danger in disclosing your defense too early is that the CRA, given the time to do so, may be able to disprove it. If

they are faced with the defense only at trial, they may not be able to respond effectively because of lack of time or witnesses.

2. Alternatively, I could make submissions to the prosecutor. This appeared to be viable because, in my view, the investigator had not done a proper financial analysis. Because of this, it could be worthwhile to go over her head and speak to her supervisor. Michael was told that, since I did not know what data the CRA had, anything he said could be twisted by them and put together with what they had to make a stronger case. It is my practice not to make submissions like this unless the client gives me specific instructions to that effect, and is prepared to take the risk.

After consideration of the alternatives, Michael said he had not evaded any taxes and couldn't believe that they were going to prosecute him. Against my advice, he instructed me to discuss the matter with the investigator and her supervisor.

When I met with them, they informed me that the CRA would prosecute on the figures from their investigation, and no submissions I might make would be entertained. In a strange twist, this statement was, at my request, actually put in writing. The follow up letter stated they would see us in criminal court.

Having worked with special investigators at head office level in my days at National Revenue, I thought this was very unusual conduct. Enforcement always welcomes discussion, especially in a case such as this where we alleged that their financial analysis was seriously flawed. Their response ended any possibility that criminal charges would not be laid.

In due course, Michael was served with a subpoena listing his alleged tax crimes. The charges were even expanded to include assisting other taxpayers to make false charitable donations. This came from two elderly women who, years before, had been his clients and had lost all the money they invested through Michael.

It was clear that the prosecution intended to use the testimony of these former clients to paint Michael as a cad at trial. I'm not aware that "cad" has any true legal standing, but that's the way this case was shaping up.

Michael was also charged with making false and deceptive statements in his T1 personal income tax returns. As well, they threw in a charge of defrauding Her Majesty of an amount greater than $5,000 by preparing and filing false T1 income tax returns and false charitable donation receipts on behalf of his clients. They also alleged that he had not reported income of well over $500,000. In short, they threw in everything but the kitchen sink. It was really quite vindictive.

I requested disclosure of all the CRA's documents, including the prosecution report.

Reams of information were delivered to my offices – boxes upon boxes of charts, documents and investigator analysis printouts. This is not uncommon in a criminal investigation.

My tax team – ex-CRA analysts and auditors – did an analysis of the documentation and, together with a forensic accountant, took the CRA's data and figures apart. This included a review of business and CRA audit records, and our own preparation of a summary of financial expenses and statements based on the information and business records.

Right away we could see that the CRA had made a number of glaring errors. They often do.

One huge mistake was that, in calculating the amount of tax evaded, they had worked mainly from a bank reconciliation. Their normal procedure is to also do a search and seizure to obtain the taxpayer's receipts and other documentation. This allows for a proper comparison. In Michael's case they had not done so. This failure demonstrated a rush to judgment. In other words, the prosecution was so anxious to put Michael behind bars that a basic investigative technique was omitted.

This mistake gave me a good opening to attack their calculations.

To make matters worse, they brought in outside legal counsel to act for the CRA. He was a seasoned litigator and very aggressive.

He wanted a 2-year jail term plus a very large fine, and continually pressed me to have Michael plead guilty. I told him that we would not entertain a guilty plea because, in my opinion, the CRA had made numerous errors, and the amount of tax they claimed to be evaded was seriously overstated.

The prosecutor, who was not a tax lawyer, did not believe me, so my team continued reviewing working papers and receipts and other data to refute the prosecution's findings and prepare for trial.

When our forensic analysis was finally completed, we had hard evidence that would reduce the CRA's assessment of over $500,000 in unreported income down to a very small amount. My feeling was that, at trial, it would be possible to reduce this figure even more. The problem was that some items in the charge would stick because Michael didn't have all his receipts, invoices and other information required by the court to show that in fact he had not evaded any tax.

Now that I was ready, I was confident much of the CRA's case could be proven wrong.

On the day of the trial, a hostile crowd of people filled the court-room. There were cries of "Michael, you are going to go to jail!" and other nasty comments. They resembled a movie lynch mob, albeit in a more restrained Canadian style. Clearly, they were out for his blood – thus the fury of the thwarted over-taxed opportunist. When their scheme failed, they all became victims. A classic case of "the lady doth protest too much."

Prosecuting counsel, sensing that I was well-prepared and that the battle would be hard fought, asked me once again if we wanted to make a deal.

With our own tax analysis in hand, I had the right cards to play if and when the client decided to seek a settlement.

Michael was shaken by the hostile crowd and gave me firm instructions to make the best possible deal I could in the circumstances.

I met with the prosecutor and his client (the CRA) and tabled my figures. They were very detailed. It took the prosecutor and the CRA some time to review it all. But review them they did. And they agreed with me. Michaels' assessment would be reduced so that most of the $500,000 in alleged undeclared income would go away, and the fine would be small.

Nonetheless the prosecutor still wanted Michael to serve jail time. In court, citing his past conduct, he presented a very forceful argument for a jail sentence and the judge, who was from the same town, seemed inclined to agree.

It was time for me to play the ace up my sleeve. I quoted a recent Supreme Court of Canada decision that supported home confinement rather than jail time. My daughter Brigitte, also a tax lawyer who practices with me in the firm, had found the precedent, and it was right on point. In that decision the court gave a 6-month period of house arrest.

Because it was a precedent from the highest court in the land, the judge was forced to agree and, over the loud protests of the crowd, no jail time was ordered. Additionally, Michael was permitted to go to his office between 7 AM and 6 PM each day.

Before the trial, I had told Michael to pack his toothbrush and be ready to go to jail. He and his family were more than delighted that he would be going home instead.

THE GETAWAY CAR

After the decision, we had to deal with court officials with respect to the terms of his house arrest and payment of the fine. It took quite a while. Meanwhile, I was told, a large crowd was still milling about outside the court house. They knew the decision and were not happy.

It was dangerous for Michael to go out and get his truck. I directed my senior analyst, Karen, who had assisted me in court throughout the trial, to slip out and bring the vehicle around to the side door of the court house. We hoped to whisk Michael away from court without harassment.

Karen is plucky. She faced down the TV cameras and the angry crowd and made her way to Michael's truck. She got in and started it up, idling for a few moments to throw the crowd off track. Then suddenly she booted it, and came screaming out of the lot and around the corner, almost on two wheels, and screeched to a stop in front of the side door, where Michael and I were waiting. We dashed into the waiting truck and Karen took off, almost before we had the doors closed.

The media and the unhappy crowd tried to give chase, but quickly gave up.

Next morning, the local newspaper ran a front page picture of Michael's very large house. The headline said "Wealthy Local Resident Gets Away with House Arrest in Tax Evasion Case."

Michael was happy with the court's decision. He paid his fine, satisfied the judgment and is now a productive member of society with all this behind him.

As an aside, Karen still chuckles about the getaway. She keeps asking when we can do that again.

RUNNING FOR COVER

As a side anecdote to Michael's case, I confess this was not the first time that I had to flee from the press after a court case. Avoiding public pursuit is not something they teach you in law school. Perhaps I should start a course.

Years before, while representing a prominent real estate developer who had been charged with tax evasion, we found the press waiting for us outside the courthouse door, their TV cameras and microphones held at the ready.

Bert, my client in this case, was very anxious not to have anyone question him about the trial. Bert, his accountant, Roger (who has also consulted with me for over 40 years), and I began walking quickly away from the courthouse and down the street. We didn't have Karen or a getaway car to whisk us away.

It was difficult for the media to follow us since the street was under construction and there were piles of dirt and holes in the road and sidewalk. It was tough going carrying our heavy briefcases. To make matters worse, the press began chasing us with their cameras and microphones and as we walked more quickly, they in turn increased their own pace. It soon turned into a full-blown race down the street.

Just ahead I saw the door of what appeared to be a bar and restaurant, and we ducked in there, hoping not to be followed. Let me start the joke for you.

A realtor, an accountant and a lawyer walk into a bar ... .

The joke was on us. The bar turned out to be a strip club and women were performing on the stage. As we told our wives later, we had no choice but to stay. The media mob was milling around outside the front door. It was safer to stay put. The club's bouncers could keep them out.

We sat down, had lunch and a drink and watched the show. The food was quite good, and the dances were very entertaining.

After about 90 minutes the media gave up waiting and left us alone. We were able to escape unscathed. And it was a great excuse for being home late for dinner.

The Crocodile on Your Doorstep

What the Crocodile Really Wants to Say

THE CROCODILE LIKES TO choose when and where it will pounce.

One could argue that there is method to this madness, and a major economic benefit. The longer the crocodile lies in wait, the larger the ultimate kill.

Given the wide-ranging powers of collection at its disposal, the CRA can essentially swallow up everything a taxpayer owns, if it waits long enough. And by waiting it lulls the tax evader into a false sense of security.

Here, written with tongue firmly in cheek, is what I think the CRA really wants to say.

Letter to a Taxpayer

Mr. John Guy,
435 Main Street,   SIN # XXX XXX 221
Toronto, ON M4C 3H5   December 31, 2013

Dear Sir,

Re: Individual Income Tax Returns for 2006, 2007, 2008, 2009 and 2010, inclusive.

On behalf of the public treasury, we thank you for not filing your tax returns for the year(s) indicated above.

Your lack of action affords us the opportunity to assess new interest every day to your yet-to-be-defined tax balance. Each year, that interest compounds, adding in excess of 20% more to your original balance, enriching the public treasury immensely.

We are thus happy to finance your ever-growing tax contributions until such time as:

a) you choose to file, whereupon we will additionally assess a penalty for filing late, add the 20% percent premium, compounded and back-dated to the date(s) your tax payments were due, and then initiate collection action after 90 days; or

b) we tire of waiting for you to file, make our own assessment of what you owe, and then do all of the above.

Either way, at that time we will expect you to expend all of your financial assets, including the equity in your home, to retire the tax balance in full.

Don't forget, the high interest remains in effect for each day you still carry a balance.

We thank you again for your pending generous contributions to the public purse.

Yours sincerely,

M.E. Smith
Non-Compliance
Canada Revenue Agency

At the end of day, it comes down to this. If you live and work in Canada, there will be tax. It's inevitable.

We are told that tax is the price we pay for "peace, order and good government." Tax funds the public purse, which funds the infrastructure that runs our land and everything that makes a first world country first world.

If you go back to our taxpayer behavioural profiles from "Taxpayer Demographics: A Behavioural Study," you will note that the Law Abiders firmly believe it's a privilege to pay taxes. Altruistic Compliers and Rationalizers dutifully file and pay. Even the Underground Economists and Over-Taxed Opportunists acknowledge that somebody has to pay taxes to keep the country running. They just want to pay less personally. And the Outlaws – well, even they are fiercely protective of their right to access healthcare, protection of law enforcement, and carry a Canadian passport.

In short, most acknowledge that there must be tax.

Unfortunately, despite the rosy statement in the Canada Revenue Agency's 2012-2013 report to Parliament (*http://www.cra-arc.gc.ca/gncy/nnnl/2012-2013/p3-cnts-eng.html*):

- 92.1% of individuals over the age of 18 filed an income tax return on time,
- 94.5% of individuals over the age of 18 who owed taxes paid them on time and
- hundreds of thousands of individual taxpayers and their businesses find themselves with tax assessments they just can't pay all at once and on time.

Time to Pay – A New Danger Rating Scale

WHEN TAX IS OWING, THE CROCODILE comes looking for the money. He starts gently, and politely. As in a chess game, the first moves are with pawns. As the magnitude of the tax owing and the passage of time escalates, so do the moves of the game. By the time the CRA deploys its knights and bishops, you should consider your queen to be under attack, and your king in check.

To visualize the steps in the CRA collection process, I offer the Taxpayer Danger Rating Scale in Figure 4. The higher you rank on the scale, if ever you owe tax, or you owe tax now, the greater your danger.

Understanding the ways in which collection of tax can escalate into ever more dangerous waters may help you understand when and where to seek help before the CRA calls checkmate.

1. DEMANDS TO FILE

This usually starts as a polite request from the CRA to file the returns they believe are outstanding. It will be followed, in a matter of weeks, with escalating letters demanding that you file, until you receive a Final Request to File, which threatens legal action. Continue to be

Figure 4: Taxpayer Danger Rating Scale

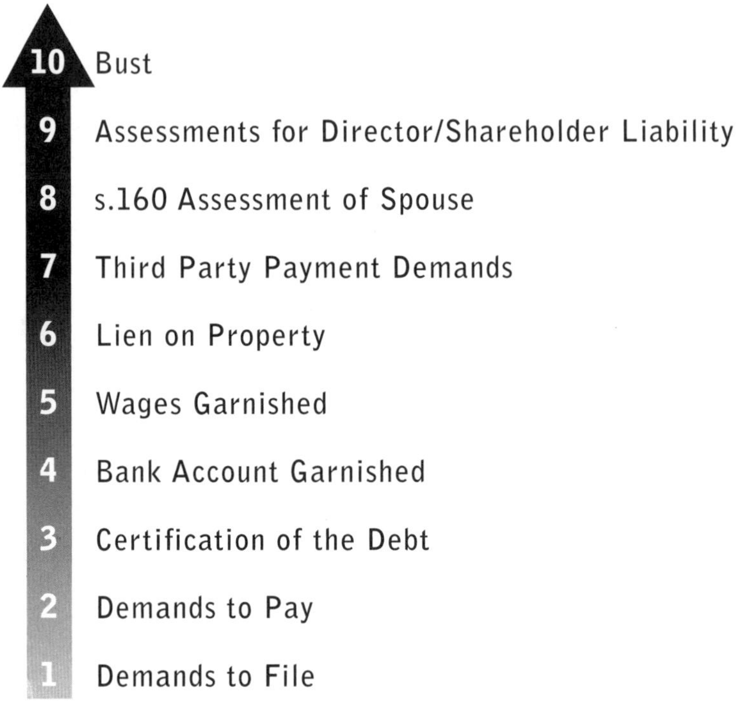

10 Bust

9 Assessments for Director/Shareholder Liability

8 s.160 Assessment of Spouse

7 Third Party Payment Demands

6 Lien on Property

5 Wages Garnished

4 Bank Account Garnished

3 Certification of the Debt

2 Demands to Pay

1 Demands to File

delinquent and the Taxman will use his own accounting strategies to "arbitrarily assess" you for the unfiled years. This assessment stands as your tax bill until such time as you file returns reflecting your true income and expenses.

Here are the dangers:

- The CRA will collect aggressively on the arbitrarily assessed balance, including taking such legal action as seizing your bank account, putting a lien on your home or garnishing wages.
- The CRA can still choose to prosecute you under section 238 of the *Income Tax Act* for failure to file.

2. DEMANDS TO PAY

When your tax balance, however small, remains unpaid, the CRA becomes progressively aggressive in its collection tactics. Demand to Pay letters and likely telephone calls from an Agent at a National Collections Centre anywhere in Canada, will come regularly for a number of months. Failure to engage with the crocodile at this stage will result in a Notice of Pending Legal Action, which is the CRA's way of telling you they are about to punt you up the scale.

3. CERTIFICATION OF THE DEBT

If your tax balance remains unpaid after repeated requests to arrange suitable terms of repayment, the Taxman may register a certificate in the federal court against the tax owing. You will be notified in writing that a federal certificate has been registered. Unless you make suitable arrangements quickly, the Taxman can, and likely will, move forward with aggressive collection which can include:

- seizing the money in your banking and investment accounts;
- securing your property against the tax debt through property liens;
- garnishing your wages; or
- demanding third party repayments from your clients/tenants/prime contractors, etc.

Over time the action will continue to escalate. If you receive a letter advising you that your tax arrears have been certified, it's time to get serious about coming to terms with the Taxman – whatever it takes.

4. BANK ACCOUNT GARNISHED

Having your bank account garnished is a tremendous violation of your personal property. One day you use your debit card at the gas station or the grocery store, and the transaction is declined. You call your bank, and the answer makes your blood run cold. The CRA has seized personal assets in payment of your tax arrears, and the first – and easiest – target is the money in your bank account. There's nothing the bank can do until you come to terms with the CRA.

Here's a summary of what the CRA can seize, why they can do it, and what it will take to get your bank account working again.

Why CRA Freezes Your Bank Account

After repeated requests, usually by telephone and by letter, for payment in full or an arrangement to pay over time, the CRA will stop playing nice and go looking for your money. The first place they look is your bank. You likely will have already received a letter that the CRA may take legal action without further notice, but you might not receive that letter before the CRA has already moved to seize your most available asset – your bank account.

How CRA Freezes Your Account

When you opened your bank account, you were asked to provide a Social Insurance Number. This number confirms that you are a Canadian resident. It also provides a database that the CRA can tap into to find out where you bank and your account numbers. The CRA also can get this information from any cheques you have sent to them as payment of tax balances. If you signed up for automatic deposit of tax refunds or social benefits payments – the CRA already knows where you bank.

Ninety-one days after the day your tax was due to be paid, or assessed, CRA is legally empowered to go to your bank and demand the surrender of funds held in your bank account. To do this, the CRA sends a Third Party Requirement to Pay (RTP) letter to your bank. The letter looks like the one in Figure 5.

Figure 5: Third Party Requirement to Pay (RTP)

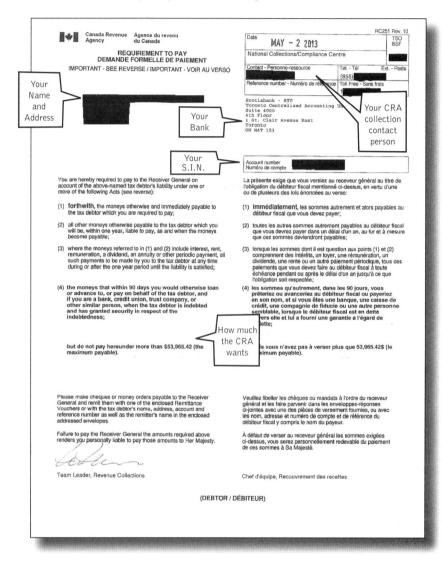

What the Bank Must Do

Once your bank receives this letter, they are required by law to send the CRA money from *any account in your name*, up to, but not in excess of, the sum indicated in the letter. Once the bank has forwarded that amount to the CRA, your account(s) are freed.

If the balance in your account(s) is less than the total demanded, the bank will forward what money there is as of the date the bank receives the RTP. Any deposits you make to the account(s) thereafter will continue to be forwarded to CRA, until the full sum demanded has been paid.

Accounts at Other Banks

An RTP sent to Scotiabank, for example, will not affect any accounts you hold at other banks (such as Royal Bank, TD Bank, CIBC, etc.). If the CRA is unaware that you have accounts at more than one bank, those accounts remain available for you to use. However, CRA often issues RTPs simultaneously to all the banks they have on file for you.

What If You Have a Joint Account?

If your bank account(s) is also in the name of another person, for instance in your name and your spouse's name, the CRA will allege that the funds in that account are subject to the RTP. Most banks will not ask any questions, but simply send all the funds in any account with your name on it. After the seizure, you can argue that some (or perhaps even all) of the money in the account belonged to the other account holder. You will have to demonstrate with a full disclosure of who put in how much money when, etc., to be successful. In the meantime the CRA will hold on to the money seized. If you think you're at any risk of a bank account seizure, maybe a joint chequing account for the mortgage and the car insurance payment isn't such a good idea.

RTP Doesn't Freeze Your Spouse's Account

Tax is a personal matter. If you owe tax, your spouse is not automatically also on the hook for your tax debt. An RTP to your bank for your tax arrears will only affect accounts that are in *your* name. Your spouse's accounts, so long as it's not a joint account with you, won't be affected.

(Note: There are ways for the CRA to try to come after your spouse for your debt, but it's not automatic. The CRA would have to prove that your spouse received the benefit of an asset from you without paying for, or earning it. Then they would have to assess your spouse under section 160 of the *Income Tax Act*. See #8 on the scale.)

Your Credit Card Usually Is Not Effected

Your bank issued you the credit card, but it was really on behalf of VISA, or MasterCard, etc. So a bank account RTP most often is specific to the bank account(s) in your name. In rare circumstances, and especially if you owe a very large amount of money, the CRA may *also* issue an RTP on credit lines or a credit card, but this would have to be specified additionally on the RTP demand.

You Can Open a New Account at a Different Bank to Access Your Money

A new account at a new (different) bank is not subject automatically to the RTP. You may choose to open a new account and deposit your cheques there. In time CRA may discover that bank account. If you write the CRA a cheque from your new bank account they are likely to discover the new account sooner than later. As a tax lawyer, I don't advise anyone to switch banks for the purpose of avoiding payment of tax. It could be deemed as "hiding" money. Pragmatically, it might work temporarily.

MoneyMart Isn't a Safe Tax Haven

Some people are so smart they stop using a bank account and cash all their cheques at the MoneyMart, or the Cash Store, etc. After a time, CRA will wise on to that and may issue an RTP to MoneyMart, who then, like the bank, is required by law to forward the proceeds of any cheque you cash to the tax authorities.

Getting CRA to Remove the Freeze on Your Bank Account

The faster you come to terms with the CRA, the faster you can get your cash flowing again and your bank account freed up. CRA will want payment in full, or your offer of suitable payment terms, usually secured by post-dated cheques, before they agree to release the RTP on your account(s). You'll need to speak to the friendly CRA collection contact specified on the RTP letter to make these arrangements. Alternatively, if you've hired someone to help fix your tax problem – a tax lawyer is a good choice – your representative will negotiate with the CRA person. You will need to ensure that your representative has a copy of the RTP letter and the collection contact's name.

Once an agreement is confirmed, the CRA will fax the letter in Figure 6 to your bank. (It's a form letter and, delightfully, it's always the same.)

Once the bank receives this fax, the RTP is supposed to be lifted immediately. It's safest to call your bank and make sure the letter has been actioned in the back rooms.

Figure 6: Requirement to Pay Cancellation Letter

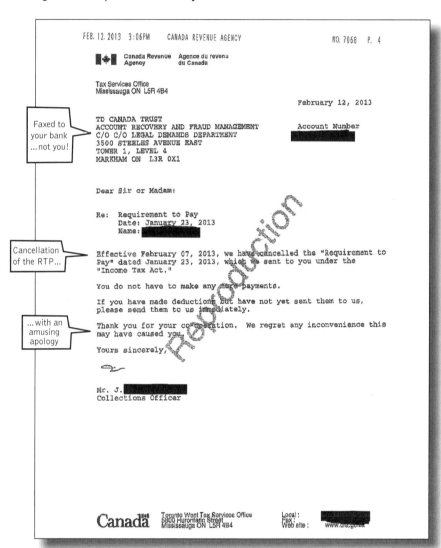

Faxed to your bank ...not you!

Cancellation of the RTP...

...with an amusing apology

FEB. 12. 2013 3:06PM   CANADA REVENUE AGENCY   NO. 7068   P. 4

Canada Revenue   Agence du revenu
Agency   du Canada

Tax Services Office
Mississauga ON L5R 4B4

February 12, 2013

TD CANADA TRUST   Account Number
ACCOUNT RECOVERY AND FRAUD MANAGEMENT
C/O C/O LEGAL DEMANDS DEPARTMENT
3500 STEELES AVENUE EAST
TOWER 1, LEVEL 4
MARKHAM ON L3R 0X1

Dear Sir or Madam:

Re: Requirement to Pay
     Date: January 23, 2013
     Name:

Effective February 07, 2013, we have cancelled the "Requirement to
Pay" dated January 23, 2013, which we sent to you under the
"Income Tax Act."

You do not have to make any more payments.

If you have made deductions but have not yet sent them to us,
please send them to us immediately.

Thank you for your co-operation. We regret any inconvenience this
may have caused you.

Yours sincerely,

Mr. J.
Collections Officer

Canada   Toronto West Tax Services Office   Local :
          5800 Hurontario Street   Fax :
          Mississauga ON L5R 4B4   Web site :   www.cra.gc.ca

What About the Money CRA Took from Your Account?

Once it's gone, it's gone, unless you eventually successfully demonstrate through an appeal or an objection that your assessment was wrong and you never owed that tax. In that event, any overpayment to your tax account will eventually be credited back to you.

5. WAGES GARNISHED

The same document that permits the CRA to require your bank to remit the funds in your accounts can be directed to your employer or prime contractor to require that payment of wages be diverted to the CRA as payment of your tax arrears.

The letter looks much the same as the one to your bank, but with a few changes (see Figure 7).

What Your Employer Must Do

Once the payroll department at your work receives this letter, your employer is required by law to send the CRA the requested percentage of your after-tax wages each and every time you are paid. The CRA has identified the employer's source deduction account, so they already know your regular wage, and thus they will be able to identify a radical change in payment that suggests your employer is trying to elude the payment demand. In that event, the CRA will make your employer liable for your tax debt. Thus your employer is very motivated to keep the Taxman happy.

All money received from your employer will be credited to your tax account to reduce your arrears.

Getting CRA to Remove the RTP on Your Wages

The faster you come to terms with the CRA, the faster you can start receiving your full wage again. However, you may find that the garnishment is a lower amount than the CRA was demanding from you as a monthly payment arrangement, in which case you may opt to let the RTP remain until your tax is paid.

Once a payment agreement is confirmed, the CRA will fax a letter to your employer similar to the example sent to the bank (see Figure 6). Yes, it will have the same amusing "apology."

Figure 7: Requirement to Pay – Employer

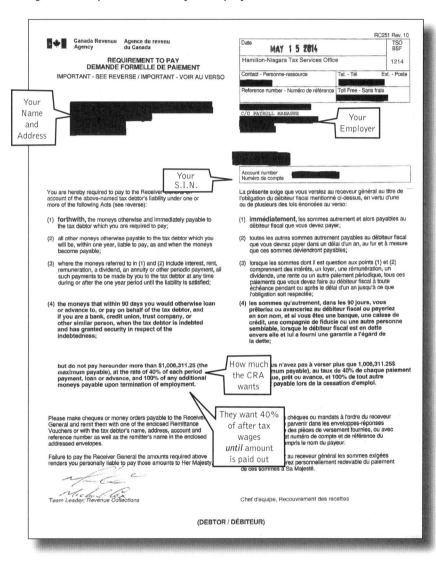

6. LIEN ON PROPERTY

When the CRA registers a lien against your home, it's a frontal attack on your biggest asset. It's aggressive collection action and it's something that happens because a tax balance has remained unpaid for an extended period of time. Treat this as a serious matter. If you stay calm and act reasonably, there are things you can do, and ways you can use your home equity to help pay the tax arrears and protect your home.

Here are the answers to common questions about tax liens to help you understand what to do, and where to turn for help.

How Do I Know if there Is a Lien Registered Against My Home?

A title search on your property will reveal the existence of a lien.

The CRA process usually advises you by letter that a certificate has been registered in Federal Court for the arrears owing. This is normally the opening move in a plan to register a lien against your home and/or real estate property. If and when the property lien is registered, the CRA typically advises you by letter.

In some cases, though, you may not discover there's a lien until you try to sell your home, or refinance your home with a new or bigger mortgage.

Does a Tax Lien Mean I Have Lost Title to My Home?

No. The lien is a registration on the title that effectively prevents you from closing a sale or refinancing against your home equity until you make arrangements with the CRA for proceeds from any sale or home refinancing to be directed to the CRA against payment of your debt.

When your tax debt is paid in full, the lien will be removed by CRA.

Does a Lien Mean the CRA Will Take My Home?

Not immediately. A lien is registered as security against your tax debt. However, after the passage of significant time, if your tax balance remains unpaid, the CRA may register a Writ of Seizure and Sale, which is very serious enforcement action. If you still do not make arrangements for settlement of your tax debt, the CRA then has the legal authority to seize your home and sell it. Any proceeds remaining after your tax balance is discharged will be paid to you, but your home will have been liquidated to satisfy your tax debt.

Does this happen? Yes, but not without many months – even years – of prior notice. The CRA prefers you to find other means of sourcing the funds with which to pay your tax balance. By law, there is a mandatory notice period that CRA – or any other creditor – must serve to you advising of their intent to execute on the Writ of Seizure and Sale. If you still do not make arrangements to retire your tax arrears, CRA will then make arrangements to sell your home, and you will be required to leave the premises.

If CRA Has Registered a Lien, Can I Sell My Home, or Renew the Mortgage?

Yes. Even with a CRA lien, you can access the equity in your home through a secured line of credit, mortgages and even the sale of your home. However, because CRA has registered security against that equity, the proceeds of any sale or financing must be paid to the CRA to retire the arrears in full. Thereafter, any remaining proceeds are payable to you.

You will need the cooperation of the CRA to secure your home equity financing, or close the sale of your home.

If you are *borrowing* from home equity, once the bank, or other lender, confirms the amount of money you are approved to borrow, the CRA will agree to lift the lien in order for the financing to occur, on condition that its position against the property is paid out of the funds advanced.

If you are *selling* your home, CRA will agree to lift the lien on the condition that when the proceeds of the sale are transferred to your real estate lawyer, its position against the home is paid out before the balance of the proceeds are paid to you.

NOTE: Your mortgage(s) are generally registered in first position. Therefore, when you sell your home, the funds from the sale go to, in this order:

1. the bank (or the mortgagee),
2. other secured lenders, if any,
3. the CRA,
4. any other creditors who have registrations against your property, and
5. you, the seller.

What If the Tax Debt Is More than I Can Get from Selling My House?

If the sale price of your home is not enough to discharge the tax debt in full – after the mortgage(s) and secured lines of credit are paid out, of course – the CRA will be paid whatever is left. This will be applied against your tax balance to reduce it. Whatever is left unpaid remains as a tax balance you still owe to the CRA.

What If There Are Other People on Title Besides Me?

CRA can only realize proceeds from your share of the equity in the property. So if you sell, only your share of the equity can be paid out to the CRA. The CRA cannot seize your spouse's, or anyone else's equity. However ...

If you have transferred your equity (title) to someone else, without receiving payment for the share that equates to the fair market value at the time of the transfer, the CRA may consider assessing that someone else for the amount of your tax arrears.

Can I Go Bankrupt to Get Rid of the Tax Lien?

No. *And this is important.* Filing for bankruptcy, or filing a consumer proposal, does not discharge a lien against your property. If you go bankrupt on your CRA debt, the lien remains and – even worse – may accrue interest over time. Even after your discharge from bankruptcy, the lien remains in force, until you eventually sell your home. At that point, the CRA will be second in line after the mortgage holder, etc., and will receive the remaining proceeds up until your share of the equity is exhausted. After that, however, because of your bankruptcy, your tax debt is extinguished – even if your equity is not enough to pay the tax in full.

The Bottom Line: Tax liens are serious, complicated and too dangerous for a do-it-yourself solution.

7. (THIRD PARTY) PAYMENT DEMANDS TO YOUR CLIENTS

When a small business has been running a large tax balance for several years, the Taxman can suddenly get tired of waiting to be paid. Without warning he will send letters to or, even worse, visit your principal clients to serve them with Third Party Requirement to Pay letters. This is a legally binding demand that any monies due to be paid to you must instead be paid directly to the tax authority – federal or provincial. If your clients defy the order and continue to pay you, they may be held liable for the unpaid tax balances.

How does the Taxman know the names of your clients? We see a pattern in which the CRA demands to see your books and records for a "trust audit." The auditor visits your premises to check that you are reporting and filing accurate source deductions or HST remittances. At the same time he is reviewing your invoices, he is gathering the names and addresses of your clients. Then, when he determines you're not likely to be able to pay off your tax bill in full within the next 12 to 24 months, he goes straight to your clients to collect the tax. The move is calculated to choke the life out of your business and force you into bankruptcy. Then the CRA agent can close the file and collect his next promotion or salary increase.

Before you panic and fall into the bankruptcy trap, consider retaining experienced legal tax counsel.

In cases such as this, I consider the value of an injunction in the courts for a stay of collection action to permit you the time to organize your finances to address the tax debt. Where circumstances warrant, I also seek cancellation of penalties and interest through submission of an application for Taxpayer Relief. This protects your legal right to due process, as set out under section 220(3.1) of the *Income Tax Act* and/or section 281(1) of the *Excise Tax Act*.

8. SECTION 160 ASSESSMENT (OF SPOUSE)

In some cases, knowing that a large tax bill will be due even before a tax return is filed, taxpayers will transfer property to a spouse, a relative, a business colleague or even a friend in an attempt to deplete assets and prevent the CRA from seizing the home to collect on the debt.

Under section 160 of the *Income Tax Act* or Part IX (GST/HST) of the *Excise Tax Act*, if you owe tax and you transfer property to a spouse or a person who has since become your spouse, a person under 18 years of age or a person with whom you were not dealing at arm's length, the person to whom you transferred the property becomes liable for the lesser of the amount you owe, or the excess of the fair market value of the property over the consideration given for the property.

These vicarious liability rules do not apply to a transfer of property between a taxpayer and his or her spouse under a decree, order or judgment of a court, or under a written separation agreement where, at the time of transfer, the taxpayer and his or her spouse were separated and living apart as a result of the breakdown of their marriage or common-law relationship.

If you are assessed under section 160 with liability for someone else's tax debt, it means that the CRA believes it will never recover the tax from that taxpayer. Thus, the CRA has searched for every related source available to pay the tax. It's the crocodile going after the gazelle's fawns because the gazelle outran him.

The CRA may give up on the taxpayer because he or she has declared bankruptcy, has absconded, is deceased or is simply MIA.

There is no time limit on the CRA's ability to assess the recipient of property under section 160. By the time the assessment comes, spouses may be divorced or widowed. Business partnerships may long since have been dissolved. Friends may have gone their separate ways. None of this matters. The assessment can still be raised.

If you are so assessed, the Tax Crocodile will then pursue you through every stage of this Taxpayer Danger Rating Scale until you pay, declare bankruptcy, abscond, die or disappear. The only good news is that you can object to and appeal the assessment. Depending on the circumstances, you may very well be successful.

9. ASSESSMENTS FOR DIRECTOR/SHAREHOLDER LIABILITY

Directors of a corporation have a responsibility to ensure that trust monies – payroll remittances, employer health tax (in Ontario) and Excise Tax (GST/HST, depending on your province) – are properly recorded and remitted to the tax authorities as and when due. The penalties for failure to report and failure to remit are onerous, and can inflate the balance owing to devastatingly large amounts very quickly.

If the corporation is identified as being delinquent in these remittances, or if the corporation goes out of business or declares bankruptcy, the directors of the corporation may be assessed personally with the tax bill. If there is more than one director, each will be assessed individually for the full amount(s) owing. Each director will be pursued by CRA through every stage of this Taxpayer Danger Rating Scale.

NOTE: Here's where a lot of people get caught.
The rules also apply to non-profit corporations and charities. If you are acting in the role of a director of a charity, you can be liable for its source deductions and GST/HST if the charity fails to pay them.

The CRA can also assess what it calls "de facto directors." If you are deemed to be acting in the role of a director or hold yourself out as a director, even though no formal appointment to that office was ever made in the books of the corporation or elsewhere, you can be held liable for unpaid "trust monies" – that is, GST/HST or payroll deductions.

Time Limit

There is a time limit, however, for being personally assessed. A Notice of Assessment for director's liability must be issued within 2 years of the date you have ceased to be a director. Therefore, if there is any possibility you may be responsible for past actions of the corporation and have yet to be assessed, resign immediately. It is expected that your resignation will be on the public record, which means a Notice of Change of Directors must be filed with the provincial or federal corporation registry. As soon as you have formally resigned and filed the Notice of Change, the "2-year clock" starts running. You will not be liable unless the CRA assesses the corporation and then issues you a Notice of Assessment within this 2-year period. If you can prove the existence of a letter of resignation as a director, you may still be able to avoid the assessment, even if the letter was never sent to the corporate registry.

Due Diligence Defense

While there can be a due diligence defense for failure to comply, it's quite difficult to escape personal liability. The onus of proof to establish a good due diligence defense will be on the offending director. Being unaware of the corporation's financial situation does not relieve a director from liability. It is important that a director exercises a reasonable degree of care, diligence and skill, and be prudent. Otherwise, he or she will personally be on the hook to pay the GST/HST or source deductions that were not remitted as required.

If you are the shareholder of a corporation and you receive remuneration as dividends, you may be assessed personally if the corporation also has unpaid corporate tax. In order to be eligible to pay out dividends, the corporation must have taxable income on the balance sheet. So if you pay yourself in dividends, there will be corporate tax payable.

10. BUST

If your tax bill has grown so large that, even with cancellation of accrued interest and penalties, you have no ability to pay it down in 24 months, or even at the outset 36 months, you owe it to yourself to explore the options available under the *Bankruptcy and Insolvency Act* (BIA).

Debt Relief Under the BIA: Two Options

A Consumer Proposal allows you to propose to repay your unsecured creditors – which would include the CRA and/or the provincial tax authorities – an agreed upon sum of money divided into monthly payments for up to 60 months. This sum is usually more than the total of what creditors would expect to receive in a bankruptcy. (Otherwise, why would your creditors accept your proposal? Bankruptcy is faster for them.) You must be able to demonstrate that you can meet the monthly payment without fail. If your creditors do not accept your proposal, you may opt to file for bankruptcy – or walk away. A Consumer Proposal is prepared by a trustee in bankruptcy, who presents it to your creditors on your behalf.

If you owe more than $250,000, you would file a Division I proposal. In this scenario, if your creditors reject the proposal, you are obligated to file for bankruptcy.

Bankruptcy is a legal declaration that you are insolvent. A trustee determines the liquidation value of your assets, which are turned over to the trustee to sell in order realize that money and use it to pay off your creditors. You are required to fulfill certain requirements by the trustee, and 50% of any income you earn in excess of the provincial minimums must be paid to the trustee for distribution to your creditors. This will continue for as long as it takes before you are discharged from your bankruptcy – typically 9 months to 21 months, but the term may be longer based on a number of factors.

As soon as the trustee files your Notice of Intent for a Proposal or Bankruptcy, all creditors are stayed from collection action against you, including the CRA. This means the CRA must immediately stand down on any bank or wage garnishments that they have levied against you for your tax arrears. Interest also stops accruing on your balances.

Here are the most important facts to understand about bankruptcy.

1. There is no free ride. You will be required to pay some amounts to your creditors, and any assets of value will likely be liquidated by the trustee.

2. A bankruptcy involves *all* your unsecured debts, not just your tax debt.

3. If the equity in your home is low – typically 25% or less – likely you will not be required to sell your home. If only one spouse in a matrimonial home ownership is declaring bankruptcy, only 50% of the home equity will be calculated in the valuation of your assets. Your spouse will have the opportunity to buy out your share of the equity at fair market value.

4. Filing for bankruptcy, or filing a consumer proposal or Division I proposal, does not discharge a CRA lien against your property. After the bankruptcy, the lien remains and – even worse – accrues interest over time. Even after your discharge from bankruptcy, the lien remains in force, until you eventually sell your home. At that point, the CRA will be second in line after the mortgage holder, etc., and will receive the remaining proceeds up until your share of the equity is exhausted. After that, however, because of your bankruptcy, your tax debt is extinguished – even if your equity is not enough to pay the tax in full.

5. If you are a sole proprietor, bankrupting your business is achieved through your personal bankruptcy.

6. Tax balances for trust monies – source deductions, GST/HST, PST, EHT, EI and CPP – will be assessed personally to the directors of a corporation should the business go bankrupt or be deemed in danger of bankruptcy. These balances can then only be discharged through the director's personal bankruptcy. The tax authorities will rigorously pursue collection of these tax balances, and may oppose your bankruptcy discharge, extending the time in which you must continue to pay your surplus income to the trustee for months or even years.

7. There is a mandatory period during which you remain a bankrupt until you are discharged and then fully clear of your debts. Any default on the terms of your bankruptcy will extend the time before you are discharged, or may invalidate the bankruptcy – which permits your creditors to pursue you anew.

8. While you are a bankrupt, you cannot hold office as a director of a corporation. You can, however, continue to operate your business. The value of your shares, however, will vest in the trustee.

9. The trustee is an officer of the court and is a licensed insolvency professional. As such he or she is obliged to represent both sides, meaning you and your creditor. They are not permitted to cut you a deal. They must diligently and honestly take stock of your assets and recover as much as is realistically possible to present as payment to your creditors.

10. Your tax lawyer acts only for you. In this stressful situation, and especially at the time of the creditor's meeting, you need someone in your corner to make sure you get the best possible terms.

Notwithstanding the foregoing, there are times when a proposal or bankruptcy is a wise financial choice. I review all scenarios with clients at this stage, and engage in serious tax planning to determine the pros and cons, and map out what assets can be safely preserved. Depending on the facts, what I call a "phoenix manoeuvre" could be utilized to mitigate the damage.

That said, the decision to discharge tax arrears through a creditor proposal or bankruptcy pretty much concedes the game to the crocodile.

Smack the Crocodile Between the Eyes

THE TAXPAYER DANGER SCALE from "Time to Pay" exposes the tactics that the crocodile has at his discretion to eat you for lunch, financially speaking.

Most Canada Revenue Agency (CRA) collections agents use their powers sparingly, and will consider a reasonable request for a temporary stay of collection escalation while I work with a taxpayer to reorganize his or her finances to address payment of the tax debt.

Then again sometimes you run into a grandstander – a collector who is new on the file, new to the CRA or simply determined, for whatever reason, to bring home a fresh kill.

These would-be heroes will renege on payment arrangement agreements, move without warning to seize bank accounts or issue Third Party Payment demands to your client list, or your tenants, without the benefit of discussion with counsel.

In rare cases, agents have been caught on the record threatening overly aggressive actions against a taxpayer unless the taxpayer terminates his relationship with legal counsel. It's easier for the crocodile to eat its prey without having to first fight past a protector.

In one such case, when the client advised us, Philippe DioGuardi wrote to the Tax Services Office manager to advise of the threat, and the unsuitability of it. He also suggested that if the CRA did not properly admonish the agent and modify his behaviour, legal action could ensue for interfering with a client's relationship with legal counsel.

A few short days later a letter arrived from the CRA (see Figure 8). It is framed and mounted on the wall of the DioGuardi Tax Law firm and is shown to clients.

Reluctantly, I have deleted the offender's name, although I feel he deserves to be named, shamed and put on the list of the Order of Bloodsuckers. CRA collection agents beware. Should one of you attempt to so harass a client of the firm again, I may start an online wall of shame to publish your activities. I will ask taxpayers to add their own posts on the wall.

Figure 8: CRA Reins In Overly Aggressive Agent

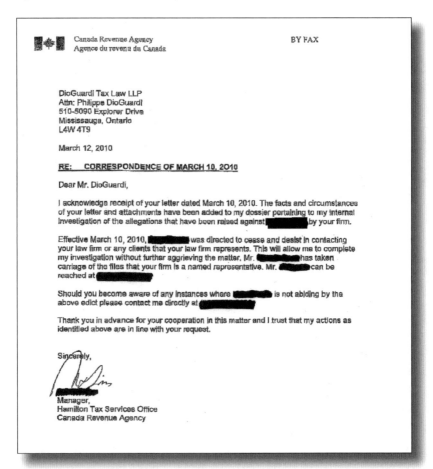

Chilling Out the
Tax Collector

FROM THE CASE FILES
OF PAUL DIOGUARDI

JIM HAD RUN A SUCCESSFUL HVAC business for many years. He lived in central Ontario, and his business employed enough people to be a significant employer in the town. When the Canada Revenue Agency (CRA) threatened to seize his operating account and shut down the business, it was a crisis, not just for Jim, but for everyone who worked for him

Several years earlier, Jim had suffered a terrible illness. He had required several serious surgeries. His medical condition, and the serial surgeries, temporarily impaired his short-term memory, and left him unable to ensure that his business was fulfilling its obligations to customers and to the tax authorities.

Fortunately, Jim was supported by two minority partners in the business, and the chartered accountant who had managed his financial and tax matters for many years.

Alas, during Jim's illness and recovery, payroll remittances fell off the table. His support team either didn't realize it, or were unable to manage the cash flow to file and pay on time. Eventually the CRA came looking for the money. Barely out of the hospital and back on his feet, Jim entered into intense negotiations with the tax collectors, and he thought he had negotiated a deal whereby he would pay down the principal on the arrears over a period of time. He understood that the CRA would secure its position through a lien on the building his business owned, and the hugely onerous interest and penalties would be addressed through a section 220(3.1) request for Taxpayer Relief. Jim believed that the considerate CRA agent on his file would make that submission for him.

Jump forward 5 years and Jim's file was transferred across the province to a new tax office and a new collections agent. By now the remaining balance owing – almost entirely comprised of interest and penalties – had grown to enormous proportions. The CRA wanted payment in full immediately, or they would close his business to close the file and write off the debt.

The new collections agent called Jim on the Friday of a holiday weekend. In Ontario, especially central Ontario, which is the lake district of the province, holiday weekends are sacrosanct. The agent left a peremptory message stating that if Jim did not remit payment by a certain date, she would garnish his accounts and "put him out of business."

Jim didn't get the message until the following Tuesday morning. He called the agent in a panic, but she was gone for several weeks on holiday. As far as Jim knew, the CRA was moving to seize his corporation's bank account, which would indeed put him out of business.

That's when he came to DioGuardi. We reviewed the situation and determined that, among a number of other facts, a submission for relief of interest and penalties had never been filed.

Our preliminary discussions with the CRA, and the aggressive agent, were unable to secure a stay of collection action while we reviewed the assessments and presented a reasonable tender of payment on the arrears. It was essential that Jim's business continue to operate. He had major new contracts that would boost cash flow and permit retirement of the tax arrears. He also had an extremely worthy case for taxpayer relief.

Any reasonable creditor would accept these terms of repayment. Unfortunately the CRA agent on his file was determined not to be reasonable. She was, in my opinion, a "nasty piece of goods."

We took the CRA to court.

First we sought immediate injunctive relief, requesting that the court order the CRA to suspend collection until such time as we could agree on a reasonable tender of payment. We argued that it was against the laws of natural justice to arbitrarily shut down a business, and put many people out of work, when the taxpayer:

- was prepared to make an arrangement to retire the arrears,
- had a viable business that could reasonably be expected to honour the terms of an arrangement, and
- was still within the 10-year limit to present a submission for relief of interest and penalties which, if granted, would elimi-nate the lion's share of the arrears outstanding.

The judge was most thoughtful in her deliberations. At length, she concluded that the CRA should stay its collection enforcement until such time as the taxpayer had submitted a request for relief under section 220(3.1) and had received a decision.

We were elated. This gave Jim the breathing space he needed, because the opportunities under section 220(3.1) permitted a first submission, a request for a second review of an unfavourable deci-sion, and the opportunity for judicial review of any decisions on the second review request. The whole process, from beginning to end, would take years.

The CRA was devastated. They were forced to "chill" while we prepared and submitted a very robust submission under section 220(3.1). I'll cut to the chase. The first request received partial relief. A request for a second review achieved more substantial relief. In the interim, Jim secured serious refinancing to make a huge payment against his arrears, which reduced his tax balances owing to amount composed entirely of interests and penalties. By moving DioGuardi into play as his knight, Jim was able to hold the CRA in check long enough to arrange his affairs and keep his business alive.

The game need not always go to the crocodile.

Round Two:
The Widow Wins
Fairness

IN ANOTHER INSTANCE, WE WERE able to achieve a remarkable result on behalf of a retired widow in round two of the taxpayer relief process.

A group of siblings came to the firm one day with a very large box of tax documents, letters to Members of Parliament, the Minister of Finance and representations prepared by both past accountants and lawyers.

Their story was harrowing. Their mother had been left widowed suddenly when their father was killed in very sad accident. Her several children were all adults, and had rallied around their mother to help her continue to run the family business. She had never been in business, and so focused her energies on sales and revenues. The details of tax reporting were beyond her ability, and she was unable to address these needs immediately.

Eventually, she managed to gather the books and records and take them to a reputable chartered accountant firm. She was assured that her tax returns would be prepared and filed for assessment. Since she heard no more, she was confident that the matter had been managed.

Imagine her surprise when, some years down the road, the Canada Revenue Agency (CRA) raised its own assessments, and sent her a tax bill for hundreds of thousands of dollars, more than half of which was comprised of non-filing penalties and arrears interests.

The situation was all the more distressing because the widow, now elderly, was no longer running the business, was in poor health, and would certainly be unable to discharge a tax balance of that magnitude in her lifetime.

She sought out the chartered accounting firm and discovered that not only had her tax returns never been prepared or filed, but the source documents had been misplaced. That's accountant-speak for "lost."

Eventually she found more reliable accounting help, who recreated invoices and expenses to the best of their ability, and filed accurate tax returns to counter the CRA's arbitrary assessment. She was reassessed. She liquidated assets to pay the principal portion of the assessment, but the penalties and interest remained unpaid, and were huge.

Mildly sympathetic, the CRA made her aware of provisions under the *Income Tax Act* and, with the assistance of her family, she wrote to the CRA to seek relief. "Unfortunately," came back the answer, "the two taxation years for which most of the tax (and therefore the penalties and interest) were assessed was beyond the 10-calendar-year cut-off. Relief could not be granted. Please pay. And by the way we will register liens against your properties so that, when you are deceased, your estate will be forced to pay." The CRA also garnished her statutory pensions.

The situation was monstrous. That's when the family sought our assistance.

As tax lawyers, we aren't miracle workers. On the other hand we do practice at the leading edge. We were aware of a landmark case before the courts that was on appeal. This case, *Bozzer v. R.* (2011 DTC 5106), challenged the interpretation of the "10-calendar-year cut-off" as expressed in section 220(3.1) of the *Income Tax Act*. *Bozzer* cited an ambiguity in the wording of section 220(3.1) that suggested that a taxpayer could seek relief of any penalties and interest assessed under the *Act* within 10 calendar years. The CRA had interpreted this, in their decisions, to mean that only the last 10 taxation years were subject to the provisions of section 220(3.1). Bozzer's position was that the 10-year cut-off referred to the year *in which* the taxpayer was assessed, not the year *for which* the taxpayer was assessed.

We agreed with the *Bozzer* interpretation. Therefore, we argued with the CRA that the widow's request for fairness could indeed be considered because, while the taxation years at issue where beyond the 10-year window, the assessments for those tax years had been raised by the CRA within the last 10 calendar years.

On this basis we presented submissions under section 220(3.1) for relief of the penalties and interests assessed on the widow's delinquent tax returns.

The CRA quickly responded that the tax years at issue did not qualify for relief. We responded that the CRA's interpretation of section 220(3.1) was not correct and that our request for relief must be considered. Concurrently we submitted to the Minster of National Revenue our position with respect to the interpretation of section 220(3.1) and advised that if the CRA continued to reject our relief request for review, we would take the matter to Judicial Review.

We received in what, for the federal bureaucracy, was a very short time, a letter from the Minister advising that until the *Bozzer* matter had been decided by the court, our request for taxpayer relief on behalf of our client would be held in suspense. Neither rejected, nor reviewed, but waiting.

This was a small win. Unfortunately it brought no immediate relief to my client, who was living on a restricted income without the benefit of her statutory pension benefits. But we were still in the game.

In 2011, the court decided in favour of *Bozzer*. It was an inspired decision from the judge, who wrote that the ambiguity in the wording of section 220(3.1) opened the door to an interpretation that could reasonably be argued to include assessments raised within the last 10 calendar years.

The CRA soon after confirmed that the widow's submission would be reviewed. It was, with less than the desired results. A small amount of relief was given, but my client still was required to pay hundreds of thousands of dollars in penalties and interest, an amount that was ever growing as interest compounded daily.

We moved on to the second review. We cited *Bozzer*, and the circumstances of the widow's sudden bereavement, her advanced age, poor health and the neglect of duty on the part of the licensed professional who had accepted the assignment to file her tax returns and had failed to do so.

The CRA took many months to review this second request. At length, the answer was received. All arrears interest on tax balances was relieved. The decision was worth over $100,000 dollars.

However, the CRA cited, the *Bozzer* decision had related specifically to arrears interest on tax balances assessed within 10 calendar years. The penalties for late filing, and accrued interest thereto, would be treated as related to the taxation year, not the year of assessment, and therefore would not be cancelled.

We were delighted to have achieved so much. The remaining balance was small compared to the arrears interest. We carried our flag high and bravely into one last round. We appealed the decision to the court.

The judge, while in sympathy with the virtue of our cause and our client, ruled that, as it related to *Bozzer*, the CRA's interpretation of section 220(3.1) did not merit his intervention.

Our client was disappointed. We had taken the matter as far as the law allowed. We savoured the fact that we had secured a substantial abatement of tax for the widow and her family.

Round two went to the widow – any way you look at it. Perhaps it was a case of "you should see the other guy."

Lawyers are not allowed to comment on judges and how they reach their decisions. Nevertheless, as I said at the outset of these tales, after the age of 70 we don't have to behave unless we want to. Perhaps in this case I don't want to behave.

Had I been the judge, the widow would have been granted relief of all penalties and interest.

She had paid her fair share and then some, and had suffered beyond the laws of natural justice. CRA did not deserve a penny more than the tax principal.

Alas, there is no equity in tax law ... and no compassion in a crocodile brain.

Justice at Last – A Pyrrhic Victory

AS DISCUSSED IN "The Widow Wins Fairness," there are provisions in the *Income Tax Act* and the *Excise Tax Act* that give the Minister of National Revenue (and his or her appointed designates) the discretion to waive, cancel or reduce penalties and interest assessed in tax balances in the last 10 calendar years.

Tax bureaucrats are charged with reviewing each case carefully and making a decision to grant or deny this relief based on the individual merits of the case. The more substantial the evidentiary support – medical documentation, legal representations and the like – the easier it should be for the bureaucrat to understand the true nature of the circumstances, and exercise his or her discretion to grant relief.

In my experience, all too often tax bureaucrats pay little attention to the details and deny relief as a punishment for past, delinquent tax behaviour.

This is not in keeping with the spirit and intent of the Taxpayer Relief provisions.

The following tale, in my opinion, qualifies these tax officials for the highest place of ignominy on the wall of shame. Their behaviour was callous, uninformed and ultimately contributed to the undoing of the taxpayer. The specifics of this case are heart-rending.

George was a very successful businessman. Then a devastating series of tragedies struck him and his family.

In 1999, one of his adult daughters was diagnosed with a terminal illness. After 3 years of failing health, it took her life.

In 2000, his other daughter became seriously ill. She was forced to undergo many difficult treatments, one of which was only available in the United States. This led to a battle between the taxpayer and the Ontario Health Insurance Plan, which had denied coverage for the treatment.

To compound matters, the stress of this situation led to the breakdown of George's marriage. George was emotionally shattered.

The cumulative life stressors precipitated serious mental and emotion conditions, including severe depression.

During these years George's business crumbled. Understandably, he was also unable to devote the proper attention to managing his business affairs, including preparing and filing his tax returns. He filed late, and was assessed with interest and penalties.

He sought medical assistance for his depression. Alas, in April of 2005, just when the doctors believed that George was starting to get back on his feet, a catastrophic motor vehicle accident left him seriously injured and unable to work.

The depression returned, and led to a failed suicide attempt in June of 2005, which resulted in George being briefly hospitalized in a psychiatric facility.

Meanwhile the tax machine rolled on and interest continued to accrue on George's tax arrears.

He came to me in early 2006 to assist with a request under section 220(3.1) of the *Income Tax Act* for relief of the penalties and arrears interest.

In short order, his section 220(3.1) request was prepared and submitted. Given George's fragile emotional state we requested that the CRA review the submission on an expedited basis. A few months later we again advised CRA that a response was urgently requested, since our client was deteriorating rapidly. The stresses of his life, exacerbated by a tax debt he believed he could never pay, were taking their toll.

While awaiting a decision from the CRA in relation to his fairness request, George succumbed to his inner demons and made another attempt on his life. Tragically, this attempt was successful.

Callously, the tax juggernaut rolled on. Three months after George's death, his request for fairness was denied by the CRA.

The Fairness Committee Report underlying the CRA's decision to deny relief had noted that the taxpayer had previously received fairness relief in relation to late filing penalties for his 2000 and 2001 taxation years. The Report further observed that he was not facing financial hardship at that time and could have made the necessary payments when they came due.

It recommended that additional relief for the 2000 and 2001 taxation years be denied, as his daughter had been married and living away from home when diagnosed with her illness, and she had continued in her employment until she passed away. His other daughter had her surgery in October 2001 and was now in remission.

The CRA Report also noted that doctors' findings from the summer of 2005, after his car accident and before his psychiatric hospitalization, indicated that George looked well and was able to walk with the assistance of crutches. Based on the foregoing, the CRA determined that that relief was not warranted for the 2004 taxation year since, the CRA represented, George could have hired an accountant to handle his tax matters.

Although the deceased's estate was impecunious, I decided that there was no way the cretins who made this decision were going to get away with such a travesty of justice.

In my opinion, the Fairness Committee had failed to properly administer the policies as set forth in CRA Information Circular 92-2, which provides that:

> Penalties and interest may be waived or cancelled in whole or in part
> where they result in circumstances beyond a taxpayer's control. For
> example, one of the following extraordinary circumstances may have
> prevented a taxpayer, a taxpayer's agent, the executor of an estate,
> or an employer from making a payment when due, or otherwise

complying with the Income Tax Act: a serious illness or accident; or serious emotional mental distress, such as a death in the immediate family.

On a *pro bono* basis, I launched an appeal to the court for Judicial Review of the CRA's decision.

Thank your lucky stars that, when bad decisions are made, the problem can be referred to a court for judicial review. Judges can usually be counted on to look on such matters with an unbiased eye and deal with problems reasonably.

Grounds for Judicial Review include:

- situations where the Tax Authorities acted without jurisdiction, went beyond their authority or refused to exercise their discretion reasonably;
- failed to observe a principle of natural justice, procedural fairness or other procedure they were required by law to observe; erred in law in making a decision;
- based their decision or order on an erroneous finding of fact that they made in a perverse or capricious manner or without regard for the material before them;
- acted, or failed to act, by reason of fraud or perjured evidence; or,
- acted in any other way that was contrary to the law.

AT JUDICIAL REVIEW

When I took the matter before the Federal Court, the judge was of the view that the CRA's decision was unreasonable, and noted that, with respect to the denial of additional relief for his 2000 and 2001 taxation years, it was not clear how the fact that George's daughter lived away from home, was married, and continued to work up until her death had any bearing on the degree of emotional and mental distress that he may have suffered in conjunction with her illness and death, or on his capacity to deal with his financial affairs.

Indeed, the judge noted that the medical and psychiatric evidence provided to the CRA suggested that over the period between 2002 and 2006, the severe emotional strain that the taxpayer had been under "took a toll on his overall mental health, resulting in depression, anxiety, sleep disturbance and multiple psychosomatic problems."

The medical evidence provided in the submission indicated that the automobile accident occurred on April 11, 2005, and that the taxpayer was hospitalized for some 9 weeks thereafter. This, concluded the judge, showed that he did not leave the hospital until shortly after the date on which his 2004 income tax return was due.

Moreover, the medical evidence demonstrated that he was in very serious condition while he was in hospital. In these circumstances, the finding that George was in a position to deal with his financial affairs during the relevant period was patently wrong.

Thus I was able to convince the court that the Minister's decision to deny relief was unreasonable. The judge instructed the CRA to reconsider its decision.

The CRA complied and, ultimately, granted full relief of penalties and interest. Unfortunately, it was too late for George. It was a pyrrhic victory, at best.

Not only had the tax bureaucrats involved been wrong, but, in my view, needlessly cruel.

I was very moved by this case and the desperate lengths to which my unfortunate client was pushed. On a no-name basis I shared the facts with my old friend Maynard, a trucker who used to operate a funeral business on the side. He had one pithy comment to share: "Life's a bitch and then you die." Not quite Hobbs' "nasty, brutish and short," but it fits the situation perfectly.

At least I had been able to make these (expletive deleted here) tax agents contemplate their misdeed.

The court decision has since been referenced in practitioner's guides and has raised the bar for CRA decision-making when extreme personal circumstances are at issue.

The Strangest Tale of All

I WAS HAVING LUNCH WITH TED, an old friend from law school days. We were sitting al fresco at a café table along the Sparks Street Mall in Ottawa. It was a beautiful summer day, and the meal was topped off by a bottle of wonderful Pinot Grigio.

Over the years, I had discussed with this old friend and legal colleague my firm's running battle with the Law Society of Upper Canada over the protection of tax debtor clients. Ted had a corporate commercial practice, and seldom had to deal with collection agents from the Canada Revenue Agency (CRA). Nevertheless, being a buddy, his was a convenient shoulder for me to cry on. I had been doing so about this particular topic since 2008.

That day, however, it had not been a topic of our conversation until, over the last dregs of wine, he popped up with a provocative statement, and commenced a modern-day version of a Socratic dialogue.

"Paul," said Ted, "I believe the Law Society has been infiltrated by Revenue Canada operatives who are hiding under the mantle of the Regulator to stop you from protecting and representing your tax debtor clients."

I almost choked on the wine. The idea was preposterous! My Regulator would never knowingly sell out to the enemy.

Ted, always up for a good argument, refused to budge from his premise.

"Let's review the facts," he countered. (How lawyerly.) "You told me that, way back in 2008, one of the Law Society's lower level officials took issue with the wording in your retainer agreement, the one you use only for tax debtor clients. You have told me many times that these clients come to you at the eleventh hour, when, after years of keeping the Taxman at bay, they are out of runway. Their bank accounts have been seized, or their wages are garnished. There's a tax lien on their home. Didn't you tell me about one dreadful case where the man's wife was being harassed by telephone calls at 2 in the morning? When your clients are this desperate, they only want one thing from you. To make it go away. Am I right, Paul?"

I had to agree with his portrayal of the presenting circumstances most common for tax debtor clients. For a corporate lawyer, Ted had quite a flair for the dramatic.

"Well, then," Ted continued with his relentless lawyer logic, "as soon as you agree to represent these clients, don't you need an authorization signed by the client announcing to the CRA that you are their legal counsel?"

Again, I had to agree.

"Bingo!" said Ted. "As soon as the CRA knows you've been hired, they also know that your client has paid a retainer to secure your representation. How soon do you send in the authorization?"

"Within 48 hours," I replied. "Sometimes sooner."

"So in the normal course there's no way you would have been able to render complete service that fast. You may be the super tax lawyer, but you're not superman." (Quite the sense of humour had Ted.) "That means, if you held retainers in trust in the traditional manner, as I do, the money, for the most part, still belongs to the tax debtor, and the CRA can move in and seize it from you before you've had a chance to get very far. Has that ever happened?"

"They've tried," I acknowledged. "But they've never succeeded, because I know their game. So they just give up and go back to their usual tactics. The CRA knows by now that a seizure demand to DioGuardi is pointless. Other lawyers have not been so lucky. It could happen to you, Ted. If any of your fat cat corporate clients owes payroll arrears, or is behind on HST, or has personal tax arrears – and you know that many, many people are hiding this dirty little secret – the CRA can come after you, too, and try to seize your client's retainer. In your case they would likely succeed."

"Perhaps so," Ted acknowledged, thinking hard. "But it would take the CRA some time to figure out that I was representing the tax debtor. When it comes to you, it's like shooting fish in a barrel. You're revealed as counsel practically on the day you take the retainer. The CRA has to have you in its sights from the get-go, which makes it a piece of cake to target client retainers if you put them in your trust account, and knock you out of the box. That would leave your client defenceless. You've already told me the Tax Crocodile has tried on more than one occasion to convince your clients to 'get rid of your lawyer so we can do a deal with you.' They're looking for an easy meal and aren't above resorting to dirty tricks. A lawyer in the way is harder to digest."

Ted clearly had been a good listener, or maybe he had read my last book. In any case, he had nailed it on the head. This was the Tax Crocodile's favourite MO. While it infuriates me, I also take it as a backhand compliment to the power of the DioGuardi name. When the CRA knows DioGuardi is on the case, they know they're up against fighters and it won't be easy to finish off the tax debtor.

Ted had warmed to his theme and was rattling on apace. "I truly believe that the CRA has decided to come at you through your Regulator. Think about it. First a low level Law Society investigator takes exception to the fact that your clients agree to let you protect their retainer. Who does the Regulator assign to look into the matter? A former employee of the Tax Crocodile, who has been recruited on special assignment by the Law Society. Didn't you think it was strange that a former tax auditor was assigned to your case instead of a lawyer?"

I did think it was strange at the time, long ago in 2008, but had shrugged it off as a coincidence.

On reflection, I had to agree with Ted that the only thing this former Tax Crocodile employee investigated was the language in my special tax debtor retainer. He alleged that my clients didn't understand that their retainer could be seized by the CRA, and further they didn't understand that by signing the agreement they were surrendering title of the retainer to my care. No client was ever at risk of losing their fee. In fact, the retainer was bonded by third party private funds. To the best of my knowledge, no other lawyer is so bonded.

With respect to the former Tax Crocodile's investigation, no client had ever complained about agreeing to let me protect their retainer. They trusted me, based on my reputation and my many years of tax practice, and because the need for effective legal representation trumped everything. The complaints to the Regulator were from a handful of clients who, at the end of their representation, didn't want to have to pay the CRA, and thought they could leverage me through the Regulator to get their fees back – probably so that they could use the money to pay the CRA.

I offer here, as an aside, to any who care to listen, that the most effective way to get a reimbursement of fees from your lawyer is to speak directly to the lawyer, in writing and in person. If your request has merit, your lawyer will work out an appropriate reimbursement. Or you can hire another lawyer and tax the account, which is a formal proceeding under the *Solicitor's Act*. But if you complain to the Regulator, the Regulator will simply start an investigation that proceeds at a snail's pace through the myriad procedural stages of the bureaucracy. Most of the time your lawyer doesn't even know that you've asked the Law Society to help you get your money back. So there you are, many months later – or in the case of my complaining clients more than 6 *years* later – and you're no further ahead in your quest for reimbursement. That's my jeremiad on the subject, for whatever it's worth.

Getting back to my Socratic dialogue with Ted.

"So," Ted continued, "in the absence of any real complaints from clients about having you protect the retainer from seizure by the CRA, the Regulator's hired gun, who was a former Tax Crocodile auditor, and was not a lawyer, challenged the propriety of your retainer agreement, which asked your client to agree that you could take title to the fee in order to protect your client's access to your legal representation. You told me he based his allegation on a policy decision by Convocation in 1982. That's 32 years ago! And that policy did not take into consideration the needs of a tax debtor practice. Surely a former Tax Crocodile would know that the CRA could seize retainers from a lawyer's trust account. Both you and I are aware of the court's decision on the *Ristimaki* appeal in 2006. The CRA seized hundreds of thousands of dollars of the client's money from the lawyer's trust account in that case. Of course Mrs. Ristimaki sued her lawyer for negligence. She deserved to win her appeal. Any lawyer who follows the evolution of the law knows that the *Ristimaki* ruling set a new standard of care for protection of a client's interest and property. It changed everything. Did this former Tax Crocodile auditor/investigator not understand how the power afforded to the CRA under section 224 of the *Income Tax Act* to seize money held by a third party can come between a lawyer and his client?"

"I think he understood section 224," I responded. "He just didn't believe that CRA would use it against a lawyer's trust account. He may have missed the *Ristimaki* ruling, although in 2008 it was still very fresh. Or perhaps, like most auditors, he just didn't read. I was adamant in my position, so this former Tax Crocodile decided to write to the head of collections at Tax Crocodile Central, expecting to hear that the CRA would never go after something as small as a lawyer's trust retainer. The CRA's response, in a letter directed to the Law Society of Upper Canada, must have been a thunder stroke. It more than vindicated that the money a tax debtor paid to hire a lawyer, if it was put in trust, could and would be seized if the tax devils knew where to find it."

Ted was laughing. "That poor little former Tax Crocodile employee must have been dumbfounded. 'Hoisted with his own petard,' as Shakespeare said. But that doesn't disprove my theory, because you told me that when this former CRA employee couldn't find a way to dislodge the protection of your tax debtor retainer, 2 years later the

Regulator brought in another, younger and more aggressive former Tax Crocodile employee.

"I expect," continued Ted, "that this new guy was to be the hatchet man. Orders issued to him from above were likely to the effect that he should finish this off. Despite the CRA's confirmation that they could and would seize retainers in a lawyer's trust account, apparently, the Law Society doesn't care. If the Law Society is of the opinion that it is acceptable for tax debtor clients to risk losing their retainers and thus their access to legal representation, leaving them alone to face the crocodile, don't you think we have proved that the Tax Crocodile is running the agenda? Why, unless it was infiltrated by agents from Crocodile Central, would the Law Society want to stop your firm from protecting your clients from the tax collector? How could the lawyers who govern our regulatory body tell you to put your clients in harm's way? You and I both know it's against the legal ethics we were taught in law school. Again I return to my theme: to my mind, there is no other explanation than that these Law Society employees, who were both former employees of the CRA, are really Revenue Canada double agents.

"And just like a Tax Crocodile," Ted went on, "this investigator hasn't let go. You tell me he has started proceedings against your son and practice associate, Philippe. By reputation and by your report, I understand that Philippe is a tough and seasoned litigator, and well able to take care of himself. Good thing, too, since the story has been sniffed out by the press, and your special bonded tax debtor retainer is now become front page news. Yet the only comments on the record come from two hugely biased sources: a spokesperson from the Law Society and an investigative accountant. The Regulator's mouth-piece made a very general comment about lawyers needing to use a trust account, and that Bylaw 9 sets out the rules for management of a trust account. She didn't once reference the special provisions in Bylaw 9 that permit exceptions to the trust account rule that validate your position. Perhaps she forgot about these provisions. Ironically, she inadvertently supported you by admitting that a lawyer could take instructions from the client as to the management of the retainer money.

"As for the accountant, well, he's an *accountant*," Ted scoffed. "Why would he have any understanding about how a lawyer must practice law in a post-*Ristimaki* world. Both 'commenters,' as I read it, overlook the dangers to the client. Both ignore, likely on purpose, the essential issue of protecting the client's right of access to legal representation.

"Bottom line – I agree with you, Paul. This proceeding has been done in a reckless and negligent way, which is not unusual for the Law Society, these days. I read recently that two lawyers were awarded $500,000 in costs when the court ruled that the Law Society had pushed forward a case that had no merit. It's not the first time that's happened. These linear bureaucrats don't much care about the consequences. It's not their money.

"In your case, I expect the hatchet man investigator from the Law Society simply wants to put your head on a pole and close the file. Sounds like CRA tactics to me. And so, I rest my case."

Ted took another sip of his Pinot Grigio.

It was my turn to talk, but I didn't say what was really in my head. It was too explosive to share. It had crossed my mind, on more than one occasion, that the Law Society has a conflict of interest when it comes to setting the rules for the handling of client retainers. Benchers of the Law Society hold three of five positions on the Board of Trustees of the Law Foundation of Ontario, giving them control over the Foundation. The Foundation receives millions of dollars a year from the interest earned on client moneys held in lawyers' trust accounts. It would receive less money if lawyers representing tax debtor clients were permitted to exercise the alternatives of existing Bylaw provisions to deposit tax debtor client retainers into their general accounts. Therefore, there was reason for me to suspect that the Law Society deliberately had failed to address protection for tax debtor clients in preference to its own economic interest over the public interest.

I took a deep breath, brushed these thoughts aside, and focused on Ted's theory of CRA infiltration.

"Ted," I said, "you must have had more wine than I. Your comments are fanciful, and overly critical. Until now we have been dealing with low-level linear bureaucrats. I believe that once the Benchers at the Law Society get wind of the facts, they will realize the gravity of the dilemma lawyers face when representing tax debtor clients in a post-*Ristimaki* world, and they will set a new policy to govern the treatment and protection of client retainers."

"Wake up, Paul." Ted barked back. "Remember your history. The Russian peasants before the revolution were always saying, 'If only our little father the Czar knew of our plight, he would speedily remedy our problems.' The Czar was never told by his advisors that the peasants were in need. When he did nothing, the peasants thought he didn't care, and so they brought him down. What makes you think the Law Society Benchers know – or care to know – about the plight of tax debtors who seek legal representation? Even if they knew, what makes you think the Benchers will bestir themselves to revisit a 32-year-old policy decision that is working just fine for them?"

"Two things," I answered boldy. "*Ristimaki*, and the CRA's letter to the Law Society. The implications of these two things cannot be ignored. I believe the Benchers can be motivated to act to protect the public."

"Here's to you then," said Ted, raising his glass in a toast and finishing off the last mouthful of wine. "You have more faith in them than I do."

I couldn't swallow my last sip of wine. It was as ashes in my mouth. I started to break out in a cold sweat. Then I woke up!

Ted's theory of CRA infiltration into the ranks of the Regulator was too fantastic to be true. Then again, if the Regulator were to forbid a lawyer to take a direction from his client asking that the retainer be protected from seizure by the CRA, the Tax Crocodile would be able to blithely step between *any lawyer* and his tax debtor client. No tax debtor would be able to retain legal representation. This would be a very serious injustice. In the adversarial tax arena, it would destroy the value of legal representation. Tax litigation, which is conducted through the courts and therefore between lawyers, would continue as usual, because at this stage there is little or no danger of seizure. Even the CRA must respect the courts. But tax debtor representation when the courts are not engaged would be dead as we know it. No lawyer could protect a client. Why hire a lawyer if there is no protection? Nothing would make the Tax Crocodile happier. All those tax debtors undefended and easy prey.

As a lawyer, I must and will protect my clients. You may remember from my earlier confession about my Uncle Paul (see "Keep On Punching") that I said fighting is in the DioGuardi genes. I will keep on punching at the real enemy – the tax collector, not the Law Society. I believe that eventually right will prevail. The Law Society will step up on the side of justice and do its duty to protect the public in general, and tax debtors specifically, from the jaws of the predatory CRA.

On these happy thoughts, I at last rolled over and fell back into a deep sleep, dreaming now of more pleasant things. Halcyon fields, comely maidens dancing in a flowering bower, and a table overflowing with nature's bounty. The stuff of any man's dreams – even an old curmudgeon like me.

Insatiable Appetite

Hungry for More

IN JUNE 2013, FORMER NATIONAL Security Agency (NSA) analyst, Edward Snowden, forever changed our expectations of privacy.

The NSA, he reported, in concert with spy agencies around the world, have been collaborating with big tech – every major provider of Internet technologies and services – to vacuum up Internet activity, cellphone calls, e-mails, text messages and online ad click-throughs.

This trove of metadata, Snowden reported, is stored in vast NSA data centres and is available to be sliced and diced for cross-reference against any of an infinite number of query algorithms.

As a NSA analyst himself, he had access to virtually any data he wanted. And that data could lead him to anyone he wanted.

Privacy is dead, he advised, and it was time for citizens to know the truth so they could choose whether to allow this surveillance to continue without suspicion, or to use the power of democracy to make it stop.

Philippe DioGuardi, who, with me, is a Senior Tax Lawyer at DioGuardi Tax Law, has devoted much time to serious research on the dangers of the Internet.

I will step aside, for the moment, and let him to take the stage to share his insights and opinions in "Inescapable Surveillance and the Loss of Privacy."

Inescapable Surveillance and the Loss of Privacy

SOFTWARE FREEDOM ACTIVIST Richard Stallman calls Facebook "a surveillance machine."

Science-fiction writer and futurist Bruce Sterling sums up the Internet this way:

> Microsoft, Apple, Cisco, Google et al, they are all ... intelligence assets posing as commercial operations. They are surveillance marketers. They give you free stuff in order to spy on you and pass that info along the value chain. Personal computers can have users, but social media has livestock.

That livestock is you.

As long as we engage in social media, we are nothing more than a juicy steak to feed the insatiable appetite of online marketers.

Inescapably, the Internet is forever.

Your online activities create an enduring record of your past – a record that can be used to compile a picture of you in the future for any of a number of reasons.

In the hands of a government agency, such as the Canada Revenue Agency (CRA), your Internet Service Provider (ISP) address is a breadcrumb trail glowing in cyberspace and leading straight to your door, to your PayPal account or to anywhere you spend money or stash money.

Such a trail led the RCMP to the home of a 19-year-old student who, in April 2014, allegedly exploited the Heartbleed bug vulnerability and hacked into the CRA's website, stealing the SIN numbers of 900 taxpayers. (See "The Tax Season Scandal of 2014.") The theft itself was identified by the deep packet inspection techniques of the security surveillance agencies monitoring traffic into and out of the CRA website.

If the spying eyes of the government are already tracking your Internet activities – and by now it's clear this is indeed the case – and those same spying eyes are monitoring activity in and out of the Canada Revenue Agency website, it's a given that the CRA can, in course of an audit or investigation, request to view the Internet records related to a taxpayer.

Canada's new Bill C-13 legislation further opens the door to this new brand of CRA audit. Without your permission, and without having to prove there's a need to monitor you, the Canada Revenue Agency, or any other public official, can request a record of your activity online and on your cellphone from your service provider. Rogers, Bell, Shaw, et al. will simply hand over the records of who you called, what you searched and, of course, what you bought online, without telling you.

It makes a stealth net worth audit easier and more accurate than ever before. The real question is, how much cyber-spying does the CRA actually do? Today? Having been in the practice of "adversarial" tax law for more than 20 years, as of the time of writing, it is my legal opinion that the CRA will consider any and every opportunity presented by technology to monitor and review the financial behaviours of taxpayers for the purposes of administering and enforcing the ITA.

That means the CRA will not hesitate to ask Google, Yahoo or Bing for the records of your Internet searches. They will compel Rogers, Shaw and Bell to surrender your cell phone records without a warrant.

In many cases, the CRA may not even have to ask! So much of what you do, or have done, is already available to anyone who wants to take the time to really search. Because anything picked up from Internet activity was given freely, it's all fully admissible in the course of an audit or investigation of a taxpayer's compliance.

I believe that there is demonstrable risk that a taxpayer's Internet records, now or at any time in the future, may be sought by the CRA in the course of a targeted review, or as part of a general review of a group of individuals who match a specified profile.

Welcome to the age of the robo-audit.

The greatest risk is that Internet searches related to tax problems or clicks on sponsored ad links headlined by such terms as "tax evasion," "breaking income tax law," "unfiled taxes" and more, when aggregated in the taxpayer's Internet history, may raise a red flag with respect to the taxpayer's behaviours and expose a taxpayer to both the random and targeted scrutiny of the CRA.

Why would the CRA *not* use information about Internet search history to profile potential candidates for audit?

Other branches of government already seek access to "big data" to profile candidates for security investigations, immigration investigations and even marital status reviews. The U.S. government clearly makes use of the data captured from Internet search engine providers, and shares their discoveries with relevant international allies.

According to an article on mashable.com by Julian Sanchez (June 13, 2013), "The IRS is all fired up to use big data to hunt for tax cheats."

Where the IRS goes, the CRA inevitably follows. The tax collectors will not be able to let so much juicy data go to waste.

The Tax Season Scandal of 2014

IT WAS AN UNBELIEVABLE HEADLINE for the 9th of April, with the 2103 T1 personal tax filing deadline only 3 weeks away.

"Canada Revenue Agency shuts down EFILE," screamed media sites across Canada.

Only a week earlier, the Minister of National Revenue, The Honourable Kerry-Lynne Findlay, had been crowing about the high acceptance rate of online tax filing. She announced that more Canadians were filing T1 tax and benefit returns online than ever before. As of March 24, 2014, the minister reported, the Canada Revenue Agency (CRA) had received over 6.7 million returns, with close to 84% of those being e-filed, compared to 80% at the same time last year. "Electronic filing is quickly becoming the norm," the minister proclaimed, citing with pride that tax filers were discovering how convenient, easy, and secure online filing was. Enrolment in direct deposit for receiving benefits and tax refunds had also increased, she said. So far, 65% of taxpayers getting a refund from their 2013 T1 return received it by direct deposit, compared to 61% at the same point in the tax cycle a year earlier.

The minister encouraged all Canadians to join the growing number of their neighbours and friends who file online. According to her news release, when combining online filing with direct deposit, taxpayers could get their refunds in as little as 8 days. Given the number of free software options available, said the minister, filing a T1 income tax and benefit return couldn't be easier or simpler.

She was also pleased at the "process savings" the CRA would realize by not having to manually process tax filings. She didn't say if the savings would be passed on to taxpayers. That, of course, being the purview of the Minister of Finance.

We must note, sadly, that the Ministry of Finance was about to be dealt a devastating blow. Ironically, so was the CRA.

Late in the day on April 7, 2014, a serious vulnerability in the SSL Internet website security software was discovered independently by Neel Mehta of Google Security, and a team of security engineers at the Finland-based computer security firm of Codenomicon. Dubbed "Heartbleed" by the ever-imaginative Internet gurus, the bug reportedly opened hundreds of thousands of websites to data theft, and let attackers not only eavesdrop on "secure" communications, but also potentially gain access to the very encryption keys being used to establish secure connections.

The Internet giants – Amazon.com, Google, and Yahoo – were affected. So, apparently, were governments and banks, among others.

By April 8, "Heartbleed" was the news of the day. Software developers were rushing out patches to fix affected web servers. Security experts were preaching doom and gloom in every major news report. Websites with SSL security encryption were being checked for leaks.

On April 9, 2014, the CRA stepped into the media frenzy and announced it was shutting down all external access to its online services, including e-filing of tax returns. The Minister of National Revenue explained that the "Heartbleed" security bug might have exposed the passwords and personal information of taxpayers who filed online, signed up for direct deposit of benefits and refunds and/ or set up personal online access to their tax accounts.

The next day, April 10, it was sorrowfully announced that the redoubtable James (Jim) Flaherty, who had resigned his post as national Minister of Finance less than a month earlier, had suffered a heart attack and died.

It was a dark few days in Canada's halls of finance.

As Canadians shared their condolences with the family of the late departed Finance Minister, DioGuardi Tax Law offered essential advice to taxpayers.

"Keep your tax matters private. Keep tax offline," wrote tax lawyer Philippe DioGuardi on the DioGuardi Tax Law Facebook® page, twitter® feed, website blog and news page.

"No one knows if your personal tax information has been compromised," Philippe DioGuardi warned taxpayers. "The CRA has been very quiet on that subject. But since the Heartbleed bug may also affect your online banking, anyone filing online *and* who registered for direct deposit has a double-trouble risk of exposure."

CRA tried to manage the scandal by graciously announcing that taxpayers would be granted an extension on the deadline to file their 2013 T1 returns, the date of that deadline to be determined when the CRA website resumed operation.

DioGuardi Tax Law, however, suggested that the CRA website shutdown was proof that the Internet is not safe for such highly personal matters as tax. "File the old-fashioned way," Philippe DioGuardi urged. "On paper, delivered to the CRA by mail or in person."

He further suggested, "When you receive your 2013 assessment, check the fees and penalties section carefully. If you find a paper filing charge or a late filing penalty, object. On paper and through the mail."

Late in the day on Sunday, April 13, 2014, the CRA announced its web portal had been "fixed" and that EFILE was back in business. Accountants, tax filing services and eager taxpayers sprang into action, happily filing returns online. Taxpayers would now have until May 5, 2014, to file their T1 personal returns. In my memory, this is the first time the filing deadline has ever been extended on a nationwide basis.

Then the other shoe dropped.

First thing Monday, April 14, the CRA announced that the SIN numbers of 900 lucky early EFILE-ers had been stolen from the CRA website. In the space of 6 short hours, hackers had breached the CRA EFILE portal and got away with the 900 SIN numbers.

CRA advised that these 900 taxpayers would be advised of the theft by – ironically – registered letter, and given directions to protect their identities and with free credit protection services for 1 year.

Seems that sauce for the goose was not safe enough to be sauce for the gander. CRA did not deem e-mail safe enough for advising e-filers that their SIN numbers were in the hands of thieves who, quite possibly, would use this sensitive personal information to steal their identities and perpetrate who-knows-what manner of fraud that could jeopardize bank accounts, credit ratings, mortgages and more.

The CRA had confirmed the DioGuardi position: tax is too private for online.

It didn't stop accountants, tax services and taxpayers themselves from rushing back to e-filing. But I do hope it gave some of them pause.

Late in the day on April 16, 2014, the Royal Canadian Mounted Police (RCMP) announced the arrest of a 19-year-old engineering student at the University of Western Ontario. A few days earlier the RCMP, who had followed the trail of an IP address, had served a search warrant on the home where the young man lived with his parents, and had taken away computer equipment. The young man, whose name I will not share here (you can find it in the newspaper archives), was charged with one count of unauthorized use of a computer and one count of mischief in relation to data, as of the time of writing. The RCMP alleged that the young man exploited the Heartbleed security bug to hack into the CRA's website and extract private taxpayer information, including the 900 SIN numbers.

The media reported that the young man, whose father, reportedly, teaches computer science at the same university, was something of a computer wunderkind, and some years before had hacked into other computers to prove a security vulnerability.

Security experts don't believe the matter is necessarily over. One expert told a national news service that he expected fallout from the Heartbleed vulnerability to go well beyond 900 stolen SINs. An identity theft expert suggested more information may have been leaked than the CRA admitted, because it is unlikely that personal details such as a usernames and basic contact information were stored separately from their SIN numbers in the CRA database.

How did the CRA realize the SIN numbers had been stolen? And how did the RCMP track an IP address to the home of a university student in London, Ontario?

An Internet security expert told the *Globe and Mail* that the theft would have been spotted by the network monitoring tools of "other federal agencies that capture and analyze transiting data packets."

We can only take that to mean CSEC (Communications Security Establishment Canada) – the Canadian counterpart of the National Security Agency in the U.S., and one of the infamous Five Eyes (FVEY) identified by Edward Snowden in his revelations of government surveillance of Internet activity.

Now we have proof that e-filed tax returns have been snooped by government surveillance agencies. How long will it be before data from other online activities are cross-referenced back through CSEC to the CRA for the "robo-audit" we discussed in the previous chapter?

My son Philippe, it seems, is a Cassandra of all things tax.

What can you do? Likely not much. The march of technology is inevitable. CRA will continue to prefer processes to people and will automate your tax life more and more.

But you can resist as long as possible, and try to keep yourself safe by printing your tax return out on paper and mailing it to the CRA.

And if you want to really drive them crazy, you can write on the bottom of your paper return, "Compliments of Paul DioGuardi."

Last Words – But Not the Final Chapter

WE HAVE TAKEN A JOURNEY together. Here is my final confession, and my prediction for what comes next.

As birth rates in Canada drop and the demographics of an aging population kick in, fewer working people will be available to pay the taxes necessary to fund retirement income and the health care that all Canadians demand as their inalienable right.

The public purse is and will become even more desperate for revenue. Tax rates may not increase, but taxation inevitably will. More things in life will be taxed.

Moreover, tax will become the punishment used to dictate politically correct behaviour. Didn't sort your garbage into the correct three (or five or six) different bins? You'll be charged a garbage tax. Need to wash the children's soccer shirts in the middle of the day? You'll be charged a tax for prime time hydro and water usage. (In Ontario this is already in practice.) Don't update your windows to stem heat loss? You'll be charged a heat loss tax.

In "Tax Credits and Crocodile Traps" I discussed the dangers of tax credits. Every credit has a string attached to something else in the system. You will be required to reveal more details of your actions to qualify for tax credits. The more you reveal, the more opportunity for the bureaucrats to scrutinize your behaviour and find a way to tax it.

Collection of all tax will become ever more aggressive. Privileges will be suspended or revoked if you have tax arrears outstanding. Imagine losing your driver's license or passport for non-payment of tax. Cash-strapped European nations, such as Italy, are already reviewing proposals to enact such legislation.

God forbid the day comes that you are turned away from a doctor's office or emergency room for non-payment of tax.

Yet it all may come to pass. The surveillance necessary for such enforcement is already an integral part of our lives.

Your cellular phone, your tablet computer and your laptop capture every detail of every waking moment. More incredibly, you actively participate in the data collection when you snap a photograph, tweet your opinion, or post your whereabouts on Facebook.

There are no secrets now.

Thanks to Edward Snowden, we also know that our governments have for years been collecting and sorting what we say, tweet, post and e-mail. Each and every one of us has a security agency profile, and while we believe we have nothing to hide, one day, at random or on purpose, someone will connect the dots and *presto*! You're under the microscope.

New technologies have added smart fridges, washing machines and cars that already feed into the metadata maw reports on what you eat, how often you wash with hot water and how fast you drive. Wristwatches will upload your vital signs to a healthcare system, who may look back down the data trail to see how often you do or don't exercise, so they can manage resources to treat your future injuries or chronic care needs.

It's no accident that Google added Nest Labs to its arsenal. Now you can be watched from within the privacy of your own home.

At least Homer Simpson had the insight and instinct to rip off and smash his "Oogle specs." (*The Simpsons,* season 25, episode 11: "Specs and the City"), but I doubt the civilized world will exhibit as much human decency.

I anticipate the tax authorities will waste no time in harnessing this vast trove of personal data in pursuit of revenues. Reviews of your income and expenses can be conducted by reviewing data logged by your fridge, your car, your home thermostat and, of course, your smart phone.

Life as a tax lawyer will become ever more fascinating. I look forward to sharing new tales with you as this techno-future unfolds.

In the meantime,

never

smile at a crocodile.